I0009979

Mobile Deep Learning with TensorFlow Lite, ML Kit and Flutter

Build scalable real-world projects to implement end-to-end
neural networks on Android and iOS

Anubhav Singh
Rimjhim Bhadani

BIRMINGHAM - MUMBAI

Mobile Deep Learning with TensorFlow Lite, ML Kit and Flutter

Copyright © 2020 Packt Publishing

All rights reserved. No part of this book may be reproduced, stored in a retrieval system, or transmitted in any form or by any means, without the prior written permission of the publisher, except in the case of brief quotations embedded in critical articles or reviews.

Every effort has been made in the preparation of this book to ensure the accuracy of the information presented. However, the information contained in this book is sold without warranty, either express or implied. Neither the authors, nor Packt Publishing or its dealers and distributors, will be held liable for any damages caused or alleged to have been caused directly or indirectly by this book.

Packt Publishing has endeavored to provide trademark information about all of the companies and products mentioned in this book by the appropriate use of capitals. However, Packt Publishing cannot guarantee the accuracy of this information.

Commissioning Editor: Pravin Dhandhre
Acquisition Editor: Ali Abidi
Content Development Editor: Nathanya Dias
Senior Editor: Ayaan Hoda
Technical Editor: Utkarsha S. Kadam
Copy Editor: Safis Editing
Project Coordinator: Aishwarya Mohan
Proofreader: Safis Editing
Indexer: Manju Arasan
Production Designer: Deepika Naik

First published: April 2020

Production reference: 1030420

Published by Packt Publishing Ltd.
Livery Place
35 Livery Street
Birmingham
B3 2PB, UK.

ISBN 978-1-78961-121-2

www.packt.com

Packt.com

Subscribe to our online digital library for full access to over 7,000 books and videos, as well as industry leading tools to help you plan your personal development and advance your career. For more information, please visit our website.

Why subscribe?

- Spend less time learning and more time coding with practical eBooks and Videos from over 4,000 industry professionals

- Improve your learning with Skill Plans built especially for you

- Get a free eBook or video every month

- Fully searchable for easy access to vital information

- Copy and paste, print, and bookmark content

Did you know that Packt offers eBook versions of every book published, with PDF and ePub files available? You can upgrade to the eBook version at www.packt.com and as a print book customer, you are entitled to a discount on the eBook copy. Get in touch with us at customercare@packtpub.com for more details.

At www.packt.com, you can also read a collection of free technical articles, sign up for a range of free newsletters, and receive exclusive discounts and offers on Packt books and eBooks.

Contributors

About the authors

Anubhav Singh is the founder of The Code Foundation, an AI-focused start-up that works on multimedia processing and natural language processing, with the goal of making AI accessible to everyone. An International rank holder in the Cyber Olympiad, he's continuously developing software for the community in domains that don't get a lot of attention. Anubhav is a Venkat Panchapakesan Memorial Scholarship awardee and an Intel Software Innovator. Anubhav loves talking about what he's learned and is an active community speaker for Google Developer Groups all over the country and can often be found guiding learners on their journey in machine learning.

Rimjhim Bhadani is a lover of open source. She has always believed in making development resources accessible to everyone at minimal costs. She is a big fan of mobile application development and has developed a number of projects, most of which aim to solve major and minor daily life challenges. She has been an Android mentor at Google Code-in and an Android developer for Google Summer of Code. Supporting her vision to serve the community, she is one of six Indian students to be recognized as a Google Venkat Panchapakesan Memorial Scholar and one of three Indian students to be awarded the Grace Hopper Student Scholarship in 2019.

About the reviewer

Subhash Shah is an experienced solutions architect. With 14 years of experience in software development, he now works as an independent technical consultant. He is an advocate of open source development and its utilization in solving critical business problems. His interests include microservices architecture, enterprise solutions, machine learning, integrations, and databases. He is an admirer of quality code and **test-driven development** (TDD). His technical skills include translating business requirements into scalable architecture and designing sustainable solutions. He is a co-author of *Hands-On High Performance with Spring 5, Hands-On AI for Banking,* and *MySQL 8 Administrator's Guide,* all from Packt Publishing. He has also been a technical reviewer for other books.

Packt is searching for authors like you

If you're interested in becoming an author for Packt, please visit `authors.packtpub.com` and apply today. We have worked with thousands of developers and tech professionals, just like you, to help them share their insight with the global tech community. You can make a general application, apply for a specific hot topic that we are recruiting an author for, or submit your own idea.

Table of Contents

Preface

Deep learning is rapidly becoming the most popular topic in the industry. This book introduces trending deep learning concepts and their use cases with an industrial- and application-focused approach. You will cover a range of projects covering tasks such as mobile vision, facial recognition, smart AI assistants, and augmented reality.

With the help of eight projects, you will learn to integrate deep learning processes into the iOS and Android mobile platforms. This will help you to transform deep learning features into robust mobile apps efficiently. This book gets you hands-on with selecting the right deep learning architectures and optimizing mobile deep learning models while following an application-oriented approach to deep learning on native mobile apps. We will later cover various pretrained and custom-built deep learning model-based APIs, such as the ML Kit through Google Firebase. Further on, the book will take you through examples of creating custom deep learning models with the help of TensorFlow Lite using Python. Each project will demonstrate how to integrate deep learning libraries into your mobile apps, right from preparing the model through to deployment.

By the end of this book, you'll have the skills to build and deploy advanced deep learning mobile applications on both iOS and Android.

Who this book is for

This book caters to app developers who wish to leverage the power of deep learning to make better user experiences or who want to bring powerful intelligent features into their applications. At the same time, it also works well for deep learning practitioners who wish to deploy their deep learning models to cross-platform mobile applications.

A basic understanding of how mobile applications work and a good understanding of Python is required for making the best use of this book. Having a high school-level understanding of mathematics is advisable.

What this book covers

Chapter 1, *Introduction to Deep Learning for Mobile*, talks about the emerging importance of deep learning on mobile devices. It covers the basic concepts of machine learning and deep learning, also introducing you to the various options available for integrating deep learning with Android and iOS. The chapter also introduces implementations of deep learning projects using native and cloud-based learning methodologies.

Chapter 2, *Mobile Vision – Face Detection Using On-Device Models*, introduces you to mobile vision and mobile vision models available in ML Kit. You will learn how to create a face detection model in Keras and understand how to convert that to be used for mobile devices. The model uses the Google Cloud Vision API for face detection.

Chapter 3, *Chatbot Using Actions on Google*, helps you to create your own customized chatbot by extending the functionality of Google Assistant. The project provides a good understanding of how to build a product that uses engaging voice and text-based conversational interfaces using Actions on Google and Dialogflow's API.

Chapter 4, *Recognizing Plant Species*, provides an in-depth discussion on how to build a custom Tensorflow Lite model that is able to perform visual recognition tasks using image processing. The model developed runs on mobile devices and is primarily used to recognize different plant species. The model uses a deep **Convolutional Neural Network (CNN)** for visual recognition.

Chapter 5, *Generating Live Captions from a Camera Feed*, presents a method of using a camera feed to generate natural language captions in real time. In this project, you'll create your own camera application that uses a customized pretrained model generated by the image caption generator. The model uses a CNN and **Long Short-Term Memory (LSTM)** for caption generation.

Chapter 6, *Building an Artificial Intelligence Authentication System*, presents you with ways to authenticate users and create a mechanism to identify rare and suspicious user interactions. Upon identification of rare events, that is, those that differ from the majority of data, the user is not allowed to log in, receiving a message saying that a malicious user was detected. This could be of great use when the application in question contains highly secured data, such as confidential emails or virtual banking vaults. The project uses an LSTM-based model on network request headers to perform classification of anomalous logins.

Chapter 7, *Speech/Multimedia Processing – Generating Music Using AI*, explores ways to generate music using AI. You will be introduced to multimedia processing. The chapter demonstrates the methods used to generate music after training on samples. The project uses recurrent neural networks and an LSTM-based model to generate MIDI music files.

Chapter 8, *Reinforced Neural Network-Based Chess Engine*, discusses Google's DeepMind and how reinforced neural networks can be used for machine-assisted gameplay on the Android platform. You will first create a Connect4 engine to get an intuition for building a self-learning, game-playing AI. Then, you will develop a chess engine based on deep reinforcement learning and host it on **Google Cloud Platform** (**GCP**) as an API. Then, you'll use the API for the chess engine to perform gameplay on mobile devices.

Chapter 9, *Building an Image Super-Resolution Application*, presents a method of generating super-resolution images with the help of deep learning. You will learn a third method of handling images on Android/iOS, and how to create TensorFlow models that can be hosted on DigitalOcean and then included in Android/iOS apps. With this model being highly resource-intensive, you will be instructed on how to host the model on the cloud. The project uses generative adversarial networks.

Chapter 10, *Road Ahead*, briefly covers the most popular applications for deep learning in mobile apps today, the current trends, and what is expected to transpire in this field in the future.

To get the most out of this book

You'll need a working Python 3.5+ installation on your local system. It is a good idea to install Python as part of the Anaconda distribution. To build the mobile apps, you'll need a working installation of Flutter 2.0+. Furthermore, you'll often require both TensorFlow 1.x and 2.x throughout the book; hence, having two Anaconda environments is essential:

Software/hardware covered in the book	OS requirements
Jupyter Notebook	Any OS with an updated web browser (preferably Google Chrome/Mozilla Firefox/Apple Safari).Minimum RAM requirement: 4 GB; however, 8 GB is recommended.
Microsoft Visual Studio Code	Any OS with more than 4 GB of RAM; however, 8 GB is recommended.
Smartphone with developer access	Android/iOS with at least 2 GB of RAM; however, 3 GB is recommended.

All the software tools you'll need in this book are freely available. However, you'll have to add your credit/debit card details to your account to activate GCP or DigitalOcean platforms.

If you are using the digital version of this book, we advise you to type the code yourself or access the code via the GitHub repository (link available in the next section). Doing so will help you avoid any potential errors related to the copying and pasting of the code.

Deep learning on Flutter mobile applications is at a very early stage of development. Upon reading this book, if you write blogs and make videos on how to perform machine learning or deep learning on mobile apps, you'll be contributing strongly to the growing ecosystem of both app developers and machine learning practitioners.

Download the example code files

You can download the example code files for this book from your account at `www.packt.com`. If you purchased this book elsewhere, you can visit `www.packtpub.com/support` and register to have the files emailed directly to you.

You can download the code files by following these steps:

1. Log in or register at `www.packt.com`.
2. Select the **Support** tab.
3. Click on **Code Downloads**.
4. Enter the name of the book in the **Search** box and follow the onscreen instructions.

Once the file is downloaded, please make sure that you unzip or extract the folder using the latest version of:

- WinRAR/7-Zip for Windows
- Zipeg/iZip/UnRarX for Mac
- 7-Zip/PeaZip for Linux

The code bundle for the book is also hosted on GitHub at `https://github.com/PacktPublishing/Mobile-Deep-Learning-Projects`. In case there's an update to the code, it will be updated on the existing GitHub repository.

We also have other code bundles from our rich catalog of books and videos available at `https://github.com/PacktPublishing/`. Check them out!

Download the color images

We also provide a PDF file that has color images of the screenshots/diagrams used in this book. You can download it from `https://static.packt-cdn.com/downloads/9781789611212_ColorImages.pdf`.

Conventions used

There are a number of text conventions used throughout this book.

`CodeInText`: Indicates code words in text, database table names, folder names, filenames, file extensions, pathnames, dummy URLs, user input, and Twitter handles. Here is an example: "Notice that the `dialogflow` variable here is an object of the `actions-on-google` module."

A block of code is set as follows:

```
dependencies:
  flutter:
    sdk: flutter
  firebase_ml_vision: ^0.9.2+1
  image_picker: ^0.6.1+4
```

Bold: Indicates a new term, an important word, or words that you see onscreen. For example, words in menus or dialog boxes appear in the text like this. Here is an example: "To proceed to the console, click on the **Start Building** or **Go to Actions Console** buttons."

Warnings or important notes appear like this.

Tips and tricks appear like this.

Get in touch

Feedback from our readers is always welcome.

General feedback: If you have questions about any aspect of this book, mention the book title in the subject of your message and email us at customercare@packtpub.com.

Errata: Although we have taken every care to ensure the accuracy of our content, mistakes do happen. If you have found a mistake in this book, we would be grateful if you would report this to us. Please visit www.packtpub.com/support/errata, selecting your book, clicking on the Errata Submission Form link, and entering the details.

Piracy: If you come across any illegal copies of our works in any form on the Internet, we would be grateful if you would provide us with the location address or website name. Please contact us at copyright@packt.com with a link to the material.

If you are interested in becoming an author: If there is a topic that you have expertise in and you are interested in either writing or contributing to a book, please visit authors.packtpub.com.

Reviews

Please leave a review. Once you have read and used this book, why not leave a review on the site that you purchased it from? Potential readers can then see and use your unbiased opinion to make purchase decisions, we at Packt can understand what you think about our products, and our authors can see your feedback on their book. Thank you!

For more information about Packt, please visit packt.com.

Introduction to Deep Learning for Mobile

1

In this chapter, we will explore the emerging avenues of deep learning on mobile devices. We will briefly discuss the basic concepts of machine learning and deep learning, and we'll introduce the various options available for integrating deep learning with Android and iOS. This chapter also introduces implementations of deep learning projects using native and cloud-based learning methodologies.

In this chapter, we will cover the following topics:

- Growth of **artificial intelligence** (**AI**)-powered mobile devices
- Understanding machine learning and deep learning
- Introducing to some common deep learning architectures
- Introducing to reinforcement learning and **natural language processing** (**NLP**)
- Methods of integrating AI on Android and iOS

Growth of AI-powered mobile devices

AI is becoming more mobile than it used to be, as smaller devices are being packed with more computational power. Mobile devices, which were simply used to make phone calls and send text messages, have now been transformed into smartphones with the introduction of AI. These devices are now capable of leveraging the ever-increasing power of AI to learn user behavior and preferences, enhance photographs, carry out full-fledged conversations, and much more. The capabilities of an AI-powered smartphone is expected to only grow day by day. According to Gartner, by 2022, 80% of smartphones will be AI-enabled.

Changes in hardware to support AI

To cope with the high computational powers of AI, there have been regular changes and enhancements in hardware support of cellphones to provide them with the ability to think and act. Mobile manufacturing companies have been constantly upgrading hardware support on mobile devices to provide a seamless and personalized user experience.

Huawei has launched the Kirin 970 SoC, which enables on-device AI experiences using a specially dedicated neural network processing unit. Apple devices are fitted with an AI chip called *neural engine*, which is a part of the A11 Bionic chip. It is dedicated to machine learning and deep learning tasks such as facial and voice recognition, recording animojis, and object detection while capturing a picture. Qualcomm and MediaTek have released their own chips that enable on-device AI solutions. Exynos 9810, announced by Samsung, is a chip that is based on neural networks such as Snapdragon 845 of Qualcomm. The 2018 Samsung devices, Galaxy S9 and S9+, included these chips based on the country where they are marketed. With it's Galaxy S9, the company made it pretty evident that it would integrate AI to improve the functioning of the device's camera and translation of text in real time. The latest Samsung Galaxy S10 series is powered by the Qualcomm Snapdragon 855 to support on-device AI computations.

Google Translate Word Lens and the Bixby personal assistant have been used to develop the feature. With the technologies in place, it is possible for the device to translate up to 54 languages. The phones, which are smart enough to decide between a sensor of f/2.4 and f/1.5, are well suited for capturing photographs in low-light conditions. Google Pixel 2 leverages the power of machine learning to integrate eight image processing units using its coprocessor, Pixel Visual Core.

Why do mobile devices need to have AI chips?

The incorporation of AI chips has not only helped to achieve greater efficiency and computational power, but it has also preserved the user's data and privacy. The advantages of including AI chips on mobile devices can be listed as follows:

- **Performance**: The CPUs of mobile devices in the current date are unsuitable to the demands of machine learning. Attempts to deploy machine learning models on these devices often results in slow service and a faster battery drain, leading to bad user experience. This is because the CPUs lack the efficiency to do enormous amounts of small calculations as required by the AI computations. AI chips, somewhat similar to **Graphical Processing Units (GPU)** chips that are responsible for handling graphics on devices, provide a separate space to perform calculations exclusively related to machine learning and deep learning processes. This allows the CPU to focus its time on other important tasks. With the incorporation of specialized AI hardware, the performance and battery life of devices have improved.

- **User privacy**: The hardware also ensures the increased safety of the user's privacy and security. In traditional mobile devices, data analysis and machine learning processes would require chunks of the user's data to be sent to the cloud, posing a threat to the user's data privacy and security of mobile devices. With the on-device AI chips in action, all of the required analyses and calculations can be performed offline on the device itself. This incorporation of dedicated hardware in mobile devices has tremendously reduced the risks of a user's data getting hacked or leaked.

- **Efficiency**: In the real world, tasks such as image recognition and processing could be a lot faster with the incorporation of AI chips. The neural network processing unit by Huawei is a well-suited example here. It can recognize images with an efficiency of 2,000 pictures per second. The company claims that this is 20 times faster than the time taken by a standard CPU. When working with 16-bit floating-point numbers, it can perform 1.92 teraflops, or 1 trillion floating operations every second. The neural engine by Apple can handle around 600 billion operations per second.

- **Economy**: On-device AI chips reduce the need to send data off into the cloud. This capability empowers users to access the services offline and save data. Therefore, people using the applications are saved from paying for the servers. This is advantageous to users as well as developers.

Let's look at a brief overview of how AI on mobile devices has impacted the way we interact with our smartphones.

Improved user experience with AI on mobile devices

The use of AI has greatly enhanced user experience on mobile devices. This can be broadly categorized into the following categories.

Personalization

Personalization primarily means modifying a service or a product to suit a specific individual's preferences, sometimes related to clusters of individuals. On mobile devices, the use of AI helps to improve user experience by making the device and apps adapt to a user's habits and their unique profile instead of generic profile-oriented applications. The AI algorithms on mobile devices leverage the available user-specific data, such as location, purchase history, and behavior patterns, to predict and personalize present and future interactions such as a user's preferred activity or music during a particular time of the day.

For instance, AI collects data on the user's purchase history and compiles it with the other data that is obtained from online traffic, mobile devices, sensors embedded in electronic devices, and vehicles. This compiled data is then used to analyze the user's behavior and allow brands to take necessary actions to enhance the user engagement rate. Therefore, users can leverage the benefits of AI-empowered applications to get personalized results, which will reduce their scrolling time and let them explore more products and services.

The best examples out there are recommendation systems running through shopping platforms such as Walmart, Amazon, or media platforms such as YouTube or Netflix.

 In the year 2011, Amazon reported a 29% sales increase to $12.83 billion, which was up from $9.9 billion. With its most successful recommendation rate, 35% of Amazon's sales come from customers who followed the recommendations generated by its product recommendation engine.

Virtual assistants

A virtual assistant is an application that understands voice commands and completes tasks for the user. They are able to interpret human speech using **Natural Language Understanding** (**NLU**) and generally respond via synthesized voices. You might use a virtual assistant for nearly all of the tasks that a real personal assistant would do for you, that is, making calls to people on your behalf, taking notes that you dictate, turning on or turning off the lights in your home/office with the help of home automation, play music for you, or even simply talk to you about any topic you'd like to talk about! A virtual assistant might be able to take commands in the form of text, audio, or visual gestures. Virtual assistants adapt to user habits over time and get smarter.

Leveraging the power of NLP, a virtual assistant can recognize commands from spoken language, and identify people and pets from images that you upload to your assistant or keep in any online album that is accessible to them.

The most popular virtual assistants on the market right now are Alexa by Amazon, Google Assistant, iPhone's Siri, Cortana by Microsoft, and Bixby running on Samsung devices. Some of the virtual assistants are passive listeners and respond only when they receive a specific wake up command. For example, Google Assistant can be activated using "Hey Google" or "OK Google", and can then be commanded to switch off the lights using "Switch off the bedroom lights" or can be used to call a person from your contacts list using "Make a call to <contact name>". In Google IO '18, Google unveiled the Duplex phone-calling reservation AI, demonstrating that Google Assistant would not only be capable of making a call, but it could also carry on a conversation and potentially book a reservation in a hair salon all by itself.

The use of virtual assistants is growing exponentially and is expected to reach 1.8 billion users by 2021. 54% of users agreed that virtual assistants help make daily tasks simpler, and 31% already use assistants in their daily lives. Additionally, 64% of users take advantage of virtual assistants for more than one purpose.

Facial recognition

The technology that is powerful enough to identify or verify a face or understand a facial expression from digital images and videos is known as facial recognition. This system generally works by comparing the most common and prominent facial features from a given image with the faces stored in a database. Facial recognition also has the ability to understand patterns and variations based on an individual's facial textures and shape to uniquely recognize a person and is often described as a biometric AI-based application.

Initially, facial recognition was a form of computer application; however, recently, it is being widely used on mobile platforms. Facial recognition, accompanied by biometrics such as fingerprint and iris recognition, finds a common application in security systems on mobile devices. Generally, the process of facial recognition is performed in two steps—feature extraction and selection is the first, and the classification of objects is the second. Later developments have introduced several other methods, such as the use of the facial recognition algorithm, three-dimensional recognition, skin texture analysis, and thermal cameras.

Face ID, introduced in Apple's iPhone X, is a biometric authentication successor to the fingerprint-based authentication system found in several Android-based smartphones. The facial recognition sensor of Face ID consists of two parts: a `Romeo` module and a `Juliet` module. The `Romeo` module is responsible for projecting over 30,000 infrared dots on to the face of the user. The counterpart of this module, the `Juliet` module, reads the pattern formed by the dots on the user's face. The pattern is then sent to an on-device `Secure Enclave` module in the CPU of the device to confirm whether the face matches with the owner or not. These facial patterns cannot be directly accessed by Apple. The system does not allow the authorization to work when the eyes of the user are closed, which is an added layer of security.

The technology learns from changes in a user's appearance and works with makeup, beards, spectacles, sunglasses, and hats. It also works in the dark. The **Flood Illuminator** is a dedicated infrared flash that projects invisible infrared light on to the user's face to properly read the facial points and helps the system to function in low-light conditions or even complete darkness. Contrary to iPhones, Samsung devices primarily rely on two-dimensional facial recognition accompanied by an iris scanner that works as a biometric recognition in Galaxy Note 8. The leading premium smartphone seller in India, OnePlus, also depends on only two-dimensional facial recognition.

 The global market for software taking benefit of facial recognition is expected to grow from $3.85 billion USD in 2017 to $9.78 billion USD by 2023. The Asia Pacific region, which holds around 16% of its market share, is the fastest-growing region.

AI-powered cameras

The integration of AI in cameras has empowered them to recognize, understand, and enhance scenes and photographs. AI cameras are able to understand and control the various parameters of cameras. These cameras work on the principles of a digital image processing technique called **computational photography**. It uses algorithms instead of optical processes seeking to use machine vision to identify and improve the contents of a picture. These cameras use deep learning models that are trained on a huge dataset of images, comprising several million samples, to automatically identify scenes, the availability of light, and the angle of the scene being captured.

When the camera is pointed in the right direction, the AI algorithms of the camera take over to change the settings of the camera to produce the best quality image. Under the hood, the system that enables AI-powered photography is not simple. The models used are highly optimized to produce the correct camera settings upon detection of the features of the scene to be captured in almost real time. They may also add dynamic exposure, color adjustments, and the best possible effect for the image. Sometimes, the images might be postprocessed automatically by the AI models instead of being processed during the clicking of the photograph in order to reduce the computational overhead of the device.

Nowadays, mobile devices are generally equipped with dual-lens cameras. These cameras use two lenses to add the bokeh effect (which is Japanese for "blur") on pictures. The **bokeh** effect adds a blurry sense to the background around the main subject, making it aesthetically pleasing. AI-based algorithms assist in simulating the effect that identifies the subject and blurs the remaining portion producing portrait effects.

The Google Pixel 3 camera works in two shooting modes called **Top Shot** and **Photobooth**. The camera initially captures several frames before and after the moment that the user is attempting to capture. The AI models that are available in the device are then able to pick the best frame. This is made possible by the vast amount of training that is provided to the image recognition system of the camera, which is then able to select the best-looking pictures, almost as if a human were picking them. **Photobooth** mode allows the user to simply hold the device toward a scene of action, and the images are automatically taken at the moment that the camera predicts to be a picture-perfect moment.

Predictive text

Predictive text is an input technology, generally used in messaging applications, that suggests words to the user depending on the words and phrases that are being entered. The prediction following each keypress is unique rather than producing a repeated sequence of letters in the same constant order. Predictive text can allow an entire word to be inputted by a single keypress, which can significantly speed up the input process. This makes input writing tasks such as typing a text message, writing an email, or making an entry into an address book highly efficient with the use of fewer device keys. The predictive text system links the user's preferred interface style and their level of learned ability to operate the predictive text software. The system eventually gets smarter by analyzing and adapting to the user's language. The T9 dictionary is a good example of such text predictors. It analyzes the frequency of words used and results in multiple most probable words. It is also capable of considering combinations of words.

Quick Type is a predictive text feature that was announced by Apple in its iOS 8 release. It uses machine learning and NLP, which allows the software to build custom dictionaries based on the user's typing habits. These dictionaries are later used for predictions. These prediction systems also depend on the context of the conversation, and they are capable of distinguishing between formal and informal languages. Additionally, it supports multiple languages around the world, including U.S. English, U.K. English, Canadian English, Australian English, French, German, Italian, Brazilian Portuguese, Spanish, and Thai.

Google also introduced a new feature that would help users compose and send emails faster than before. The feature, called Smart Compose, understands the text typed in so that AI can suggest words and phrases to finish sentences. The Smart Compose feature helps users to save time while writing emails by correcting spelling mistakes and grammatical errors, along with suggesting the words that are most commonly typed by users. Smart Reply is another feature, similar to reply suggestions in LinkedIn messaging, which suggests replies that can be sent on a single click, according to the context of the email received by the user. For example, if the user receives an email congratulating them of an accepted application, it is likely that the Smart Reply feature would give options to reply with—"Thank you!," "Thanks for letting me know," and "Thank you for accepting my application." Users can then click on the preferred reply and send a quick response.

In the 1940s, Lin Yutang created a typewriter in which actuating keys suggested the characters following the selected ones.

Most popular mobile applications that use AI

In recent times, we have seen a great surge in the number of applications incorporating AI into their features for increased user engagement and customized service delivery. In this section, we will briefly discuss how some of the largest players in the domain of mobile apps have leveraged the benefits of AI to boost their business.

Netflix

The best and the most popular example of machine learning in mobile apps is Netflix. The application uses linear regression, logistic regression, and other machine learning algorithms to provide the user with a perfect personalized recommendation experience. The content that is classified by actors, genre, length, reviews, years, and more is used to train the machine learning algorithms. All of these machine learning algorithms learn and adapt to the user's actions, choices, and preferences. For example, John watched the first episode of a new television series but didn't really like it, so he won't watch the subsequent episodes. The recommendation systems involved in Netflix understand that he does not prefer TV shows of that kind and removes them from his recommendations. Similarly, if John picked the eighth recommendation from the recommendations lists or wrote a bad review after watching a movie trailer, the algorithms involved try to adapt to his behavior and preferences to provide extremely personalized content.

Seeing AI

Seeing AI, developed by Microsoft, is an intelligent camera app that uses computer vision to audibly help blind and visually impaired people to know about their surroundings. It comes with functionalities such as reading out short text and documents for the user, giving a description about a person, identifying currencies, colors, handwriting, light, and even images in other apps using the device's camera. To make the app this advanced and responsive in real time, developers have used the idea of making servers communicate with Microsoft Cognitive Services. OCR, barcode scanner, facial recognition, and scene recognition are the most powerful technologies brought together by the application to provide users with a collection of wonderful functionalities.

Allo

Allo was an AI-centric messaging app developed by Google. As of March 2019, Allo has been discontinued. However, it was an important milestone in the journey of AI-powered apps at Google. The application allowed users to perform an action on their Android phones via their voice. It used Smart Reply, a feature that suggested words and phrases by analyzing the context of the conversation. The application was not just limited to text. In fact, it was equally capable of analyzing images shared during a conversation and suggesting replies. This was made possible by powerful image recognition algorithms. Later, this Smart Reply feature was also implemented in the Google inbox and is now present in the Gmail app.

English Language Speech Assistant

English Language Speech Assistant (ELSA), which is rated among the top five AI-based applications, is the world's smartest AI pronunciation tutor. The mobile application helps people improve their pronunciation. It is designed as an adventure game, differentiated by levels. Each level presents a set of words for the user to pronounce, which is taken as input. The user's response is examined carefully to point out their mistakes and help them improve. When the application detects a wrong pronunciation, it teaches the user the correct one by instructing them about the correct movements of the lips and the tongue so that the word is said correctly.

Socratic

Socratic, a tutor application, allows a user to take pictures of mathematical problems and gives answers explaining the theory behind it, with details of how it should be solved. The application is not just limited to mathematics. Currently, it can help a user in 23 different subjects, including English, physics, chemistry, history, psychology, and calculus. Using the power of AI to analyze the required information, the application returns videos with step-by-step solutions. The application's algorithm, combined with computer vision technology, has the capability to read questions from images. Furthermore, it uses machine learning classifiers trained on millions of sample questions, which helps with the accurate prediction of concepts involved in solving a question.

Now, let's take a deeper look at machine learning and deep learning.

Understanding machine learning and deep learning

It is important to understand a few key concepts of machine learning and deep learning before you are able to work on solutions that are inclusive of the technologies and algorithms associated with the domain of AI. When we talk about the current state of AI, we often mean systems where we are able to churn a huge amount of data to find patterns and make predictions based on those patterns.

While the term "artificial intelligence" might bring up images of talking humanoid robots or cars that drive by themselves to a layman, to a person studying the field, the images might instead be in the form of graphs and networks of interconnected computing modules.

In the next section, we will begin with an introduction to machine learning.

Understanding machine learning

In the year 1959, Arthur Samuel coined the term **machine learning**. In a gentle rephrasing of his definition of machine learning, the field of computer science that enables machines to learn from past experiences and produce predictions based on them when provided with unknown input is called machine learning.

A more precise definition of machine learning can be stated as follows:

- A computer program that improves its performance, P, on any task, T, by learning from its experience, E, regarding task T, is called a machine learning program.
- Using the preceding definition, in an analogy that is common at the moment, T is a task related to prediction, while P is the measure of accuracy achieved by a computer program while performing the task, T, based upon what the program was able to learn, and the learning is called E. With the increase of E, the computer program makes better predictions, which means that P is improved because the program performs task T with higher accuracy.

- In the real world, you might come across a teacher teaching a pupil to perform a certain task and then evaluating the skill of the pupil at performing the task by making the pupil take an examination. The more training that the pupil receives, the better they will be able to perform the task, and the better their score will be in the examination.

In the next section, let's try to understand deep learning.

Understanding deep learning

We have been hearing the term **learning** for a long time, and in several contexts where it usually means gaining experience at performing a task. However, what would **deep** mean when prefixed to "learning"?

In computer science, deep learning refers to a machine learning model that has more than one layer of learning involved. What this means is that the computer program is composed of multiple algorithms through which the data passes one by one to finally produce the desired output.

Deep learning systems are created using the concept of neural networks. Neural networks are compositions of layers of neurons connected together such that data passes from one layer of neurons to another until it reaches the final or the output layer. Each layer of neurons gets data input in a form that may or may not be the same as the form in which the data was initially provided as input to the neural network.

Consider the following diagram of a neural network:

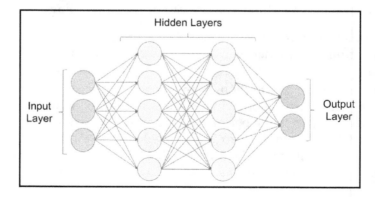

A few terms are introduced in the preceding screenshot. Let's discuss each one of them briefly.

The input layer

The layer that holds the input values is called the input layer. Some argue that this layer is not actually a layer but only a variable that holds the data, and hence is the data itself, instead of being a layer. However, the dimensions of the matrix holding the layer are important and must be defined correctly for the neural network to communicate to the first hidden layer; therefore, it is conceptually a layer that holds data.

The hidden layers

Any layer that is an intermediary between the input layer and the output layer is called a hidden layer. A typical neural network used in production environments may contain hundreds of input layers. Often, hidden layers contain a greater number of neurons than either the input or the output layer. However, in some special circumstances, this might not hold true. Having a greater number of neurons in the hidden layers is usually done to process the data in a dimension other than the input. This allows the program to reach insights or patterns that may not be visible in the data in the format it is present in when the user feeds it into the network.

The complexity of a neural network is directly dependent on the number of layers of neurons in the network. While a neural network may discover deeper patterns in the data by adding more layers, it also adds to the computational expensiveness of the network. It is also possible that the network passes into an erroneous state called **overfitting**. On the contrary, if the network is too simple, or, in other words, is not adequately deep, it will reach another erroneous state called **underfitting**.

 You can learn more about overfitting and underfitting at `https://towardsdatascience.com/overfitting-vs-underfitting-a-conceptual-explanation-d94ee20ca7f9`.

The output layer

The final layer in which the desired output is produced and stored is called the output layer. This layer often corresponds to the number of desired output categories or has a single neuron holding the desired regression output.

The activation function

Each layer in the neural network undergoes the application of a function called the **activation function**. This function plays the role of keeping the data contained inside neurons within a normalized range, which would otherwise grow too large or too small and lead to errors in the computation relating to the handling of large decimal coefficients or large numbers in computers. Additionally, it is the activation function that enables the neural network to handle the non-linearity of patterns in data.

Introducing some common deep learning architectures

After a brief revision of the key terms, we are now ready to dive deeper into the world of deep learning. In this section, we will be learning about some famous deep learning algorithms and how they work.

Convolutional neural networks

Inspired from the animal visual cortex, a **convolutional neural network** (**CNN**) is primarily used for, and is the de facto standard for, image processing. The core concept of the convolutional layer is the presence of kernels (or filters) that learn to differentiate between the features of an image. A kernel is usually a much shorter matrix than the image matrix and is passed over the entire image in a sliding-window fashion, producing a dot product of the kernel with the corresponding slice of matrix from the image to be processed. The dot product allows the program to identify the features in the image.

Consider the following image vector:

```
[[10, 10, 10, 0, 0, 0],
 [10, 10, 10, 0, 0, 0],
 [10, 10, 10, 0, 0, 0],
 [0, 0, 0, 10, 10, 10],
 [0, 0, 0, 10, 10, 10],
 [0, 0, 0, 10, 10, 10]]
```

The preceding matrix corresponds to an image that looks like this:

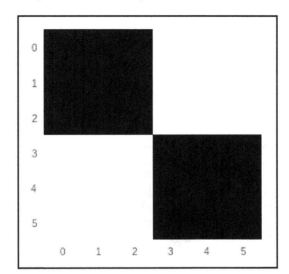

On applying a filter to detect horizontal edges, the filter is defined by the following matrix:

```
[[1,  1,  1],
 [0,  0,  0],
 [-1, -1, -1]]
```

The output matrix produced after the convolution of the original image with the filter is as follows:

```
[[  0,  0,   0,   0],
 [ 30, 10, -10, -30],
 [ 30, 10, -10, -30],
 [  0,  0,   0,   0]]
```

There are no edges detected in the upper half or lower half of the image. On moving toward the vertical middle of the image from the left edge, a clear horizontal edge is found. On moving further right, two unclear instances of a horizontal edge are found before another clear instance of a horizontal edge. However, the clear horizontal edge found now is in the opposite color as the previous one.

Thus, by simple convolutions, it is possible to uncover patterns in the image files. CNNs also use several other concepts, such as pooling.

It is possible to understand pooling from the following screenshot:

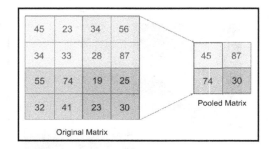

In the simplest terms, pooling is the method of consolidating several image pixels into a single pixel. The pooling method used in the preceding screenshot is known as **max pooling**, wherein only the largest value from the selected sliding-window kernel is kept in the resultant matrix. This greatly simplifies the image and helps to train filters that are generic and not exclusive to a single image.

Generative adversarial networks

Generative adversarial networks (**GANs**) are a fairly new concept in the field of AI and have come as a major breakthrough in recent times. They were introduced by Ian Goodfellow in his research paper, in 2014. The core idea behind a GAN is the parallel run of two neural networks that compete against each other. The first neural network performs the task of generating samples and is called the **generator**. The other neural network tries to classify the sample based on the data previously provided and is called the **discriminator**. The functioning of GANs can be understood with the following screenshot:

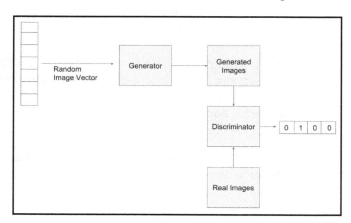

Here, the random image vector undergoes a generative process to produce fake images that are then classified by the discriminator that has been trained with the real images. The fake images with higher classification confidence are further used for generation, while the ones with lower confidence are discarded. Over time, the discriminator learns to correctly recognize fake images, while the generator learns to produce images that resemble the real images increasingly after each generation.

What we have at the end of the learning is a system that can produce near-real data, and also a system that can classify samples with very high precision.

We will learn more about GANs in the upcoming chapters.

 For an in-depth study of GANs, you can read the research paper by Ian Goodfellow at `https://arxiv.org/abs/1406.2661`.

Recurrent neural networks

Not all data in the world exists independently of time. Stock market prices and spoken/written words are just a few examples of data that is bound to a time series. Therefore, the sequence of data has a temporal dimension, and you might assume that being able to use it in the manner befitting to data, which comes with the passage of time instead of a chunk of data that remains constant, would be more intuitive and would produce better prediction accuracy. In many cases, this has been found to be true and has led to the emergence of neural network architectures that can take time as a factor while learning and predicting.

One such architecture is the **recurrent neural network** (**RNN**). The major characteristic of such a network is that it not only passes data from one layer to another in a sequential manner, but it also takes data from any previous layer. Recall from the *Understanding machine learning and deep learning* section the diagram of a simple **artificial neural network** (**ANN**) with two hidden layers. The data was being fed into the next layer by the previous layer only. In an RNN with, say, two hidden layers, it is not mandatory for the input to the second hidden layer be provided only by the first hidden layer, as would be the case in a simple ANN.

This is depicted by the dashed arrows in the following screenshot:

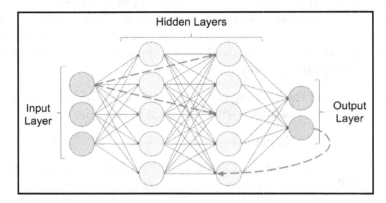

RNNs, in contrast to simple ANNs, use a method called **backpropagation through time** (**BPTT**) instead of the classic backpropagation in ANNs. BPTT ensures that time is well represented in the backward propagation of the error by defining it in functions relating to the input that has to recur in the network.

Long short-term memory

It is very common to observe **vanishing** and **exploding** gradients in RNNs. These are a severe bottleneck in the implementation of deep RNNs where the data is present in a form where relationships between features are more complex than linear functions. To overcome the vanishing gradient problem, the concept of **long short-term memory** (**LSTM**) was introduced by German researchers Sepp Hochreiter and Juergen Schmidhuber, in 1997.

LSTM has proved highly useful in the fields of NLP, image caption generation, speech recognition, and other domains, where it broke previously established records after it was introduced. LSTMs store information outside the network that can be recalled at any moment, much like a secondary storage device in a computer system. This allows for delayed rewards to be introduced to the network. A spiritual analogy of LSTMs has been made, which calls it the "karma" or reward that a person receives for their actions carried out in the past.

We shall be diving deeper into LSTMs and CNNs in the upcoming chapters of this book.

Introducing reinforcement learning and NLP

In this section, we shall be studying the basic concepts of reinforcement learning and NLP. These are some very important topics in the field of AI. They may or may not use deep learning networks for their implementations, but they are quite often implemented using deep networks. Therefore, it is crucial to understand how they function.

Reinforcement learning

Reinforcement learning is a branch of machine learning that deals with creating AI "agents" that perform a set of possible actions in a given environment in order to maximize a reward. While the other two branches of machine learning—supervised and unsupervised machine learning—usually perform learning on a dataset in the format of a table, reinforcement learning agents mostly learn using a decision tree to be made in any given situation such that the decision tree eventually leads to the leaf that has the maximum reward.

For example, consider a humanoid robot that wishes to learn to walk. It could first start by shoving both of its legs in front of itself, in which case it would fall, and the reward, which, in this case, is the distance covered by the humanoid robot, would be 0. It will then learn to add a certain amount of delay between the previous leg being put forward and the next leg being put forward. Due to this certain amount of delay, it could be that the robot is able to take $x1$ steps before, once again, both feet simultaneously push outward and it falls down.

Reinforcement learning deploys the concept of **exploration**, which means the search for a better solution, and **exploitation**, which means the usage of previously gained knowledge. Continuing our example, since $x1$ is greater than 0, the algorithm learns to put approximately the same certain amount of delay between the strides. Over time, with the combined effect of exploitation and exploration, reinforcement learning algorithms become very strong, and the humanoid, in this case, is able to learn not only how to walk but also run.

NLP

NLP is a vast field of AI that deals with the processing and understanding of human languages through the use of computer algorithms. NLP comprises several methods and techniques that are each geared toward a different part of human language understanding, such as understanding meaning based on the similarity of two text extracts, generating human language responses, understanding questions or instructions made in human languages, and the translation of text from one language to another.

NLP has found vast usage in the current world of technology with several top tech companies running toward excellence in the field. There are several voice-based user assistants, such as Siri, Cortana, and Google Assistant, that heavily depend upon accurate NLP in order to perform their functions correctly. NLP has also found usage in customer support with automated customer support platforms that reply to the most frequently made queries without the need of a human representative answering them. These NLP-based customer support systems can also learn from the responses made by the real representative while they interact with customers. One such major system in deployment can be found in the **Help** section of the DBS DigiBank application created by the Development Bank of Singapore.

Extensive research is underway in this domain, and it is expected to dominate every other field of AI in the upcoming days. In the next section, let's take a look at what the currently available methods of integrating deep learning with mobile applications are.

Methods of integrating AI on Android and iOS

With the ever-increasing popularity of AI, mobile application users expect apps to adapt to the information that is provided and made available to them. The only way to make applications adaptive to the data is by deploying fine-tuned machine learning models to provide a delightful user experience.

Firebase ML Kit

Firebase ML Kit is a machine learning **Software Development Kit** (**SDK**) that is available on Firebase for mobile developers. It facilitates the hosting and serving of mobile machine learning models. It reduces the heavy tasks of running machine learning models on mobile devices to API calls that cover common mobile use cases such as face detection, text recognition, barcode scanning, image labeling, and landmark recognition. It simply takes input as parameters in order to output a bunch of analytical information. The APIs provided by ML Kit can run on the device, on the cloud, or on both. The on-device APIs are independent of network connections and, consequently, work faster compared to cloud-based APIs. The cloud-based APIs are hosted on the Google Cloud Platform and uses machine learning technology to provide a higher level of accuracy. If the available APIs do not cover the required use case, custom TensorFlow Lite models can be built, hosted, and served using the Firebase console. The ML Kit acts as an API layer between the custom models, making it easy to run. Let's look at the following screenshot:

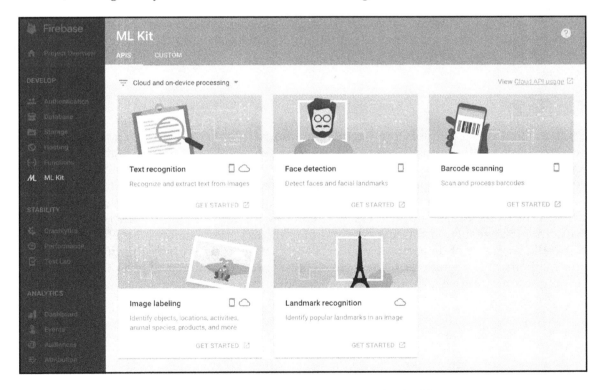

Here, you can see what the dashboard for Firebase ML Kit looks like.

Core ML

Core ML, a machine learning framework released by Apple in iOS 11, is used to make applications running on iOS, such as Siri, Camera, and QuickType more intelligent. Delivering efficient performance, Core ML facilitates the easy integration of machine learning models on iOS devices, giving the applications the power to analyze and predict from the available data. Standard machine learning models such as tree ensembles, SVMs, and generalized linear models are supported by Core ML. It contains extensive deep learning models with over 30 types of neuron layers.

Using the Vision framework, features such as face tracking, face detection, text detection, and object tracking can be easily integrated with the apps. The Natural Language framework helps to analyze natural text and deduce its language-specific metadata. When used with Create ML, the framework can be used to deploy custom NLP models. The support for GamePlayKit helps in the evaluation of learned decision trees. Core ML is highly efficient as it is built on top of low-level technologies such as Metal and Accelerate. This allows it to take advantage of the CPU and GPU. Moreover, Core ML does not require an active network connection to run. It has high on-device optimizations. This ensures that all of the computations are done offline, within the device itself, minimizing memory footprint and power consumption.

Caffe2

Built on the original **Convolution Architecture for Fast Embedding (Caffe)**, which was developed at the University of California, Berkeley, Caffe2 is a lightweight, modular, and scalable deep learning framework developed by Facebook. It helps developers and researchers deploy machine learning models and deliver AI-powered performance on Android, iOS, and Raspberry Pi. Additionally, it supports integration in Android Studio, Microsoft Visual Studio, and Xcode. Caffe2 comes with native Python and C++ APIs that work interchangeably, facilitating easy prototyping and optimizations. It is efficient enough to handle large sets of data, and it facilitates automation, image processing, and statistical and mathematical operations. Caffe2, which is open source and hosted on GitHub, leverages community contributions for new models and algorithms.

TensorFlow

TensorFlow, an open source software library developed by Google Brain, facilitates high-performance numerical computation. Due to its flexible architecture, it allows easy deployment of deep learning models and neural networks across CPUs, GPUs, and TPUs. Gmail uses a TensorFlow model to understand the context of a message and predicts replies in its widely known feature, Smart Reply. TensorFlow Lite is a lightweight version of TensorFlow that aids the deployment of machine learning models on Android and iOS devices. It leverages the power of the Android Neural Network API to support hardware acceleration.

The TensorFlow ecosystem, which is available for mobile devices through TensorFlow Lite, is illustrated in the following diagram:

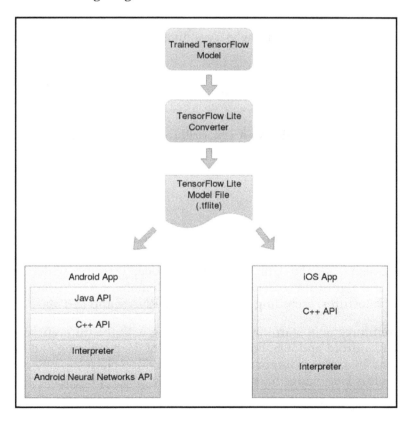

In the preceding diagram, you can see that we need to convert a TensorFlow model into a TensorFlow Lite model before we can use it on mobile devices. This is important because TensorFlow models are bulkier and suffer more latency than the Lite models, which are optimized to run on mobile devices. The conversion is carried out through the TF Lite converter, which can be used in the following ways:

- Using Python APIs: The conversion of a TensorFlow model into a TensorFlow Lite model can be carried out using Python, with any of the following lines of code:

```
TFLiteConverter.from_saved_model(): Converts SavedModel
directories.
TFLiteConverter.from_keras_model(): Converts tf.keras models.
TFLiteConverter.from_concrete_functions(): Converts concrete
functions.
```

- Using the command-line tool: The TensorFlow Lite converter is available as a CLI tool as well, albeit it is somewhat less diverse in its capabilities than the Python API version:

```
tflite_convert \
  --saved_model_dir=/tf_model \
  --output_file=/tflite_model.tflite
```

We will demonstrate the conversion of a TensorFlow model into a TensorFlow Lite model in the upcoming chapters.

Summary

In this chapter, we learned about the growth of AI in mobile devices, which provides machines with the ability to reason and make decisions without being explicitly programmed. We also studied machine learning and deep learning, which are inclusive of the technologies and algorithms associated with the domain of AI. We looked at various deep learning architectures, including CNNs, GANs, RNNs, and LSTMs.

We introduced reinforcement learning and NLP, along with the different methods of integrating AI on Android and iOS. Basic knowledge of deep learning and of how we can integrate it with mobile apps is important for the upcoming chapters, where we shall be extensively using this knowledge to create some real-world applications.

In the next chapter, we will learn about face detection using on-device models.

2
Mobile Vision - Face Detection Using On-Device Models

In this chapter, we will build a Flutter application that is capable of detecting faces from media uploaded from the gallery of a device or directly from the camera using the ML Kit's Firebase Vision Face Detection API. The API leverages the power of pre-trained models hosted on Firebase and provides the application, the ability to identify the key features of a face, detect the expression, and get the contours of the detected faces. As the face detection is performed in real time by the API, it can also be used to track faces in a video sequence, in a video chat, or in games that respond to the user's expression. The application, coded in Dart, will work efficiently on Android and iOS devices.

In this chapter, we will be covering the following topics:

- Introduction to image processing
- Developing a face detection application using Flutter

Let's begin with a brief introduction into how image recognition works!

Technical requirements

You require Visual Studio Code with Flutter and the Dart plugin, and will need to setup the Firebase console. The GitHub repository for this chapter is at `https://github.com/PacktPublishing/Mobile-Deep-Learning-Projects/tree/master/Chapter2`.

Introduction to image processing

In this chapter, we shall be detecting faces in images. In the context of artificial intelligence, the action of processing an image for the purpose of extracting information about the visual content of that image is called image processing.

Image processing is an emerging field, thanks to the surge in the number of better AI-powered cameras, medical imagery-based machine learning, self-driving vehicles, analysis of people's emotions from images, and many other applications.

Consider the use of image processing by a self-driving vehicle. The vehicle needs to make decisions in as close to real time as possible to ensure the best possible accident-free driving. A delay in the response of the AI model running the car could lead to catastrophic consequences. Several techniques and algorithms have been developed for fast and accurate image processing. One of the most famous algorithms in the domain of image processing is the **convolutional neural network (CNN)**.

We will not be developing a complete CNN in this chapter, however, we have briefly discussed CNNs in `Chapter 1`, *Introduction to Deep Learning for Mobile*. Later, we shall build a face detection Flutter app using a pre-trained model that's present on the device.

Understanding images

Before we delve into the processing of images, let's discuss the anatomy of an image from the perspective of computer software. Consider the following simple image:

The preceding image is a 10 x 10 pixel image (zoomed in); the top two rows of pixels are purple, the next six rows of pixels are red and the last two rows of pixels are in yellow.

However, the computer does not see the colors in this image. The computer sees this image in the format of a matrix of pixel densities. We are dealing with an RGB image here. RGB images are composed of three layers of colors—namely red, green, and blue. Each of these layers is represented by a matrix in the image. The elements of each matrix correspond to the intensity of the color represented by that matrix in each pixel of the image.

Let's examine the preceding image in a program. One of the two rows of pixels that is purple is represented by the following array:

```
[[255, 0, 255],
[255, 0, 255],
[255, 0, 255],
[255, 0, 255],
[255, 0, 255],
[255, 0, 255],
[255, 0, 255],
[255, 0, 255],
[255, 0, 255],
[255, 0, 255]]
```

In the preceding matrix, the first column of 255 represents the color red. The second column represents green and the third column represents blue. Thus, the first pixel of the image on the top left corner is a combination of red, green, and blue. Both red and blue are at their full intensities, while green is entirely missing. Thus, as expected, the combined color produced is purple, which is essentially red and blue mixed in equal proportions. If we observe any pixel from the red region of the image, as expected, we get the following array:

```
[ 255, 0, 0 ]
```

Similarly, from the yellow region, since the color yellow is a combination of red and green in equal proportions, the pixel is represented by this:

```
[ 255, 255, 0 ]
```

Now, if we turn off the red and green components of the image, keeping only the blue channel on, we get the following image:

This is very much according to our previous observation that only the top two rows of pixels contain the blue component and the rest of the image has no blue component, hence it is depicted in black, which indicates the absence of intensity, or 0 intensity of blue.

Manipulating images

In this section, we shall be discussing how some common manipulations on images can be done to aid with image processing. Often, some simple manipulations on images can lead to quicker and better predictions.

Rotation

Let's say we wish to rotate the image in our example by 90 degrees. If we examine the first row of pixels from the top after the rotation, we would expect that the first two pixels of the row would be purple, the middle six would be red, and the last two would be yellow. In the analogy of rotation of matrices, this might be seen as a transpose operation wherein the rows are converted to columns and vice versa. The image then looks like this:

And, as expected, the first row of pixels is represented by the following matrix:

```
[[255,    0, 255],
 [255, 0, 255],
 [255, 0,   0],
 [255, 0,   0],
 [255, 0,   0],
 [255, 0,   0],
 [255, 0,   0],
 [255, 0,   0],
 [255, 255,   0],
 [255, 255,   0]]
```

In this matrix, the first two elements represent purple, followed by six red, and the last two yellow.

Grayscale conversion

It is often useful to completely remove the color information from an image before performing machine learning on it. The reason is that color is sometimes not a contributing factor in the prediction being asked for. For example, in a system that detects digits in an image, the shape of the digit matters, whereas the color of the digit does not contribute to the solution.

Grayscale images, in simple terms, is a measure of how much light is visible in an area of the image. Usually, the most dominant light-colored elements are completely removed to display contrast with the less visible areas.

The formula for converting RGB to grayscale is as follows:

$$Y = R * 0.299 + G * 0.587 + B * 0.114$$

Y is the final value that the pixel being converted to grayscale would hold. The R, G, and B are the values of red, green, and blue for that particular pixel. The output produced is as follows:

Let's now dive into developing a face detection application!

Developing a face detection application using Flutter

With the basic understanding of how a CNN works from Chapter 1, *Introduction to Deep Learning for Mobile,* and how image processing is done at the most basic level, we are ready to proceed with using the pre-trained models from Firebase ML Kit to detect faces from the given images.

We will be using the Firebase ML Kit Face Detection API to detect the faces in an image. The key features of the Firebase Vision Face Detection API are as follows:

- Recognize and return the coordinates of facial features such as the eyes, ears, cheeks, nose, and mouth of every face detected.
- Get the contours of detected faces and facial features.
- Detect facial expressions, such as whether a person is smiling or has one eye closed.
- Get an identifier for each individual face detected in a video frame. This identifier is consistent across invocations and can be used to perform image manipulation on a particular face in a video stream.

Let's begin with the first step, adding the required dependencies.

Adding the pub dependencies

We start by adding the pub dependencies. A **dependency** is an external package that is required for a particular functionality to work. All of the required dependencies for the application are specified in the `pubspec.yaml` file. For every dependency, the name of the package should be mentioned. This is generally followed by a version number specifying which version of the package we want to use. Additionally, the source of the package, which tells pub how to locate the package, and any description that the source needs to find the package can also be included.

 To get information about specific packages, visit `https://pub.dartlang.org/packages`.

The dependencies that we will be using for this project are as follows:

- `firebase_ml_vision`: A Flutter plugin that adds support for the functionalities of Firebase ML Kit
- `image_picker`: A Flutter plugin that enables taking pictures with the camera and selecting images from Android or iOS image library

Here's what the `dependencies` section of the `pubspec.yaml` file will look like after including the dependencies:

```
dependencies:
  flutter:
    sdk: flutter
```

```
firebase_ml_vision: ^0.9.2+1
image_picker: ^0.6.1+4
```

In order to use the dependencies that we have added to the `pubspec.yaml` file, we need to install them. This can simply be done by running `flutter pub get` in the Terminal or clicking **Get Packages**, which is located on the right side of the action ribbon at the top of the `pubspec.yaml` file. Once we have installed all the dependencies, we can simply import them into our project. Now, let's look at the basic functionality of the application that we will be working on in this chapter.

Building the application

Now we build the application. The application, named **Face Detection**, will consist of two screens. The first one will have a text title with two buttons, allowing the user to choose an image from the device's picture gallery or take a new image using the camera. After this, the user is directed to the second screen, which shows the image that was selected for face detection highlighting the detected faces. The following screenshot shows the flow of the application:

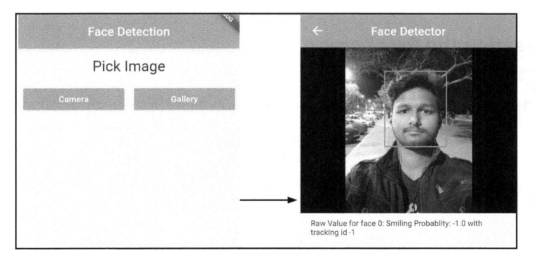

The widget tree of the application looks like this:

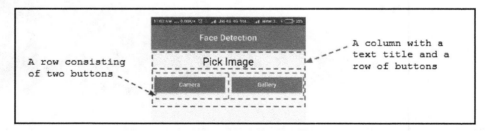

Let's now discuss the creation and implementation of each of the widgets in detail.

Creating the first screen

Here we are creating the first screen. The user interface of the first screen will contain a text title, **Pick Image**, and two buttons, **Camera** and **Gallery**. This can be thought of as a column containing the text title and a row with two buttons, as shown in the following screenshot:

In the following sections, we will build each of these elements, called **widgets**, and then bring them together under a **scaffold**.

In English, **scaffold** means a structure or a platform that provides some support. In terms of Flutter, a scaffold can be thought of as a primary structure on the device screen upon which all the secondary components, in this case widgets, can be placed together.

In Flutter, every UI component is a **widget**. They are the central class hierarchy in the Flutter framework. If you have worked previously with Android Studio, a widget can be thought of as a TextView or Button or any other view component.

Building the row title

Then is building the row title. We start by creating a stateful widget, FaceDetectionHome, inside the face_detection_home.dart file. FaceDetectionHomeState will contain all the methods required to build the first screen of the application.

Let's define a method called buildRowTitle() to create the text header:

```
Widget buildRowTitle(BuildContext context, String title) {
    return Center(
        child: Padding(
            padding: EdgeInsets.symmetric(horizontal: 8.0, vertical: 16.0),
            child: Text(
                title,
                style: Theme.of(context).textTheme.headline,
            ), //Text
        ) //Padding
    ); //Center
}
```

The method is used to create a widget with a title using the value that is passed in the title string as an argument. The text is aligned to the center horizontally by using Center() and is provided a padding of 8.0 horizontally and 16.0 vertically using EdgeInsets.symmetric(horizontal: 8.0, vertical: 16.0). It contains a child, which is used to create the Text with the title. The typographical style of the text is modified to textTheme.headline to change the default size, weight, and spacing of the text.

 Flutter uses the **logical pixel** as a unit of measure, which is the same as **device-independent pixel (dp)**. Further, the number of device pixels in each logical pixel can be expressed in terms of **devicePixelRatio**. For the sake of simplicity, we will just use numeric terms to talk about width, height, and other measurable properties.

Building the row with button widgets

Next is building the row with button widgets. After placing our text title, we will now create a row of two buttons that will enable the user to pick an image either from the gallery or take a new image from the camera. Let's do this in the following steps:

1. We start by defining `createButton()` to create buttons with all the required properties:

```
Widget createButton(String imgSource) {
    return Expanded(
        child: Padding(
            padding: EdgeInsets.symmetric(horizontal: 8.0),
            child: RaisedButton(
                color: Colors.blue,
                textColor: Colors.white,
                splashColor: Colors.blueGrey,
                onPressed: () {
                    onPickImageSelected(imgSource);
                },
                child: new Text(imgSource)
            ),
        )
    );
}
```

The method returns a widget, that is, `RaisedButton`, after providing a horizontal padding of `8.0`. The color of the button is set to `blue` and the color of the button text is set to `white`. `splashColor` is set to `blueGrey` to indicate that the button is clicked by producing a rippling effect.

The code snippet inside `onPressed` is executed when the button is pressed. Here, we make a call to `onPickImageSelected()`, which is defined in a later section of the chapter. The text that is displayed inside the button is set to `imgSource`, which, here, can be the gallery or the camera. Additionally, the whole code snippet is wrapped inside `Expanded()` to make sure that the created button completely occupies all the available space.

2. Now we use the `buildSelectImageRowWidget()` method to build a row with two buttons to list the two image sources:

```
Widget buildSelectImageRowWidget(BuildContext context) {
    return Row(
        children: <Widget>[
            createButton('Camera'),
            createButton('Gallery')
```

```
        ],
    );
}
```

In the preceding code snippet, we call the previously defined
createButton() method to add **Camera** and **Gallery** as image source buttons
and add them to the children widget list for the row.

3. Now, let's define onPickImageSelected(). This method uses
   the image_picker library to direct the user either to the gallery or the camera to
   get an image:

```
void onPickImageSelected(String source) async {
    var imageSource;
    if (source == 'Camera') {
        imageSource = ImageSource.camera;
    } else {
        imageSource = ImageSource.gallery;
    }
    final scaffold = _scaffoldKey.currentState;
    try {
        final file = await ImagePicker.pickImage(source:
imageSource);
        if (file == null) {
            throw Exception('File is not available');
        }
        Navigator.push(
            context,
            new MaterialPageRoute(
                builder: (context) => FaceDetectorDetail(file)),
            );
        } catch (e) {
        scaffold.showSnackBar(SnackBar(
        content: Text(e.toString()),
        ));
    }
}
```

First, imageSource is set to either camera or gallery using an if-else block. If
the value passed is Camera, the source of the image file is set to
ImageSource.camera; otherwise, it is set to ImageSource.gallery.

Once the source of the image is decided pickImage() is used to pick the correct
imageSource. If the source was Camera, the user will be directed to the camera
to take an image; otherwise, they will be directed to choose an image from the
gallery.

To handle the exception if the image was not returned successfully by `pickImage()`, the call to the method is enclosed inside a `try-catch` block. If an exception occurs, the execution is directed to the `catch` block and a snackbar with an error message being shown on the screen by making a call to `showSnackBar()`:

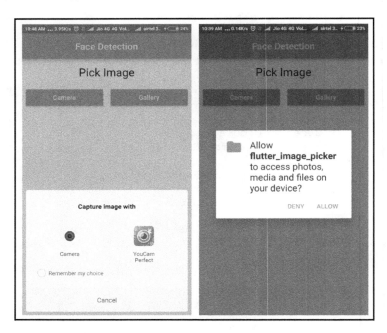

After the image has been chosen successfully and the `file` variable has the required `uri`, the user migrates to the next screen, `FaceDetectorDetail`, which is discussed in the section, *Creating the second screen*, and using `Navigator.push()` it passes the current context and the chosen file into the constructor. On the `FaceDetectorDetail` screen, we populate the image holder with the selected image and show details about the detected faces.

Creating the whole user interface

Now, we create the whole user interface, all of the created widgets are put together inside the `build()` method overridden inside the `FaceDetectorHomeState` class.

In the following code snippet, we create the final scaffold for the first screen of the application:

```
@override
Widget build(BuildContext context) {
    return Scaffold(
        key: _scaffoldKey,
        appBar: AppBar(
            centerTitle: true,
            title: Text('Face Detection'),
        ),
        body: SingleChildScrollView(
            child: Column(
                children: <Widget>[
                    buildRowTitle(context, 'Pick Image'),
                    buildSelectImageRowWidget(context)
                ],
            )
        )
    );
}
```

The text of the toolbar is set to `Face Detection` by setting the title inside the `appBar`. Also, the text is aligned to the center by setting `centerTitle` to `true`. Next, the body of the scaffold is a column of widgets. The first is a text title and the next is a row of buttons.

 The whole code inside `FaceDetectorHome.dart` can be viewed at `https://github.com/PacktPublishing/Mobile-Deep-Learning-Projects/blob/master/Chapter2/flutter_face_detection/lib/face_detection_home.dart`.

Creating the second screen

Next, we create the second screen. After successfully obtaining the image selected by the user, we migrate to the second screen of the application, where we display the selected image. Also, we mark the faces that were detected in the image using Firebase ML Kit. We start by creating a stateful widget named `FaceDetection` inside a new Dart file, `face_detection.dart`.

Getting the image file

First of all, the image that was selected needs to be passed to the second screen for analysis. We do this using the `FaceDetection()` constructor.

 Constructors are special methods that are used for initializing the variables of a class. They have the same name as the class. Constructors do not have a return type and are called automatically when the object of the class is created.

We declare a `file` variable and initialize it using a parameterized constructor as follows:

```
File file;
FaceDetection(File file){
 this.file = file;
}
```

Now let's move on to the next step.

Analyzing the image to detect faces

Now, we analyze the image to detect faces. We will create an instance of the `FirebaseVision` face detector to detect the faces using the following steps:

1. First, we create a global `faces` variable inside the `FaceDetectionState` class, as shown in the following code:

   ```
   List<Face> faces;
   ```

2. Now we define a `detectFaces()` method, inside which we instantiate `FaceDetector` as follows:

   ```
   void detectFaces() async{
       final FirebaseVisionImage visionImage =
   FirebaseVisionImage.fromFile(widget.file);
       final FaceDetector faceDetector =
   FirebaseVision.instance.faceDetector(FaceDetectorOptions( mode:
   FaceDetectorMode.accurate, enableLandmarks: true,
   enableClassification: true));
       List<Face> detectedFaces = await
   faceDetector.processImage(visionImage);
       for (var i = 0; i < faces.length; i++) {
           final double smileProbablity =
   detectedFaces[i].smilingProbability;
           print("Smiling: $smileProb");
   ```

```
        }
        faces = detectedFaces;
    }
```

We first create a `FirebaseVisionImage` instance called `visionImage` of the image file that was selected using the `FirebaseVisionImage.fromFile()` method. Next, we create an instance of `FaceDetector` by using the `FirebaseVision.instance.faceDetector()` method and store it in a variable called `faceDetector`. Now we call `processImage()` using the `FaceDetector` instance, `faceDetector`, which was created earlier, and pass in the image file as a parameter. The method call returns a list of detected faces, which is stored in a list variable called `detectedFaces`. Note that `processImage()` returns a list of type `Face`. `Face` is an object whose attributes contain the characteristic features of a detected face. A `Face` object has the following attributes:

- `getLandmark`
- `hashCode`
- `hasLeftEyeOpenProbability`
- `hasRightEyeOpenProbability`
- `headEulerEyeAngleY`
- `headEylerEyeAngleZ`
- `leftEyeOpenProbability`
- `rightEyeOpenProbability`
- `smilingProbability`

Now we iterate through the list of faces using a `for` loop. We can get the value of `smilingProbablity` for the ith face using `detectedFaces[i].smilingProbability`. We store it in a variable called `smileProbablity` and print its value to the console using `print()`. Finally, we set the value of the global `faces` list to `detectedFaces`.

 The `async` modifier added to the `detectFaces()` method enables asynchronous execution of the method, which means that a separate thread, different from the main thread of execution, is created. An `async` method works on callback mechanisms to return the value computed by it once the execution has been completed.

To make sure that the faces are detected as soon as the user migrates to the second screen, we override `initState()` and call `detectFaces()` from inside it:

```
@override
void initState() {
    super.initState();
    detectFaces();
}
```

`initState()` is the first method that is called after the widget is created.

Marking the detected faces

Next, marking the detected faces. After detecting all the faces present in the image, we will paint rectangular boxes around them with the following steps:

1. First we need to convert the image file into raw bytes. To do so, we define a `loadImage` method as follows:

    ```
    void loadImage(File file) async {
        final data = await file.readAsBytes();
        await decodeImageFromList(data).then(
            (value) => setState(() {
            image = value;
            }),
        );
    }
    ```

    The `loadImage()` method takes in the image file as input. Then we convert the contents of the file into bytes using `file.readAsByte()` and store the result in data. Next, we call `decodeImageFromList()`, which is used to load a single image frame from a byte array into an `Image` object and store the final result value in the image. We call this method from inside `detectFaces()`, which was defined earlier.

2. Now we define a `CustomPainter` class called `FacePainter` to paint rectangular boxes around all the detected faces. We start as follows:

    ```
    class FacePainter extends CustomPainter {
        Image image;
        List<Face> faces;
        List<Rect> rects = [];
        FacePainter(ui.Image img, List<Face> faces) {
            this.image = img;
            this.faces = faces;
    ```

```
for(var i = 0; i < faces.length; i++) {
    rects.add(faces[i].boundingBox);
}
            }
        }
    }
```

We start by defining three global variables, `image`, `faces`, and `rects`. `image` of type `Image` is used to get the byte format of the image file. `faces` is a `List` of `Face` objects that were detected. Both `image` and `faces` are initialized inside the `FacePainter` constructor. Now we iterate through the faces and get the bounding rectangles of each of the face using `faces[i].boundingBox` and store it in the `rects` list.

3. Next, we override `paint()` to paint the `Canvas` with rectangles, as follows:

```
@override
void paint(Canvas canvas, Size size) {
    final Paint paint = Paint()
        ..style = PaintingStyle.stroke
        ..strokeWidth = 8.0
        ..color = Colors.red;
    canvas.drawImage(image, Offset.zero, Paint());
    for (var i = 0; i < faces.length; i++) {
        canvas.drawRect(rects[i], paint);
    }
}
```

We start by creating an instance of the `Paint` class to describe the style to paint the `Canvas`, that is, the image we have been working with. Since we need to paint rectangular borders, we set `style` to `PaintingStyle.stroke` to paint just the edges of the shape. Next, we set `strokeWidth`, that is, the width of the rectangular border, to 8. Also, we set the `color` to red. Finally, we paint the image using `cavas.drawImage()`. We iterate through each of the rectangles for the detected faces inside the `rects` list and draw rectangles using `canvas.drawRect()`.

Displaying the final image on the screen

After successfully detecting faces and painting rectangles around them, we will
now display the final image on the screen. We first build the final scaffold for our second
screen. We will override the `build()` method inside `FaceDetectionState` to return the
scaffold as follows:

```
@override
Widget build(BuildContext context) {
    return Scaffold(
        appBar: AppBar(
        title: Text("Face Detection"),
        ),
        body: (image == null)
        ? Center(child: CircularProgressIndicator(),)
        : Center(
            child: FittedBox(
                child: SizedBox(
                    width: image.width.toDouble(),
                    height: image.width.toDouble(),
                    child: CustomPaint(painter: FacePainter(image, faces))
                ),
            ),
        )
    );
}
```

We start by creating the `appBar` for the screen, providing a title, `Face Detection`. Next,
we specify the `body` of the scaffold. We first check the value of the `image` that stores the
byte array of the image selected. Till the time it is null we are sure that the process of
detecting faces is in progress. Therefore, we use a `CircularProgressIndicator()`. Once
the process for detecting faces is over the user interface is updated to show a `SizedBox`
with the same width and height as the selected image. The `child` property of the
`SizedBox` is set to `CustomPaint`, which uses the `FacePainter` class we created earlier to
paint rectangular borders around the detected faces.

The whole code in `face_detection.dart` can be viewed at https://github.com/PacktPublishing/Mobile-Deep-Learning-Projects/blob/master/Chapter2/flutter_face_detection/lib/face_detection.dart.

Creating the final MaterialApp

At last, we create the final `MaterialApp`. We create the `main.dart` file, which provides the point of execution for the whole code. We create a stateless widget called `FaceDetectorApp`, which is used to return a `MaterialApp` specifying the title, theme, and home screen:

```
class FaceDetectorApp extends StatelessWidget {
  @override
  Widget build(BuildContext context) {
    return new MaterialApp(
      debugShowCheckedModeBanner: false,
      title: 'Flutter Demo',
      theme: new ThemeData(
        primarySwatch: Colors.blue,
      ),
      home: new FaceDetectorHome(),
    );
  }
}
```

Now we define the `main()` method to execute the whole application by passing in the instance of `FaceDetectorApp()` as follows:

```
void main() => runApp(new FaceDetectorApp());
```

 The whole code inside `main.dart` can be viewed at https://github.com/PacktPublishing/Mobile-Deep-Learning-Projects/blob/master/Chapter2/flutter_face_detection/lib/main.dart

Summary

In this chapter, we examined the concept behind image processing and how we can integrate it with our Android- or iOS-based application made using Flutter to perform face detection. The chapter started with adding relevant dependencies to support the functionalities of Firebase ML Kit and the `image_picker` library. The required UI components with the necessary functionalities were added. The implementation mainly covered image file selection using the Flutter plugin and how images can be processed once they are selected. An example of on-device Face Detector model usage was presented, along with an in-depth discussion of the method by which the implementation was carried out.

In the next chapter, we will be discussing how you can create your own AI-powered chatbot that can double-up as a virtual assistant using the Actions on Google platform.

3
Chatbot Using Actions on Google

In this project, we will cover the implementation of conversational chatbots using Dialogflow API, and how to make them perform different actions on Google Assistant with the help of Actions on Google. This project will provide you with a good understanding of how to build a product that uses engaging voice and text-based conversational interfaces.

We will implement a chatbot that will ask for the user's name and then generate a lucky number for the user. We will also look into how a chatbot can be made available on the Google Assistant platform using Actions on Google.

The following topics will be covered in this chapter:

- Understanding the tools available for creating chatbots
- Creating a Dialogflow account
- Creating a Dialogflow agent
- Understanding the Dialogflow Console
- Creating your first Action on Google
- Creating Actions on a Google project
- Implementing a Webhook
- Deploying a Webhook to Cloud Functions for Firebase
- Creating an Action on Google release
- Creating the UI for the conversational application
- Integrating the Dialogflow agent
- Adding audio interactions with the assistant

Technical requirements

For the mobile application, you will need Visual Studio Code with the Flutter and Dart plugin, as well as the Firebase console set up and running.

The code files for this chapter can be found in this book's GitHub repository at `https://github.com/PacktPublishing/Mobile-Deep-Learning-Projects/tree/master/Chapter3`.

Understanding the tools available for creating chatbots

If you're looking to build a conversational experience for users using a chatbot, you'll have a large number of options to build upon. There are several platforms available with different sets of features, each unique in terms of the services they offer.

One genre of chatbots that has been on a constant rise in the last decade, and has successfully paved the way for chatbots to be more readily accepted into professional websites and industry, is artificially intelligent chatbots. What sort of intelligence do these bots offer? What business objectives do they solve?

Let's try to answer both of these questions with a scenario.

Say you own a department store, and employ several employees at your store so that they can guide your customers to the right departments. One day, you realize that these employees were actually adding to the crowding of the store. In order to replace them, you come up with an app that is able to respond to questions such as, *Where can I find some cereal?* with answers such as *The groceries section is toward the north-west of the store, right beside the Fruits section!*.

The chatbot thus exhibits the ability to understand the requirement of the user, which in this case is to find **cereal**. Then, the chatbot was able to determine the relationship between **cereal** and **groceries**. From its knowledge of the inventory of the store, it is able to direct the user to the right department. To be able to come up with associations, and even with translations of words from one language to another, deep learning plays a critical role in the inner workings of chatbots.

In the following sections, we shall explore various artificial intelligence-enabled tools that can be used to create chatbots and deploy them on mobile phones.

Wit.ai

Made by Facebook, the `Wit.ai` platform offers a suite of APIs around **Natural Language Processing (NLP)** and speech-to-text services. The `Wit.ai` platform is completely open source and offers some state-of-the-art services in the domains of NLP. It can be easily integrated with mobile apps and wearables, and can even be used for home automation. The speech to text services offered by the platform makes it very suitable for creating applications that use a voice interface.

Developers can easily design complete conversations and even add personality to their chatbots. `Wit.ai` supports conversations and speech to text services in more than 130 languages, which makes it a great choice for applications that focus on worldwide linguistic accessibility.

To find out more about the platform, visit `https://wit.ai/`.

Dialogflow

Dialogflow, renamed from `Api.ai`, provides deep neural network-based natural language processing for creating conversational interfaces that seamlessly integrate with multiple platforms, such as Facebook Messenger, Slack, WhatsApp, Telegram, and so on.

Dialogflow projects run on the Google Cloud and are able to draw benefits from all the Google Cloud offerings related to building conversations, such as getting the user's location, deploying webhooks on Firebase or App Engine, and initiating actions in the Google-developed apps on both Android and iOS. You can learn more about the platform at `https://dialogflow.com/`.

Now, let's delve deeper into Dialogflow and its capabilities, in order to learn how to develop a Google Assistant-like application for mobile devices.

How does Dialogflow work?

In the previous section, we were briefly introduced to some tools we can use to develop chatbot and conversational interfaces using text and voice, as required. We came across Dialogflow, which we will be discussing in depth in this section. We will also use it to quickly develop an industry-grade chat solution.

Before we begin developing a Dialogflow chatbot, we need to understand how Dialogflow works and learn about a few of the terminologies related to Dialogflow.

The flow of information in an application using Dialogflow can be seen in the following diagram:

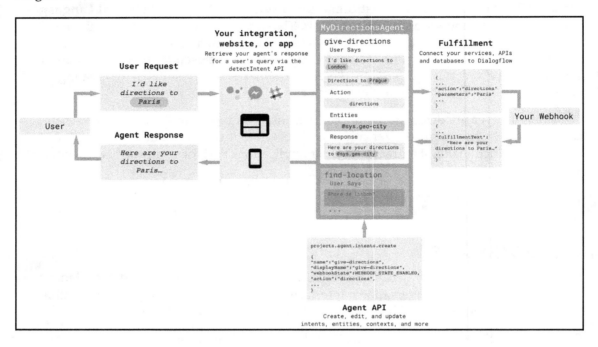

Let's discuss the terms that were introduced in the preceding diagram:

- **User**: The user is the person using the chatbot/application, and is responsible for making a **user request**. A **user request** is simply a spoken word or sentence made by the user that has to be interpreted by the chatbot. An appropriate response needs to be generated against it.
- **Integration**: Integration is a software component that is responsible for passing user requests to the chatbot logic and the **agent response** to the user. This integration could be to an app or website that you've created, or to an existing service such as Slack, Facebook Messenger, or simply a script which makes calls to the Dialogflow chatbot.

- **Agent**: The chatbot we develop using the Dialogflow tool is called an agent. The responses that are generated by the chatbot are known as **agent responses**.
- **Intent**: This is a representation of what a user is trying to do in their user request. The natural language input made by the user has to be matched with an intent to determine the kind of response to be generated for any specific request.
- **Entities**: In a user request, the user might, at times, use words or phrases that might be required for processing the response. These are extracted from the user request in the form of entities and then used as required. For example, if the user says "Where can I get some mangoes?" the chatbot is supposed to extract the word **mangoes** in order to search its available database or the internet to come up with a proper response.
- **Context**: To understand **context** in Dialogflow, consider the following scenario, where you talk to a chatbot without the capability of maintaining context: You ask your chatbot "Who is the prime minister of India?" and it generates the appropriate response. Next, you ask your chatbot "What is his age?" Your chatbot does not know who "his" refers to here. Thus, context is the state of the conversation that is maintained over a **chat session** or a part of the session unless the context is overridden by something new in the conversation with the chatbot.
- **Fulfillment**: Fulfillment is a software component that handles the business logic within the chatbot. It is an API that can be accessed through webhooks, takes input about the entities that are passed to it, and generates a response that is then used by the chatbot to generate the final agent response.

With the basic terminology and workflow of Dialogflow covered, we shall now build a basic Dialogflow agent that can provide responses to user requests.

Creating a Dialogflow account

To start using Dialogflow, you need to create an account on the Dialogflow website. To do this, follow these steps:

1. Visit `https://dialogflow.com` to begin the account creation process.

You will need a Google Account to create a Dialogflow account. If you have not created one already, visit `https://accounts.google.com`.

2. On the home page of the Dialogflow website, click on **Sign up for free** to create an account or **Go to console** to open the Dialogflow Console:

3. Upon clicking **Sign in with Google**, you'll be asked to log in with your Google Account. You shall be asked for Account Permissions to use Dialogflow and then to accept the Terms and Conditions.

Now, we can start creating a Dialogflow agent.

Creating a Dialogflow agent

As we discussed in the *How does Dialogflow work?* section, the agent is the chatbot we are creating in the Dialogflow platform.

Once your account has been successfully created, you'll be presented with the landing screen of the Dialogflow Console, prompting you to **Create an agent**:

1. Click on the **Create an agent** prompt. You'll be taken to a screen that looks similar to the following:

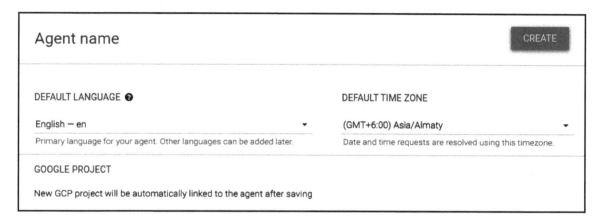

3. Fill in the name for the agent. We shall name it **DemoBot**.
4. Link any existing Google Project to the chatbot. If you do not already have an eligible Google Project, a new project will be created when you click on the **Create** button.

 You need to have a billing enabled on Google Project to create Dialogflow chatbots. To find out how to create a Google Project, go to `https://cloud.google.com/billing/docs/how-to/manage-billing-account`.

Understanding the Dialogflow Console

The Dialogflow Console is the graphical user interface for managing chatbots, intents, entities, and all the other features offered by Dialogflow.

After creating an agent, you should be able to see the following screen:

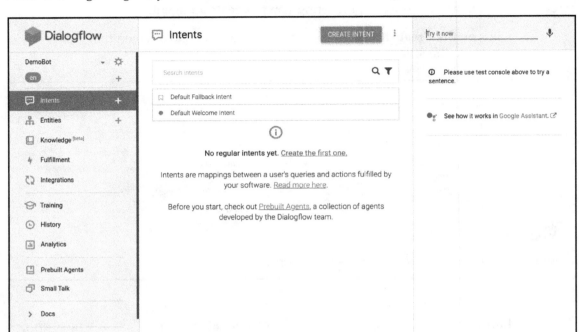

The Dialogflow Console prompts you to create a new Intent. Let's create a new Intent that recognizes the user's name and uses it to generate a lucky number for the user.

Creating an Intent and grabbing entities

Now, we shall create an intent that takes input from the user and determines the user's name. Then, the intent extracts the value of the name and stores it in an entity, which will be passed to the webhook later for processing. Follow these steps to do so:

1. Click on **Create Intent** button on the top right of the screen. The Intent creation form opens up.
2. We must provide a name for the intent, say, **luckyNum**. Then, scroll down to the **Training phrases** section and add a training phrase: name is John.

3. Grab the required entity and select the word **John**. A drop-down list will appear that matches the word with any predefined entity. We shall use the `@sys.person` entity to grab the name and store it as the **userName** parameter, as shown in the following screenshot:

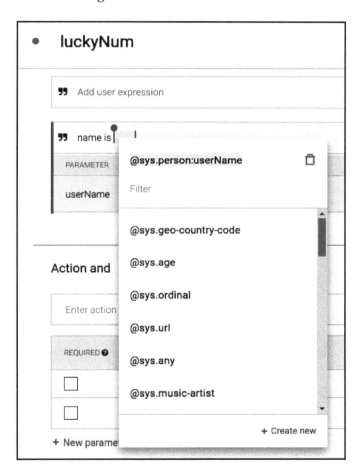

4. Scroll down to the **Actions and parameters** section and add the **userName** parameter, as shown in the following screenshot:

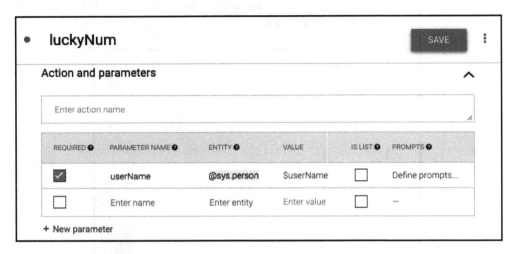

5. Now, whenever the user query is similar to name is something, something will be extracted into the **$userName** variable. This can now be passed to the webhook or Firebase Cloud Function to generate a response according to its value.

Now, let's add an action so that the Dialogflow agent can be accessed over Google Assistant.

Creating your first action on Google

Before we create an Action on Google, let's try to understand what an Action is. You might have heard about the Google Assistant, which is essentially comparable to Siri or Cortana. It is built around the concept of the virtual assistant, a piece of software that is capable of performing tasks for users based upon their direction, either in the form of text or voice.

Each task that the Google Assistant can perform is called an **Action**. Thus, tasks that are performed when the user makes requests similar to "show me the shopping list" or "make a call to Sam" are actions in which a function, say, showShoppingList() or makeCall(Sam), is executed with the appropriate arguments attached to it.

The Actions on Google platform make it possible for us to create chatbots that act as an Action on the Google Assistant. Once invoked, we can have a conversation until it's ended by the user.

Invoking the Action is performed within the Google Assistant, which matches the invocation request to the list of Actions in its directory and launches the appropriate action. Then, the next few interactions the user makes are with the action. Thus, the Google Assistant acts as an aggregator for several such actions and provides a method of invocation to them.

Why would you want to build an action on Google?

What sort of business benefit does the Actions on Google platform offer to developers who are interested in building chatbots? Consider the following screenshot:

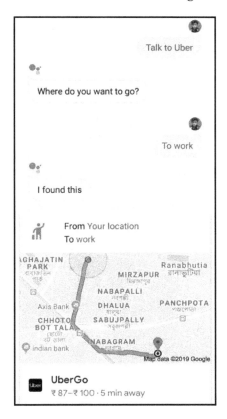

Merely by talking to the Google Assistant, the user is able to get Uber options. This is because the Talk to Uber invocation matched with the chatbot that was developed by Uber and was made available through the Actions on Google platform, which is responding to the Talk to Uber user request.

Thus, Uber is able to push its availability and interactivity by offering a text-free interface (if using voice input) and benefits from the state-of-the-art NLP algorithms that have been put into the Google Assistant, thus eventually enhancing its sales.

Publishing the chatbot you create to Actions on Google effectively allows you to provide a conversational interface for your business. You can use webhooks (which we shall cover later in this chapter, to manage the business logic. Now, let's create an Action on Google and link it to our chatbot.

Creating Actions on a Google project

In this section, we will create an Actions on Google Project and then integrate it with the Google Assistant app. This will allow the chatbot we've built to be accessible through the Google Assistant app, which is available on billions of devices globally.

Let's begin by creating the Actions on Google project:

1. In your browser, open `https://developers.google.com/actions/` to open up the Actions on xGoogle home page, where you can read all about the platform and also be introduced to its documentation.
2. To proceed to the console, click on the **Start Building** or **Go to Actions Console** button. You'll be taken to the Actions on Google console, where you'll be prompted to create a project.
3. On proceeding with project creation, you'll be able to see a dialogue box, as shown in the following screenshot:

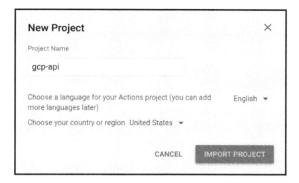

You must select the same Google Project that you created the Dialogflow chatbot agent in.

4. Click on **Import Project** to add an Action for your Dialogflow chatbot to the Google Assistant. On the next screen that loads, choose the **Conversational** template to create our Action.

5. You'll then be brought to the Actions on Google Console, which looks like this:

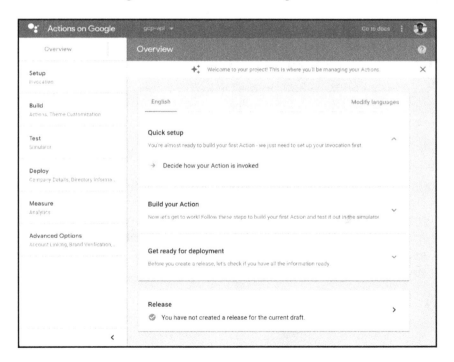

On the top bar, you'll be able to see the Project ID for your Google Project that the Action is being built in. On the left vertical navigation bar, all the different steps that you'll need to follow in order to complete your setup for the Action will be listed. On the right main content section, a quick walkthrough is provided for setting up your first Action.

6. Click on **Decide how your Action is invoked**. You'll need to provide a unique invocation string for your Action. For the sample in this chapter, we used the **Talk to Peter please** invocation. You will need to select a somewhat different invocation.

    After setting an invocation successfully, the walkthrough asks you to add an Action.

7. Click on the **Add Action(s)** link to begin the process of Action creation.
8. In the **Create Action** dialogue box that appears, choose **Custom intent** on the left listing and then click on the **Build** button. This will take you back to the Dialogflow interface.

Now, you need to enable Actions on Google to access your chatbot's intents.

Creating an integration to the Google Assistant

By default, the chatbot you have built in the Dialogflow console does not allow the Actions on Google project to access the intents available in it. We can enable access to intents by following these steps:

1. On the Dialogflow interface, click on the **Integrations** button on the left navigation pane.
2. On the page that loads, you'll be provided with integration options with different services that are supported by Dialogflow, which includes all major social chat platforms, along with Amazon's Alexa and Microsoft's Cortana.
3. On your screen, you should see the **Integration Settings** button for the Google Assistant. Click on that button. A dialogue box will open, as shown in the following screenshot:

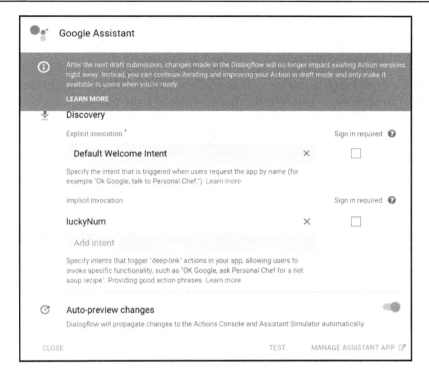

The dialog box in the preceding screenshot allows you to quickly define integration settings between your Dialogflow agent and your Actions on Google project.

4. Under **Default Invocation**, set the **Default Welcome Intent** as the intent that will be the first to run when the user begins an interaction with your chatbot through the Google Assistant.

5. In **Implicit Invocation**, specify the **luckyNum** intent we created earlier. This will be used to generate the lucky number for the user.

6. Enabling **Auto-preview changes** is a good idea since it allows you to propagate the integration settings automatically to the Actions on Google Console and the Google Assistant Test Simulator (which we'll discuss shortly) in order to test our application before creating a release for it.

Now, let's provide a meaningful prompt for **Default Welcome Intent** in order to ask the user to enter their name, so that when the user responds, their input is similar to the training phrase of the **luckyNum** intent, thereby invoking it:

1. Click on the **Intents** button. Then, click on **Default Welcome Intent**. Scroll down to the **Responses** section of the Intent editing page and remove all responses there. Since the **luckyNum** intent is expecting the user to say something similar to `My name is XYZ`, the apt question for it would be `What is your name?`. Thus, we'll set the response here as `Hi, what is your name?`.

   Notice that the **Responses** section has a new navigation pill in its tabbed navigation named Google Assistant. This allows us to specify a different response for this intent when it's invoked from the Google Assistant.

2. Click on the tab and enable the User response from the **DEFAULT** tab as the first response. We're doing this since we do not want to specify a different response that's specific to the Google Assistant in our chatbot.

3. Scroll up to the **Events** section and check that it looks similar to the following screenshot:

4. If any of the preceding two Events are missing, you can include them by simply typing them in and selecting them from the auto-suggest box that appears.

5. Click on **Save** at the top right of the middle section of the Dialogflow Console.

Now, we're ready to create our business logic in order to generate the lucky number for the user. First, we'll create a webhook for the **luckyNum** intent and then deploy it to Cloud Functions for Firebase.

Implementing a Webhook

In this section, we will enable the webhooks for the **luckyNum** intent and prepare the webhook code for the logic of the **luckyNum** intent. Follow these steps to do so:

1. Open the Intent editing page for the **luckyNum** intent and scroll down to the **Fulfillment** section. Here, turn on the **Enable webhook call for this intent** option.

   Now, this intent will look for the response to be generated from the webhook.

2. Open a text editor of your choice to create the code for the webhook so that it's in JavaScript and will run on the Node.js platform provided by Firebase:

   ```
   'use strict';
   ```

   The preceding line ensures that we use a set of coding standards that have been defined in ECMAScript 5 that provide several useful modifications to the JavaScript language, thus making it more secure and less confusing.

3. Modules in JavaScript are imported into the project using the `require` function. Include the `actions-on-google` module, along with the `firebase-functions` module, since the script will be deployed to Firebase:

   ```
   // Import the Dialogflow module from the Actions on Google client
   library.
   const {dialogflow} = require('actions-on-google');

   // Import the firebase-functions package for deployment.
   const functions = require('firebase-functions');
   ```

4. Instantiate a new client object for the Dialogflow agent we've built:

   ```
   // Instantiate the Dialogflow client.
   const app = dialogflow({debug: true});
   ```

   Notice that the Dialogflow variable here is an object of the `actions-on-google` module.

5. Set the Intent that the webhook responds to as `luckyNum` and we pass it to the `conv` variable:

```
app.intent('luckyNum', (conv, {userName}) => {

 let name = userName.name;
 conv.close('Your lucky number is: ' + name.length );

});
```

The `app` variable holds the state information of the conversation being handled and the `userName` parameter that we extracted from the `luckyNum` intent. Then, we declare the variable name and set it to the name key of the `userName` variable. This is done because the `userName` variable is a JavaScript object. You can view this in the Test console on the right-hand section by typing in a matching invocation for the `luckyNum` intent, such as `My name is Max`.

6. Set the webhook so that it responds to all HTTPS POST requests and export it as a Dialogflow Fulfillment via Firebase:

```
// Set the DialogflowApp object to handle the HTTPS POST request.
exports.dialogflowFirebaseFulfillment =
functions.https.onRequest(app);
```

The script we have developed in this section needs to deployed to a server for it to respond. We shall use Cloud Functions for Firebase to deploy this script and use it as the webhook endpoint for the chatbot.

Deploying a webhook to Cloud Functions for Firebase

Now that we're done creating the logic of the webhook, it is pretty simple to deploy it using Cloud Functions on Firebase. Follow these steps to do so:

1. Click on the **Fulfillment** button on the left navigation of the Dialogflow Console. Enable the **Inline Editor** to be able to add your webhook and deploy it directly to Cloud Functions.

You will have to clear out the default boilerplate code that is in the Inline Editor to do this.

2. Paste the code in the editor from the previous section into the `index.js` tabbed navigation pill and click on **Deploy**.

 Remember that the environment that's being used for deployment is Node.js, so `index.js` is the file that shall contain all your business logic. The `package.json` file manages the required packages for your project.

Using Cloud Functions comes with the advantage of the simplicity and minimal setup that goes into deploying your webhook. On the other hand, the restriction of having just `index.js` set prevents you from splitting your webhook logic into several files, which is typically done in large chatbot applications. Now, you're ready to create a release for your Action.

Creating an Action on Google release

Finally, we're at the stage where we can create a release for our Actions on Google chatbot. But before doing so, it is important to test out the chatbot in the Google Assistant Test Simulator:

1. Click on the **Simulator** button on the left navigation pane of the Actions on Google Console to enter the simulator. In the simulator, you'll be shown an interface similar to using Google Assistant on your phone. A suggested input will contain the invocation method for your action.

2. Enter the invocation for your action in the simulator, which in our case is `Talk to Peter Please`. This will produce an output from the **Default Welcome Intent** asking for your name. Upon entering your name as the response, similar to `My name is Sammy`, you'll be shown your lucky number, like this:

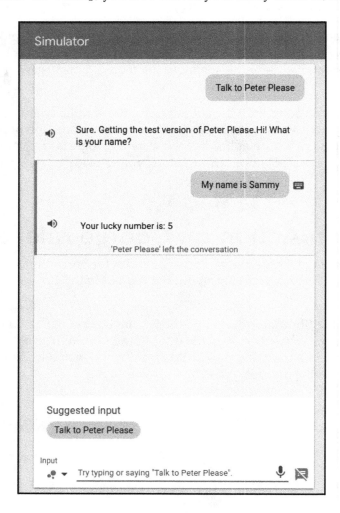

Now that we know our chatbot is working fine, along with its integration to Action on Google, let's create a release for it:

1. Click on **Overview** in the Actions on Google Console and you'll be able to see the **Get ready for deployment** prompt.
2. The Actions Test console asks you to enter some required information for your Action. These are usually the descriptions in short and long format, details of the developer, a privacy policy, terms and conditions for the action, and logos. After filling everything in successfully, click on **Save**.
3. Click on **Release** from the left navigation bar under the **Deploy** category to open the Releases page. Here, choose the **Alpha** release option and click on **Submit for release**.

The deployment will take a few hours to go through. After it has been deployed, you will be able to test your action on any device that has logged in to the Google Account that the Action has been built in. After successfully creating and deploying the Dialogflow agent, we will now develop a Flutter application with the capability to interact with the agent. The single-screen application will have a user interface very similar to any basic mobile chat app with a text box to type messages, which are the queries for the Dialogflow agent, and a send button to send each query to the agent. The screen will also contain a list view to show all the queries from the user and responses from the agent. Additionally, there will be a mic option beside the **Send** button so that the user can utilize speech to text functionality to send queries to the agent.

Creating the UI for the conversational application

We will start by creating the basic user interface for the application using some hardcoded texts to test if the UI is updating properly or not. Then, we will integrate the Dialogflow agent so that it can answer queries and tell the user their lucky number, followed by the addition of a mic option so that we can utilize the speech to text functionality.

The overall widget tree of the application will look as follows:

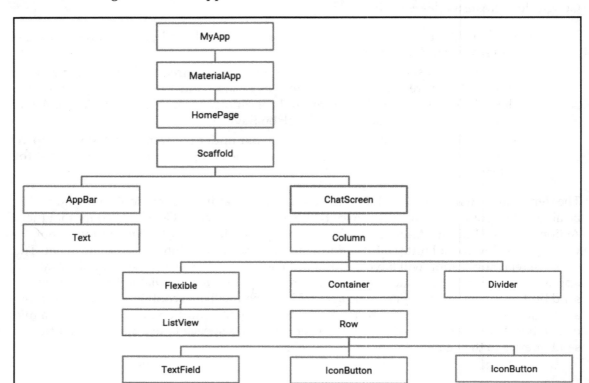

Now, let's discuss the implementation of each of these widgets in detail.

Creating the Text Controller

First of all, let's create a StatefulWidget called **ChatScreen** in a new dart file called `chat_screen.dart`. Now, follow these steps:

1. Create a text box—`TextField`, in Flutter terms—that will allow the user to enter their input text. To create the `TextField`, we need to define `createTextField()`:

```
Widget createTextField() {
    return new Flexible(
        child: new TextField(
            decoration:
```

```
                              new InputDecoration.collapsed(hintText: "Enter your
        message"),

                          controller: _textController,
                          onSubmitted: _handleSubmitted,
                      ),
              );
        }
```

The onSubmitted property works as a callback for the text field to handle the text inputs when the user indicates that they are done entering the text into the text field. The property is triggered when the *Enter* button on the keyboard is pressed.

In the preceding TextField widget, a call to _handleSubmitted() is made when the user has finished entering the text. _handleSubmitted() will be described in detail later.

We also specify the decoration property as collapsed in order to remove the default borders that might appear in the text field. We also specify a hintText property as Enter your message. To listen to the changes and update the TextField, we also attach an instance of TextEditingController. The instance can be created by executing the following code:

```
final TextEditingController _textController = new TextEditingController();
```

Unlike Java, Dart does not have keywords such as public, private, or protected to define the scope of usage of a variable. Instead, it uses an underscore, _, before an identifier name to specify that the identifier is private to a class.

2. Next, create a send button that can be used to send queries to the agent inside the createSendButton() function:

```
Widget createSendButton() {
    return new Container(
        margin: const EdgeInsets.symmetric(horizontal: 4.0),
        child: new IconButton(
            icon: new Icon(Icons.send),
            onPressed: () =>
_handleSubmitted(_textController.text),
        ),
    );
}
```

In Flutter, a graphical icon resembling a send button can easily be added using the `Icons` class. For this, we create a new instance of `Icon` and specify `Icons.send` in order to use the widget for the send button. This is used as an argument for the `icon` property. We also set the `onPressed` property, which is called when the user taps the send button. Here, again, we make a call to `_handleSubmitted`.

 `=>`, sometimes referred to as an arrow, is a shorthand notation that's used to define methods containing one line. A method defined as `fun() { return 10; }` can be written as `fun() => return 10;`.

3. The text field and the send button should appear side by side, so wrap them in a single row by adding them as children to a `Row` widget. The wrapped up `Row` widget is placed at the bottom of the screen. We create this widget inside `_buildTextComposer()`:

```
Widget _buildTextComposer() {
    return new IconTheme(
        data: new IconThemeData(color: Colors.blue),
        child: new Container(
            margin: const EdgeInsets.symmetric(horizontal: 8.0),
            child: new Row(
                children: <Widget>[
                    createTextField(),
                    createSendButton(),
                ],
            ),
        ),
    );
}
```

The `_buildTextComposer()` function returns an `IconTheme` widget with a `Container` as its child. The Container contains a Row widget consisting of a text field and the send button we created in *Steps 1* and *2*.

In the next section, we shall be building the `ChatMessage` widget, which is used to display the user-chatbot interactions.

Creating ChatMessage

The query from the user and the response from the agent can be thought of as two different parts of a single component. We will create two different containers for them and then add them inside a single unit called `ChatMessage`. This will ensure that each query, along with its answer, appears in the same order as they were input by the user. We will start by creating a stateful widget called `ChatMessage` inside a new dart file called `chat_message.dart`. The following image shows the division of a `ChatMesage` into a **query** and a **response**:

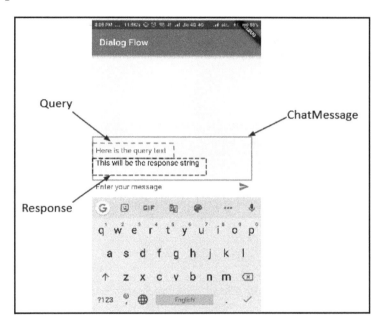

To create the UI of the screen, follow these steps:

1. Create a container with some text that will display the query entered by the user on the screen:

```
new Container(
    margin: const EdgeInsets.only(top: 8.0),
    child: new Text("Here is the query text",
        style: TextStyle(
            fontSize: 16.0,
            color: Colors.black45,
        ),
    ),
)
```

We start by providing a top margin of 8.0 to the container, which contains a string to be displayed whenever a query is entered by the user. We will modify this hardcoded string as a string parameter when _handleSubmitted() is called. We also modify the fontSize property's margin to 16.0 and set the color to black45 (a dark gray) to help the user differentiate between the queries and responses.

2. Create a container to show the response string:

```
new Container(
    margin: const EdgeInsets.only(top: 8.0),
    child: new Text("This will be the response string",
        style: TextStyle(
            fontSize: 16.0
        ),
    ),
)
```

The container with the top margin property of 8.0 contains a hardcoded response string. This will be modified later so that it can adapt to the responses from the user.

3. Wrap the two containers inside a single Column and return it as a container from the build() method that's overridden inside the stateful widget, that is, ChatMessage:

```
@override
Widget build(BuildContext context) {
    return new Container(
        margin: const EdgeInsets.symmetric(vertical: 10.0),
        child: new Column(
            crossAxisAlignment: CrossAxisAlignment.start,
            children: <Widget>[
                new Container(
                    margin: const EdgeInsets.only(top: 8.0),
                    child: new Text("Here is the query text",
                        style: TextStyle(
                            fontSize: 16.0,
                            color: Colors.black45,
),
),
),
new Container(
margin: const EdgeInsets.only(top: 8.0),
child: new Text("this will be the response text",
                        style: TextStyle(
```

```
                              fontSize: 16.0
                        ),
                   ),
              )
          ]
       )
    );
```

In Flutter, texts are wrapped inside a Container. Generally, these tend to overflow from the screens when they get too long to fit in the screen horizontally. This can be seen as a red mark on the corner of the screen. To avoid overflowing texts, make sure to wrap the Container with the Text inside Flexible so that the text can occupy the space available vertically and adjust itself.

4. To store and display all the strings (the queries and the responses), we will use a List of the ChatMessage type:

```
final List<ChatMessage> _messages = <ChatMessage>[];
```

This list should appear above the TextField that we created earlier to take input from the user.

5. To ensure that the fields appear properly in vertical order, we need to wrap them inside a column and return the same from the Widget build() method of ChatScreen.dart. The three children of the column are a flexible list view, a divider, and a container with the text field. The UI is created by overriding the build() method, as follows:

```
@override
Widget build(BuildContext context) {
    return new Column(
        children: <Widget>[
            new Flexible(
                child: new ListView.builder(
                    padding: new EdgeInsets.all(8.0),
                    reverse: true,
                    itemBuilder: (_, int index) =>
_messages[index],
                    itemCount: _messages.length,
                ),
            ),
            new Divider(
                height: 1.0,
            ),
            new Container(
```

```
                    decoration: new BoxDecoration(
                        color: Theme.of(context).cardColor,
                    ),
                    child: _buildTextComposer(),
                ),
            ],
        );
    }
```

The `ListView`, with the `ChatMessages` as its children, is made `Flexible` to allow it to occupy the entire space available on the screen in the vertical direction after placing the divider and the container for the text field. It is given padding of `8.0` in all four cardinal directions. Also, the `reverse` property is made true to make it scrollable in the direction of bottom to top. The `itemBuilder` property is assigned the current value of the index so that it can build the child items. Also, a value is assigned to `itemCount` that helps the list view correctly estimate the maximum scrollable content. The second child of the column creates a divider. This is a `devicePixel` thick horizontal line marking the separation of the list view and the text field. At the bottom-most position of the column, we place the container with a text field as its child. This is built by making a method call to `_buildTextComposer()`, which we defined previously.

6. Define `_handleSubmit()` inside the `ChatScreen.dart` method to correctly respond to the user's "send the message" actions:

```
void _handleSubmitted(String query) {
    _textController.clear();
    ChatMessage message = new ChatMessage(
        query: query, response: "This is the response string",
    );
    setState(() {
        _messages.insert(0, message);
    });
}
```

The string parameter of the method contains the value of the query string entered by the user. This query string, along with a hardcoded response string, is used to create an instance of `ChatMessage` and is inserted into the `_messages` list.

7. Define a constructor inside `ChatMessage` so that the parameter values, query, and response are passed and initialized properly:

```
final String query, response;
ChatMessage({this.query, this.response});
```

8. Modify the value of the `Text` property inside the container for queries and responses to query and response, respectively, in `ChatMessages.dart` so that the text that's displayed on the screen is the same as the text that was entered by the user and the response that was obtained from the action assistant:

```
//Modifying the query text
child: new Text(query,
    style:.......
)

//Modify the response text
child: new Text(response,
    style:.......
)
```

After successfully compiling the code we've written so far, the screen should look as follows:

In the preceding screenshot, you can see the dummy query text that will be written by the user and the response string from the chatbot.

The whole `chat_message.dart` file can be viewed on GitHub at `https:/` `/github.com/PacktPublishing/Mobile-Deep-Learning-Projects/blob/` `master/Chapter3/ActionsOnGoogleWithFlutter-master/lib/chat_` `message.dart`.

In the following section, we will integrate the Dialogflow agent so that we have real-time responses for user queries.

Integrating the Dialogflow agent

Now that we've created a very basic user interface for our application, we will integrate the Dialogflow agent with the application so that the text that's entered by the user is responded to in real time by the agent. Follow these steps:

1. To integrate Dialogflow in the application, we will use the Flutter plugin called `flutter_dialogflow`.

To explore this plugin, please go to `https://pub.dartlang.org/` `packages/flutter_dialogflow`.

Add the dependency to the plugin inside the `pubspec.yaml` file:

```
dependencies:
    flutter_dialogflow: ^0.1.0
```

2. Next, we need to install the dependency. This can be done either using the `$ flutter pub get` command-line argument or by clicking the option that appears on the screen. Here, we will use `dialogflow_v2` so let's import the package inside our `chat_screen.dart` file:

```
import 'package:flutter_dialogflow/dialogflow_v2.dart';
```

3. Add the `.json` file containing the GCP credentials that you downloaded while creating the Dialogflow agent on the console in the project. For this, create an `assets` folder and place the file inside it:

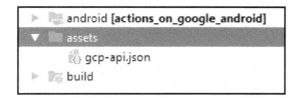

4. Add the path of the file to the `assets` section of the `pubspec.yaml` file:

```
flutter:
    uses-material-design: true
    assets:
  - assets/your_file_downloaded_google_cloud.json
```

5. Modify `_handleSubmitted()` so that it can communicate with the agent and get responses to the queries that are entered by the user:

```
Future _handleSubmitted(String query) async {
    _textController.clear();

    //Communicating with DailogFlow agent
    AuthGoogle authGoogle = await AuthGoogle(fileJson: "assets/gcp-
api.json").build();
    Dialogflow dialogflow = Dialogflow(authGoogle:
authGoogle,language: Language.english);
    AIResponse response = await dialogflow.detectIntent(query);
    String rsp = response.getMessage();
    ChatMessage message = new ChatMessage(
        query: query, response: rsp
    );
    setState(() {
        _messages.insert(0, message);
    });
}
```

First, we create an `AuthGoogle` instance called `authGoogle` by specifying the path to the `assets` folder. Next, we create an instance of the `Dialogflow` agent specifying the Google authentication instance and the language that would be used to communicate with it. Here, we've chosen English. The response is then fetched using `response.getMessage()` and is stored in the `rsp` string variable, which is then passed while creating the instance of `ChatMessage` to ensure that both strings (the input text and the response) are updated properly on the screen.

The following screenshot shows the application after the preceding modifications were made to reflect actual queries from the user and responses from the Dialogflow agent:

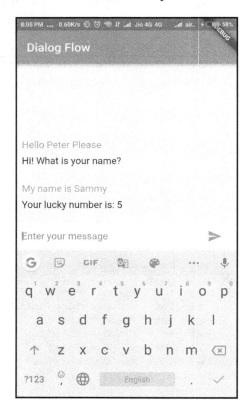

In the next section, we will be adding audio interaction capabilities to the application.

Adding audio interactions with the assistant

Now, we will add speech recognition to the application so that it can listen to the user's queries and act accordingly.

Adding the plugin

We will be using the `speech_recognition` plugin here. Let's add the dependency, as follows:

1. Add the dependency to the `pubspec.yaml` file, like so:

```
dependencies:
    speech_recognition: "^0.3.0"
```

2. Get the packages by running the following command-line argument:

```
flutter packages get
```

3. Now, since we are using the microphone of the device, we need to ask for the user's permission. To do this, we need to add the following lines of code:

On iOS, permissions are specified inside `infos.plist`:

```
<key>NSMicrophoneUsageDescription</key>
<string>This application needs to access your microphone</string>
<key>NSSpeechRecognitionUsageDescription</key>
<string>This application needs the speech recognition
permission</string>
```

On Android, the permissions are specified inside the `AndroidManifest.xml` file:

```
<uses-permission android:name="android.permission.RECORD_AUDIO" />
```

4. Now, we are ready to import the package into our `chat_screen.dart` file so that we can use it:

```
import 'package:speech_recognition/speech_recognition.dart';
```

In the next section, we will add methods that will utilize the `speech_recognition` plugin to help with audio interactions.

Adding SpeechRecognition

After adding the `speech_recognition` plugin and importing the package, we are all set to use it in our application. Let's start by adding methods that will handle speech recognition inside the application, as follows:

1. Add and initialize the required variables:

```
SpeechRecognition _speechRecognition;
bool _isAvailable = false;
bool _isListening = false;
String transcription = '';
```

`_speechRecognition` is an instance of `SpeechRecognition`. `_isAvailable` is important as it lets the platform (Android/iOS) know that we are interacting with it and that `_isListening` will be used to check whether the application is currently listening to the microphone or not.

Initially, we set the values of both `boolean` variables to false. `transcription` is a string variable that will be used to store the string that was listened to.

2. Define the `activateSpeechRecognizer()` method in order to set up the audio operations:

```
void activateSpeechRecognizer() {
    _speechRecognition = SpeechRecognition();

    _speechRecognition.setAvailabilityHandler((bool result)
        => setState(() => _isAvailable = result));

    _speechRecognition.setRecognitionStartedHandler(()
        => setState(() => _isListening = true));

    _speechRecognition.setRecognitionResultHandler((String text)
        => setState(() => transcription = text));

    _speechRecognition.setRecognitionCompleteHandler(()
        => setState(() => _isListening = false));
}
```

In the preceding code snippet, we initialized the instance of `SpeechRecognition` inside _speechRecognition. Then, we set `AvailabilityHandler` by calling the `_speechRecognition.setAvailabilityHandler()` callback function, which needs to pass back a `boolean` result that can be assigned to _isAvailable. Next, we set `RecognitionStartedHandler`, which is executed when the speech recognition service is started and sets _isListening to true to indicate that the microphone of the mobile device is currently active and is listening. Then, we set `RecognitionResultHandler` using `setRecognitionResultHandler`, which will give us back the resultant text. This is stored in the string transcription. Finally, we set `RecognitionCompleteHandler`, which sets _isListening to false when the microphone stops listening.

3. Expose the `initState()` function call, `activateSpeechRecognizer()`, inside it to set up the _speechRecognition instance, as follows:

```
@override
void initState(){
    super.initState();
    activateSpeechRecognizer();
}
```

At this point, the application is capable of recognizing audio and converting it into text. Now, we will enhance the UI so that the user can provide audio as input.

Adding the mic button

Now that we've activated the speech recognizer, we will add a mic icon beside the send button to allow the user to utilize the option for speech recognition. Follow these steps to do so:

1. First, we define the `createMicButton()` function, which is added as a third child to the `Row` widget inside _buildTextComposer():

```
Widget createMicButton() {
    return new Container(
    margin: const EdgeInsets.symmetric(horizontal: 4.0),
        child: new IconButton(
        icon: new Icon(Icons.mic),
        onPressed: () {
            if (_isAvailable && !_isListening) {
                _speechRecognition.recognitionStartedHandler();
                _speechRecognition .listen(locale: "en_US")
```

```
                                  .then((transcription) => print('$transcription'));
                  } else if (_isListening) {
                      _isListening = false;
                      transcription = '';
                      _handleSubmitted(transcription);
                      _speechRecognition
                      .stop()
                      .then((result) => setState(() => _isListening =
         result));
                  }
              }
          ),
      );
  }
```

In the preceding code snippet, we return a `Container` with a child, `IconButton`, that has the widget as `Icons.mic`. We provide a dual functionality to the button using `onPressed()` so that it can start listening to the user and, when pressed again, can stop the recording and call the `_handleSubmitted()` method by passing the recorded string for interaction with the agent.

First, we check if the microphone is available and is not already listening to the user using the `_isAvailable` and `_isListening` variables. If the condition in the `if` statement is `true`, we set the value of `_isListening` to `true`. Then, we start listening by calling the `.listen()` method on `_speechRecognition`. The `locale` parameter specifies the language, which is `en_US` here. The corresponding string is stored in the `transcription` variable.

When the mic is pressed for a second time to stop recording, the `if` condition won't be satisfied since the value of `_isListening` is set to `true`. Now, the `else` block is executed. Here, a call to `_handleSubmitted()` is made by passing the value of the transcript so that it can interact with the agent, after which the value of `_isListening` is set to `true` using the result:

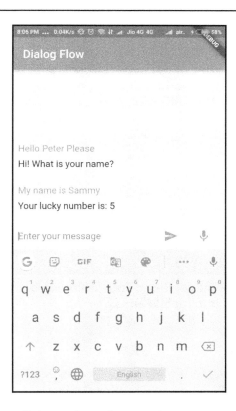

After successfully compiling all the code and wrapping ChatScreen inside a
MaterialApp instance in the main.dart file, the application will look similar to what you
can see in the preceding screenshot.

> The chat_screen.dart file can be viewed at https://github.com/
> PacktPublishing/Mobile-Deep-Learning-Projects/blob/master/
> Chapter3/ActionsOnGoogleWithFlutter-master/lib/chat_screen.dart.
>
> The whole project can be accessed at https://github.com/
> PacktPublishing/Mobile-Deep-Learning-Projects/tree/master/
> Chapter3/ActionsOnGoogleWithFlutter-master.

Summary

In this chapter, we looked at some of the most common tools that are available for creating chatbots and then proceeded with an in-depth discussion of Dialogflow to understand the basic terminology that's used. We understood how the Dialogflow Console works so that we can create our own Dialogflow agent. We did this by creating an intent that's capable of extracting the user's name and adding it as an integration to Google Assistant so that it can respond with lucky numbers.

After deploying the webhook for Cloud Functions for Firebase and creating Actions on Google release, we created a conversational Flutter application. We learned how to create a conversation application interface and integrated the Dialogflow agent to facilitate deep learning models based on the responses of the chatbot. Finally, we used a Flutter plugin to add speech recognition to the application, which again uses the deep learning-based models for converting voice into text.

In the next chapter, we'll look into defining and deploying our own custom deep learning models and integrating them into mobile apps.

Recognizing Plant Species

4

The project will provide an in-depth discussion on how to build a custom TensorFlow Lite model that is able to perform recognition of plant species from images. The model will run on mobile devices and will be primarily used to recognize different plant species. The model uses a deep **convolutional neural network** (**CNN**) for image processing developed on the Keras API of TensorFlow. This chapter also introduces you to the usage of cloud-based APIs for performing image processing. The Cloud Vision API provided by **Google Cloud Platform** (**GCP**) has been taken as an example.

By the end of this chapter, you'll understand the importance of cloud-based services for **deep learning** (**DL**) applications as well as the benefits of on-device models for performing offline and instantaneous deep learning tasks on mobile devices.

In this chapter, we will cover the following topics:

- Introducing image classification
- Understanding the project architecture
- Introducing the Cloud Vision API
- Configuring the Cloud Vision API for image recognition
- Using a **software development kit** (**SDK**)/tools to build a model
- Creating a custom TensorFlow Lite model for image recognition
- Creating a Flutter application
- Running image recognition

Technical requirements

The technical prerequisites for this chapter are as follows:

1. Anaconda with Python 3.6 and higher
2. TensorFlow 2.0
3. A GCP account with billing enabled
4. Flutter

You can find the code that we present in this chapter at our GitHub repository: `https://github.com/PacktPublishing/Mobile-Deep-Learning-Projects/tree/master/Chapter4`

Introducing image classification

Image classification is a major application domain for **artificial intelligence** (**AI**) in the modern day. We can find instances of image classification in a large number of places all around us, such as face unlocking for mobile phones, object recognition, optical character recognition, tagging of people in photos, and several others. While these task seems pretty simple when you think of it from a human's perspective, it is not as simple when it comes to computers. Firstly, the system has to recognize objects or people from an image and draw a bounding box around it/them and proceed to classification. Both these steps are compute-intensive and hard to perform for machines.

There are several challenges in image processing that researchers are trying to overcome every day, such as face recognition for people with glasses on or a newly grown beard, recognizing and tracking multiple people by their faces in crowded places, and character recognition for new styles of handwriting or entirely new languages. Deep learning has been a great tool for overcoming these challenges, with its ability to learn several invisible patterns in images.

A very common approach to deep learning for image processing is to deploy CNNs, which we have covered in an earlier chapter. To review its concepts and basic working, refer to `Chapter 2`, *Mobile Vision – Face Detection Using On-Device Models*. In this project, we will be covering how these models can be transformed into condensed models that can run efficiently on mobile devices.

You might wonder how we are going to build these models. For the sake of simplicity of syntax, strong support for the TensorFlow API, and a wide community for technical help, we will be using Python to build these models. While it is quite evident that you would need a Python runtime on your development machine, for this project, we will be opting for a quicker and more robust option—Google's Colaboratory environment. Colaboratory (or Colab, in short) provides ready-to-use runtimes with several important **machine learning (ML)** and data science-related modules that are pre-installed on the runtime. Also, Colaboratory offers support for **Graphics Processing Unit (GPU)**- and **Tensor Processing Unit (TPU)**-enabled runtimes, which makes training deep learning models a piece of a cake. We will then be deploying our TensorFlow Lite model directly on the device, a good practice for models that are geared toward working fast and that do not need regular updates.

Let's begin understanding the project architecture.

Understanding the project architecture

The project we'll be building in this chapter will include the following technologies:

- **TensorFlow** (`https://www.tensorflow.org`): To build the classification model using a CNN
- **TensorFlow Lite** (`https://www.tensorflow.org/lite`): A format of a condensed TensorFlow model that can be run efficiently on mobile devices
- **Flutter** (`https://flutter.dev`): A development library for cross-platform applications

You can read about these technologies by visiting the preceding links. A block diagram of these technologies playing their roles in this project is given in the following screenshot:

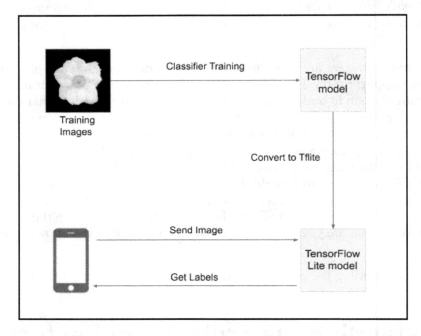

Firstly, we will be training a classification model on a dataset of several hundreds of images. For this, we will be building a TensorFlow model using Python. Then, the model has to be saved in the format of **.tflite**, which is the extension for TensorFlow Lite models. The backend side ends here and we switch to the frontend.

In the frontend, we first build an application using Flutter that can load images from a gallery that exists on the device. The predictive model residing on Firebase is downloaded and cached onto the device. The image selected from the gallery is passed to the model, which predicts the labels containing the name of the plant species being shown in the image. The storage of the model on the mobile device allows the model to be used even when offline.

On-device models are a powerful and preferred way of using deep learning on mobile applications. Several applications on the average person's mobile phone today use on-device models to bring intelligence to their applications. On-device models are often compressed forms of models developed on desktops, and may or may not be compiled into bytecode. Frameworks such as **TensorFlow Lite** perform special optimizations on **.tflite** models so that they are smaller and faster in working than when they are in their non-mobile form.

But before we start building our custom model for the task, let's take a comprehensive look at which pre-existing tools or services we have available for performing such tasks.

Introducing the Cloud Vision API

The Cloud Vision API is a popular API from the GCP suite. It has been a benchmark service for building applications using computer vision. Briefly, computer vision is the ability of computers to recognize entities in an image, ranging from human faces to roads and vehicles for autonomous driving tasks. Furthermore, computer vision can be used to automate tasks that are performed by the human visual system—such as counting the number of moving vehicles on a road, and observing changes in the physical environment. Computer vision has found a wide application in the following domains:

- Tagging of recognized faces on social media platforms
- Extracting text from images
- Recognizing objects from images
- Autonomous driving vehicles
- Medical imagery-based predictions
- Reverse image search
- Landmark detection
- Celebrity recognition

The Cloud Vision API provides easy access to some of the preceding tasks, returning labels for each recognized entity. For example, we can see that in the following screenshot, the famous Howrah Bridge, a 200-year-old engineering masterpiece, has been recognized correctly. Drawing from the information about the landmark, it is predicted that this image belongs to the city of Kolkata:

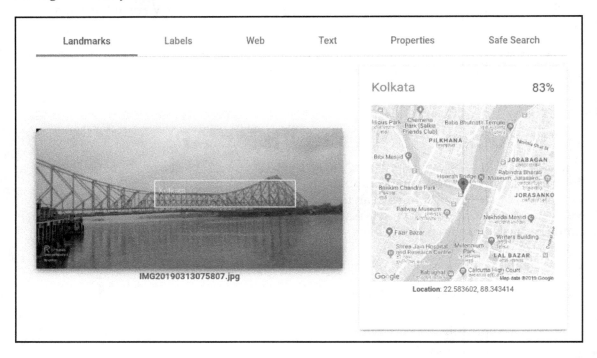

As for the labels of the preceding screenshot, the most dominant labels are for **bridge** and **suspension bridge**, which are both relevant to the bridge in consideration. As visible in the preceding screenshot, it is also possible to check for any recognized text in the image by clicking on the **Text** tab in the **Response** section. To check whether the image is good for safe searching or has some element of disturbing content in it, click on the **Safe Search** tab. For example, the image of getting a call from a famous celebrity is likely a spoof, as shown in the following screenshot:

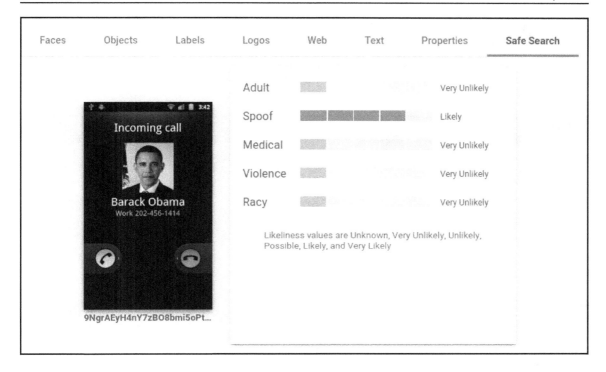

Next, we will begin with setting up a GCP account and then move on to create a sample Flutter application for using the API.

Configuring the Cloud Vision API for image recognition

In this section, we will be preparing to use the Cloud Vision API, using our Flutter application. It is mandatory to have a Google Account for this task, which we will assume that you already have. If not, you can create a Google Account free of charge by signing up at the following link: `https://accounts.google.com/signup`

If you have a Google Account at this stage, proceed to the next section.

Enabling the Cloud Vision API

To create a GCP Account, head over to the following link: `https://cloud.google.com`. After the initial signup, you will be able to see a dashboard resembling the following screenshot:

In the top-left corner, you'll be able to see the three-bars menu, which brings up a list of all the services and products available on GCP. The **Project name** is displayed on the left of the search bar. Make sure you create and enable billing for the project to progress further with this chapter. On the right, you can see the user profile information, notifications, and the Google Cloud Shell invocation icon. The center of the dashboard displays the various logs and statistics of the running services for the current user.

In order to access the Cloud Vision API and to consume it, we first need to enable it for the project and create an API key for the service. To do so, perform the following steps:

1. Click on the hamburger menu icon in the top left. This brings up a menu that resembles the one shown in the following screenshot:

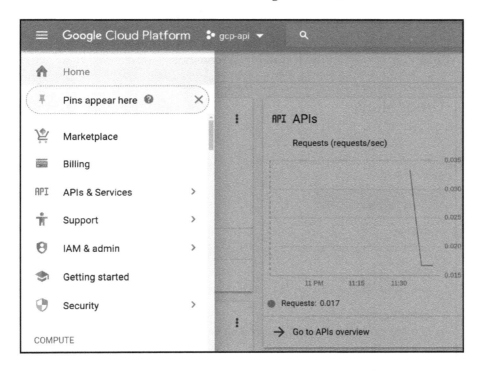

2. Click on the **APIs & Services** option. This brings up the **APIs** dashboard, which shows statistics relating to the APIs enabled on the project.
3. Click on the **Enable APIs and Services** button.
4. In the search box that appears, type **Cloud Vision API**.
5. Click on the relevant search result. The API provider will be listed as **Google**.
6. Once the API page opens up, click on **Enable**. After this, you should get an icon displaying that indicates that you have enabled this API, and the **Enable** button changes to **Manage**.

In order to be able to use the Cloud Vision API, you must create an API key for this service. We will do this in the next section.

Creating a Cloud Vision API key

Now, you'll have to create an API key for accessing the API and fetching responses from it. To do so, perform the following steps:

1. Open the left navigation menu again and hover over the **APIs & Services** menu item. A sub-menu appears—click on **Credentials**.
2. Click on the **Create Credentials** button. In the dropdown that appears, choose **API key**, as shown in the following screenshot:

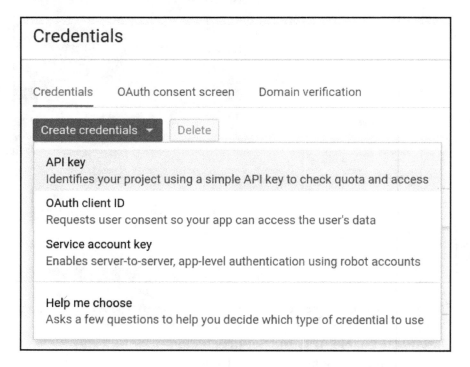

3. An API key gets created. You will need this API key while making calls to the Cloud Vision API.

The **API key** method only works for a few select APIs and services of GCP and is not very safe. You will need to use the method with Service Accounts if you want complete access to all APIs and services, and fine-grained security. To do so, you can read the following article in the official GCP documentation: https://cloud.google.com/docs/authentication/

With the API key at your disposal, you're now ready to make API calls through the Flutter app. In the next section, we will develop the predictive model on **Colaboratory** and save it as a `.tflite` model.

Using an SDK/tools to build a model

We covered the preparation for using a pre-existing service-based deep learning model for the task at hand, to predict the species of plant present in a picture. We will be training an image classifier model on samples from five different species of flowers. The model will then try to determine the species to which any image of a flower might belong. However, such models are usually trained on a generally available dataset, and would not have the specificity that might be required at times—for example, in a scientific laboratory. Hence, you must learn how to build your own models for predicting the plant species.

This can be achieved either by training a model completely from scratch or, alternatively, by extending a previously existing model. The upside to training a model completely from scratch is that you have complete control over the data being fed into the model, and whatever learning the model does during training. However, if the model is designed in such a way, it might suffer from slowness or bias. Extending a pretrained model such as the MobileNet model by the TensorFlow team comes with the benefit of being blazingly fast. A downside to the method is that it may not be as accurate as the model built from scratch, but the time-accuracy trade-off makes the MobileNet model preferable for operating on mobile devices.

 Bias is a very critical problem with ML models. Such a bias—or sampling bias, in the terminology of statistics, refers to the skew in a dataset in terms of having an equal number of samples for each category of classification in the dataset. Such categories then get fewer samples to train on and hence have a high chance of being omitted from the output predictions of the model. A good example of a biased model might be a facial recognition model trained only on the faces of small children. The model may entirely fail to recognize the faces of adults or old people.

You can learn more about identifying bias in samples in the following course by Khan Academy: `https://www.khanacademy.org/math/ap-statistics/gathering-data-ap/sampling-observational-studies/a/identifying-bias-in-samples-and-surveys`

Thus, in the upcoming sections, we will be using the MobileNet model for its capability to perform fast on mobile devices. To do so, we will be using the Keras API of TensorFlow. The language to be used for the task is Python, which, as earlier mentioned, best covers the capabilities of the TensorFlow framework. We'll assume you have basic working knowledge of Python for the upcoming section. However, it is important to understand how TensorFlow and Keras work together in this project.

We will be working in the Colaboratory environment. Let's begin by understanding the tool.

Introducing Google's Colaboratory

The Colaboratory tool provided by Google allows users to run **Notebook**-like runtimes on the computing resources provided by the company, with options to use GPUs and TPUs free of cost, for as long as the users want. The runtimes come preloaded with several Python modules relevant to ML and data science. The notebooks in Colaboratory are all able to access GCP APIs (with the proper configuration in place) directly from within the code. Each notebook has a temporary storage space of its own that gets destroyed when the runtime is disconnected. Also, it is possible to sync Colaboratory notebooks with GitHub, allowing state-of-the-art version control. Generally, Colaboratory notebooks reside on the Google Drive storage of the user. They can be shared and worked on together in real time with multiple users.

To open up Colaboratory, head over to the following link: `https://colab.research.google.com`

You will be presented with a sample, welcome notebook. Feel free to explore the welcome notebook, to get a basic understanding of how Colaboratory works. To the left of the notebook, you will be able to see the navigation tab pills, as shown in the following screenshot:

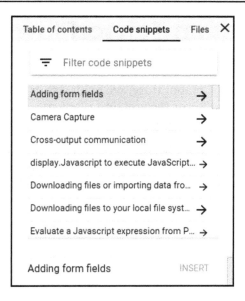

The **Table of contents** tab displays the headings and sub-headings created in the notebook, using the Markdown format to declare them. The **Code snippets** tab provides quick click-and-insert snippets of code for some common functionalities on Colaboratory. If you are not very familiar with Colaboratory and wish to perform a specific task, you might want to search the task here. The third tab, **Files**, is the storage space allocated to this notebook. The files stored here are privy to this notebook and do not show up anywhere else. Any files downloaded by using the script or created by the script are stored here. You can use the File Manager present on this screen to explore the entire directory structure of the notebook.

 On the right, the main content section is the notebook itself. To become familiar with using Colaboratory and Notebooks, we highly recommend reading the following article: `https://www.geeksforgeeks.org/how-to-use-google-colab/`

Creating a custom TensorFlow Lite model for image recognition

Once you have had a fair go at Colaboratory, we're all set up to build the custom TensorFlow Lite model for the task of recognizing plant species. To do so, we will begin with a new Colaboratory notebook and perform the following steps:

1. Import the necessary modules for the project. Firstly, we import TensorFlow and NumPy. NumPy will be useful for handling the image arrays, and TensorFlow will be used to build the CNN. The code to import the modules can be seen in the following snippet:

```
!pip install tf-nightly-gpu-2.0-preview
import tensorflow as tf
import numpy as np
import os
```

Notice the `!pip install <package-name>` command used on the first line. This is used to install packages in a running Colaboratory notebook, which, in this case, installs the latest TensorFlow release that internally implements the Keras library, which will be used to build the CNN.

 You can read more about using the `!pip install` command, and other ways to import and install new libraries to your Colaboratory runtime, here: https://colab.research.google.com/notebooks/snippets/importing_libraries.ipynb

2. To run the cell of code, hold the *Shift* key and press *Enter*. The download-and-install progress for the TensorFlow release is shown below the cell you execute your code in. It will take a few seconds, after which you will get a message similar to `Successfully installed <package_name>, <package_name>, ....`

3. Finally, we'll require the `os` module to handle the files on the filesystem.

4. Download the dataset and extract the images.

Now, we'll download the dataset from the **Uniform Resource Locator** (URL) available and extract it to a folder named /content/flower_photos, as illustrated in the following code block:

```
_URL =
"https://storage.googleapis.com/download.tensorflow.org/example_images/flow
er_photos.tgz"

zip_file = tf.keras.utils.get_file(origin=_URL,
                                   fname="flower_photos.tgz",
                                   extract=True, cache_subdir='/content',)

base_dir = os.path.join(os.path.dirname(zip_file), 'flower_photos')
```

You can explore the contents of the folder extracted by using the **Files** tab on the left panel. You'll find the folder contains a further five folders with the following names—daisy, dandelion, roses, sunflower, and tulips. These will be species of flowers we will be training our model on, and henceforth referred to as **labels**. We'll talk about these folder names again in the next step.

5. The next step is to set up generators for passing data to TensorFlow-based Keras models.

6. We'll now be creating two generator functions for feeding data into the Keras neural network. The ImageDataGenerator class of Keras provides two utility functions to feed data to a Python program, either by reading off the disk using the flow_from_directory method or by converting images to NumPy arrays, by using the flow_from_dataframe method. Here, we will be using the flow_from_directory method as we already have a folder containing the images.

 However, it has to be noted here that it was on purpose that the folder names containing the images are the same as the label to which the images belong. This is a design of the folder structure that the flow_from_directory method demands in order for it to function properly. You can read more about this method here: https://theailearner.com/2019/07/06/imagedatagenerator-flow_from_directory-method/

This can be summarized with the directory tree shown in the following screenshot:

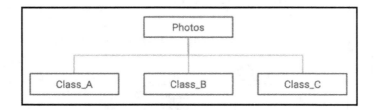

7. Then, we create an object of the `ImageDataGenerator` class and use it to create a generator for the training dataset, as shown in the following code block:

```
IMAGE_SIZE = 224
BATCH_SIZE = 64

datagen = tf.keras.preprocessing.image.ImageDataGenerator(
    rescale=1./255,
    validation_split=0.2)

train_generator = datagen.flow_from_directory(
    base_dir,
    target_size=(IMAGE_SIZE, IMAGE_SIZE),
    batch_size=BATCH_SIZE,
    subset='training')
```

The `datagen` object takes two parameters—the `rescale` and the `validation_split`. The `rescale` parameter tells the object to convert all black-and-white images to a range of 0 to 255, as is on the **Red, Green, and Blue (RGB)** scale since the MobileNet model has been trained on RGB images. The `validation_split` parameter allocates 20% (0.2 x 100) of the images from the dataset as the validation set. However, we'll need to create a generator for the validation set as well, just as we have done for the training set.

The training set generator, `train_generator`, takes the `target_size` and `batch_size` parameters, along with other parameters. The `target_size` parameter sets the dimension of the image to be generated. This is made to match the dimensions of the images in the MobileNet model. The `batch_size` parameter indicates how many images should be generated in a single batch.

8. For the validation set, we have the generator, as shown in the following code block:

```
val_generator = datagen.flow_from_directory(
    base_dir,
    target_size=(IMAGE_SIZE, IMAGE_SIZE),
    batch_size=BATCH_SIZE,
    subset='validation')
```

9. Let's take a quick look at the shape of the data being generated by these generators, as follows:

```
for image_batch, label_batch in train_generator:
  break
image_batch.shape, label_batch.shape
```

This produces the following output: `((64, 224, 224, 3), (64, 5))`, meaning that in the first batch of `train_generator`, 64 images of dimensions 224 x 224 x 3 were created, along with 64 labels of 5 one-hot encoding formatting.

10. The encoding index assigned to each label can be obtained by running the following code:

```
print(train_generator.class_indices)
```

This produces the following output: `{'daisy': 0, 'dandelion': 1, 'roses': 2, 'sunflowers': 3, 'tulips': 4}`. Notice the alphabetical order of the label names.

11. Now, we'll save these labels for future usage to deploy the model in the Flutter application, as follows:

```
labels = '\n'.join(sorted(train_generator.class_indices.keys()))

with open('labels.txt', 'w') as f:
  f.write(labels)
```

12. Next, we will create a base model and freeze layers. In this step, we'll first create a base model and then freeze all the layers of the model except the last one, like this:

```
IMG_SHAPE = (IMAGE_SIZE, IMAGE_SIZE, 3)

base_model =
tf.keras.applications.MobileNetV2(input_shape=IMG_SHAPE,
                                  include_top=False,
                                  weights='imagenet')
```

The base model is created by importing the `MobileNetV2` model provided by the TensorFlow team. The input shape is set to (64, 64, 3), and the weights from the ImageNet dataset are imported. The model might not exist on your system, in which case it will be downloaded from an external resource.

13. Then, we freeze the base model so that the weights in the `MobileNetV2` model remain unaffected by future training, as follows:

```
base_model.trainable = False
```

14. Now, we will create an extended CNN, and extend the base model to add another layer after the base model layers, like this:

```
model = tf.keras.Sequential([
    base_model,
  tf.keras.layers.Conv2D(32, 3, activation='relu'),
  tf.keras.layers.Dropout(0.2),
  tf.keras.layers.GlobalAveragePooling2D(),
  tf.keras.layers.Dense(5, activation='softmax')
])
```

We created a sequential model extending the base model, which essentially means that data is passed between the successive layers unidirectionally, one layer at a time. We also added a 2D convolutional layer with the `relu` activation function, and then a `Dropout` layer followed by a `Pooling` layer. Finally, an output layer is added with the `softmax` activation.

15. Then, the model has to be compiled in order to perform training on it, as follows:

```
model.compile(optimizer=tf.keras.optimizers.Adam(),
              loss='categorical_crossentropy',
              metrics=['accuracy'])
```

We set the loss as categorical cross-entropy and the model evaluation metric as the accuracy of prediction. `Softmax` has been found to perform best with categorical cross-entropy as the loss function, hence the choice.

16. Train and save the model. We're finally at one of the most exciting steps in ML—training. Run the following code:

```
epochs = 10

history = model.fit(train_generator,
                    epochs=epochs,
                    validation_data=val_generator)
```

The model is trained for 10 epochs, which means every sample is thrown at the neural network at least 10 times. Notice the use of `train_generator` and `val_generator` in this function. The training takes quite some time on this, even with 12GB+ of RAM and TPU acceleration available (which would be an overkill on any personal, mid-end device). You'll be able to observe the training logs below the cell that runs the preceding code.

17. We can then save the model, after which we can proceed to convert the saved model file, as follows:

```
saved_model_dir = ''
tf.saved_model.save(model, saved_model_dir)
```

18. Convert and download the model file to TensorFlow Lite. We can now convert the saved model file using the following code. This saves the model as a `model.tflite` file, like this:

```
converter =
tf.lite.TFLiteConverter.from_saved_model(saved_model_dir)
tflite_model = converter.convert()

with open('model.tflite', 'wb') as f:
  f.write(tflite_model)
```

19. We now need to download this file, for embedding it into the Flutter application that we build. We can do so using the following code:

```
from google.colab import files
files.download('model.tflite')
files.download('labels.txt')
```

Notice that we use the `files` module from the `google.colab` library. We also downloaded the `labels.txt` file that we had created in *Step 11*.

We are now ready to proceed with creating the Flutter application to demonstrate the Cloud Vision API usage, along with the usage of the embedded TensorFlow Lite model.

Creating a Flutter application

After successfully creating the TensorFlow Lite model for recognizing a wide variety of plant species, let's now create a Flutter application for running the TensorFlow Lite model on mobile devices. The application will have two screens. The first screen will contain two buttons for letting the user choose between two different models—the Cloud Vision API and the TensorFlow Lite model—that could be used to make predictions on any chosen image. The second screen will contain a **Floating Action Button** (**FAB**) to enable the user to choose images from the device's gallery, an image view to display the image chosen by the user, and a text to display the predictions using the chosen model.

The following screenshot illustrates the flow of the application:

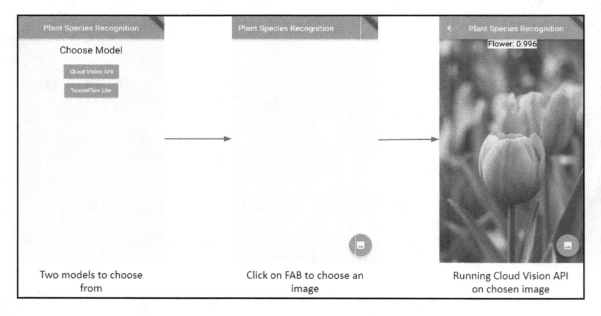

| Two models to choose from | Click on FAB to choose an image | Running Cloud Vision API on chosen image |

Now, let's look at the steps to build the application.

Choosing between two different models

Let's start by creating the first screen of the application. The first screen will consist of two different buttons, to let the user choose between the Cloud Vision API and the TensorFlow Lite model.

First of all, we create a new `choose_a_model.dart` file that will contain a `ChooseModel` stateful widget. The file will contain the code to create the first screen of the application, containing a column with some text and two raised buttons, as shown in the following screenshot:

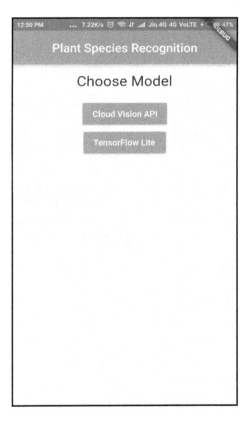

The steps to create the first screen of the application are as follows:

1. First of all, we will define some global string variables that will be used later in creating buttons for choosing the models, and saving the model chosen by the user, as follows:

```
var str_cloud = 'Cloud Vision API';
var str_tensor = 'TensorFlow Lite';
```

2. Now, let's define a method to create a simple Text widget, as follows:

```
Widget buildRowTitle(BuildContext context, String title) {
    return Center(
        child: Padding(
            padding: EdgeInsets.symmetric(horizontal: 8.0,
vertical: 16.0),
            child: Text(
                title,
                style: Theme.of(context).textTheme.headline,
            ),
        ),
    );
}
```

The method returns a widget that is aligned to the center and contains some text with the value of title passed as an argument with a **Choose a Model** string themed to a headline. The text is also provided with some horizontal and vertical padding, using the padding property with EdgeInsets.symmetric().

3. Next, we will define a createButton() method for creating buttons, as follows:

```
Widget createButton(String chosenModel) {
    return (RaisedButton(
        color: Colors.blue,
        textColor: Colors.white,
        splashColor: Colors.blueGrey,
        child: new Text(chosenModel),
            onPressed: () {
                var a = (chosenModel == str_cloud ? 0 : 1);
                    Navigator.push(
                        context,
                        new MaterialPageRoute(
                            builder: (context) =>
PlantSpeciesRecognition(a)
                        ),
                    );
                }
```

```
            )
        );
    }
```

The method returns a `RaisedButton` method with a color of `blue`, a `textColor` value of `white`, and a `splashColor` value of `blueGrey`. The button has a `Text` child that is built using the value passed in `chosenModel`. If the button for running the Cloud Vision API was clicked by the user, the value of `chosenModel` will be the Cloud Vision API, and if the button for TensorFlow Lite was clicked, it will have the value TensorFlow Lite.

When the button is pressed, we first check the value in `chosenModel`. If it is the same as `str_cloud`—that is, the Cloud Vision API—the value assigned to variable `a` is 0; otherwise, the value assigned to variable `a` is 1. The value is passed along with migration to `PlantSpeciesRecognition` using `Navigator.push()`, which is described in later sections.

4. Finally, we create the `appBar` and body of the first screen and return the `Scaffold` from the `build()` method, like this:

```
@override
Widget build(BuildContext context) {
    return Scaffold(
        appBar: AppBar(
            centerTitle: true,
            title: Text('Plant Species Recognition'),
        ),
        body: SingleChildScrollView(
            child: Column(
                mainAxisAlignment: MainAxisAlignment.center,
                children: <Widget>[
                    buildRowTitle(context, 'Choose Model'),
                    createButton(str_cloud),
                    createButton(str_tensor),
                ],
            )
        )
    );
}
```

The `appBar` contains a title of `Plant Species Recognition` that is placed at the center. The body of the `Scaffold` is a column with some text and two buttons with values of `str_cloud` and `str_tensor`, aligned to the center.

Creating the second screen

When a model is chosen by the user, the application migrates to a second screen that will let the user select an image from the device's local storage and run the chosen model on it to make predictions. We start here by creating a new file, `plant_species_recognition.dart`, containing a `PlantSpeciesRecognition` stateful widget.

Creating the user interface

We will start by creating a new file, `PlantSpeciesRecognition.dart`, containing a stateful widget named `PlantSpeciesRecognition`, and we'll override its `build()` method for placing the **user interface (UI)** components of the application:

1. Let's create a `Scaffold` with an FAB and `AppBar` with the application title that will be returned from the `build()` method. The FAB will let the user choose an image from the device's gallery to predict the species of the plant contained in the image, as follows:

```
return Scaffold(
    appBar: AppBar(
        title: const Text('Plant Species Recognition'),
    ),
    floatingActionButton: FloatingActionButton(
        onPressed: chooseImageGallery,
        tooltip: 'Pick Image',
        child: Icon(Icons.image),
    ),
);
```

In the preceding code snippet, the `AppBar` will contain `Plant Species Recognition` text. This will be displayed as the title of the application on the application bar placed on the top of the screen.

 In Flutter, `const` keywords help in freezing the state of an object. The complete state of an object described as `const` is determined during the compile time of the application itself and remains immutable. Also, the keyword is useful for small memory optimizations when used with constructors such as `Text()`. Adding a second `Text()` constructor in the code reuses the memory that was allocated for the first `Text()` constructor, thus reusing the memory space and making the application faster.

Next, we add the `floatingActionButton` property by specifying the `FloatingActionButton` class and passing in the needed parameters.

 `FloatingActionButtons` are circular buttons that hover on the top of the contents on the screen. One screen, in general, should contain one FAB that resides on the bottom-right corner and is unaffected by the scrolling of the contents.

`onPressed` is added to `chooseImageGallery` that will be called when the button is pressed. Next, we add the `tooltip` property with a `String` value of `'Pick Image'`, describing the action that the button will perform. Finally, we add `Icon(Icons.image)` as `child` to place the material icon image on the top of the FAB.

Adding the functionality

Now, let's add the functionality to allow the user to choose an image from the device's gallery. We will do this by using the `image_picker` plugin, and the whole of the code will be placed inside the `chooseImageGallery` method, as follows:

1. First, add the dependency to the `pubspec.yaml` file, specifying the name and the version number, like this:

```
dev_dependencies:
flutter_test:
sdk: flutter
image_picker: ^0.6.0
```

 For a detailed discussion on pub dependencies, refer to `Chapter 2`, *Mobile Vision – Face Detection Using On-Device Models*. Be sure to run the `Flutter` packages to include the dependency in the project. To read more about the `image_picker` plugin, visit https://github.com/flutter/plugins/tree/master/packages/image_picker.

2. Import the library in `PlantSpeciesRecognition.dart`, as follows:

```
import 'package:image_picker/image_picker.dart';
```

3. At this point, we declare the following two global variables inside `plant_species_recognition.dart`:

- `File_image`: To store the image file chosen from the gallery
- `bool _busy` (with an initial value of `false`): A flag variable to handle UI operations smoothly

4. Now, let's define the `chooseImageGallery()` method that will be called when the `FloatingActionButton` button is pressed, as follows:

```
Future chooseImageGallery() async {
    var image = await ImagePicker.pickImage(source:
ImageSource.gallery);
    if (image == null) return;
    setState(() {
        _busy = true;
    });
}
```

Here, we use the `ImagePicker.pickImage()` method to get the image from the gallery by mentioning it as the source. We store the returned value in the variable image. If the value returned from the call is `null`, we return the call since no further operations can be performed on a `null` value. Otherwise, change the value of _busy to `true` to indicate that further operations on the image are going on.

 `setState()` is a synchronous callback to notify the framework that the internal state of the object has been changed. This change might actually affect the UI of the application and, thus, the framework will need to schedule a build for the `State` object. Refer to the following link for further discussion: `https://api.flutter.dev/flutter/widgets/State/setState.html`

At this point, the application compiles successfully, and pressing the FAB launches the gallery from which an image can be chosen. However, the chosen image is not displayed on the screen, so now, let's work on this.

Displaying the chosen image on the screen

Now, let's add a widget to display the image selected in the previous section, as follows:

1. We will use a list of widgets, the image that was chosen from the gallery, and the prediction results, stacked or overlaid over each other to be displayed on the screen. Therefore, we begin by declaring an empty list of widgets that would contain all the children of the stack. Also, we declare a `size` instance to query the size of the window containing the application using the `MediaQuery` class, as follows:

```
List<Widget> stackChildren = [];
Size size = MediaQuery.of(context).size;
```

2. Now, the image is added as the first child of the stack, like this:

```
stackChildren.add(Positioned(
    top: 0.0,
    left: 0.0,
    width: size.width,
    child: _image == null ?Text('No Image Selected') :
Image.file(_image),
));
```

The `Positioned` class is used to control the position of a child of the stack; here, by specifying the values of the `top`, `left`, and `width` properties. The `top` and `left` values specify the distance of the top and left edge of the child from the top and left edge of the stack, respectively, which here is 0—that is, the top-left corner of the device's screen. The `width` value specifies the width of the child—here, the width of the window containing the application, which means the image will occupy the whole width.

3. Next, we will add the child, which would be a text saying that no image is selected if the value of `_image` is `null`; otherwise, it contains the image selected by the user.

To display the stack on the screen, we add the `stackChildren` list as the body of the `Scaffold` returned by the `build()` method, as follows:

```
return Scaffold(
    appBar: AppBar(
      title: const Text('Plant Species Recognition'),
    ),
    //Add stackChildren in body
    body: Stack(
      children: stackChildren,
    ),
    floatingActionButton: FloatingActionButton(
      onPressed: chooseImageGallery,
      tooltip: 'Pick Image',
      child: Icon(Icons.image),
    ),
);
```

In the previous code, we pass `stackChildren` inside `Stack()`, to create an overlaid structure of all the widgets contained inside the list.

4. Compiling the code at this point would produce the following result:

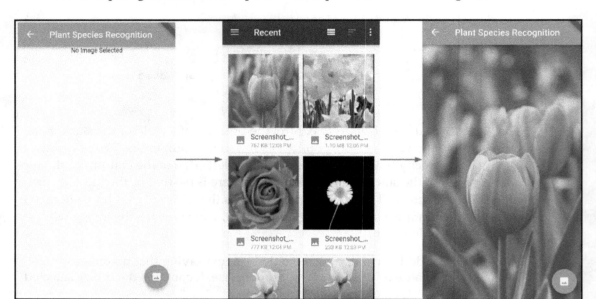

At this point, clicking on the FAB will launch the gallery, and the chosen image is displayed on the screen.

Next, we will load the TensorFlow Lite model on the device, and make HTTP requests to the Cloud Vision API to have a recognition result on the selected image.

Running image recognition

Now, the image chosen from the gallery can be used as an input for the two prediction methods of the Cloud Vision API and TensorFlow Lite model. Next, let's define methods for running both of them.

Using the Cloud Vision API

In this section, we simply define a `visionAPICall` method that is used to make an `http` `Post` request to the CloudVision API, passing in the request string encoded as `json`, which returns a `json` response that is parsed to get the values from the desired labels:

1. First of all, we define an `http` plugin dependency in the `pubspec.yaml` file, as follows:

   ```
   http: ^0.12.0+2
   ```

2. Import the plugin in `PlantSpeciesRecognition.dart` to assist in making `http` requests, like this:

   ```
   import 'package:http/http.dart' as http;
   ```

3. Now, we define the method to create a request URL and make an `http` POST request, as follows:

   ```
   List<int> imageBytes = _image.readAsBytesSync();
   String base64Image = base64Encode(imageBytes);
   ```

   To be able to send the image file for analysis along with the HTTP post request, we will need to convert the `png` file to Base64 format—that is, into a string containing just the **American Standard Code for Information Exchange (ASCII)** values. First, we use `readAsByteSync()` to read the content of _image as a list of bytes and store it in `imageBytes`. Then, we encode this list in Base64 format by passing it the `imageBytes` list as an argument for `base64Encode`.

4. Next, we create the request string, which will have the following format:

   ```
   var request_str = {
     "requests":[
       {
         "image":{
           "content": "$base64Image"
         },
         "features":[
           {
             "type":"LABEL_DETECTION",
             "maxResults":1
           }
         ]
       }
     ]
   };
   ```

While the entire string will be hardcoded, the value of the content key will vary depending on the image that is chosen by the user, and its base64-encoded format.

5. We store the URL that needs to be called in the `url` variable, like this:

```
var url =
'https://vision.googleapis.com/v1/images:annotate?key=API_KEY;
```

Be sure to replace `API_KEY` with your generated key.

6. Make an HTTP post request using the `http.post()` method, passing in the `url` and the response string, like this:

```
var response = await http.post(url, body:
json.encode(request_str));
print('Response status: ${response.statusCode}');
print('Response body: ${response.body}');
```

We also check the status code using `response.statusCode`, which should have a value of `200` if the request was successful.

7. Since the response from the server is in JSON format, we use `json.decode()` to decode it, and, further, parse it to store the desired values in the `str` variable, as follows:

```
var responseJson = json.decode(response.body);
str =
'${responseJson["responses"][0]["labelAnnotations"][0]["description"]}:
${responseJson["responses"][0]["labelAnnotations"][0]["score"].toStringAsFixed(3)}';
```

8. The whole `visionAPICall()` method, after putting everything together, will look like this:

```
Future visionAPICall() async {
List<int> imageBytes = _image.readAsBytesSync();
print(imageBytes);
String base64Image = base64Encode(imageBytes);
var request_str = {
  "requests":[
    {
      "image":{
        "content": "$base64Image"
      },
      "features":[
```

```
        {
          "type":"LABEL_DETECTION",
          "maxResults":1
        }
      ]
    }
  ]
};
var url =
'https://vision.googleapis.com/v1/images:annotate?key=AIzaSyDJFPQO3
N3h78CLOFTBdkPIN3aE9_ZYHy0';

var response = await http.post(url, body:
json.encode(request_str));
print('Response status: ${response.statusCode}');
print('Response body: ${response.body}');

var responseJson = json.decode(response.body);
str =
'${responseJson["responses"][0]["labelAnnotations"][0]["description
"]}:
${responseJson["responses"][0]["labelAnnotations"][0]["score"].toSt
ringAsFixed(3)}';
}
```

In the next section, we will cover the steps to use an on-device TensorFlow Lite model.

Using an on-device TensorFlow Lite model

Now, let's add functionality for the second choice of the user—that is, analyzing the chosen image using a TensorFlow Lite model. Here, we will be using our previously created TensorFlow Lite model. The following steps discuss in detail how to use an on-device TensorFlow Lite model:

1. We will start by adding the `tflite` dependency in the `pubspec.yaml` file, like this:

```
dev_dependencies:
flutter_test:
  sdk: flutter
image_picker: ^0.6.0
//Adding tflite dependency
tflite: ^0.0.5
```

2. Next, we configure `aaptOptions` in Android. Add the following lines of code to the `android/app/build.gradle` file, inside the `android` block:

```
aaptOptions {
        noCompress 'tflite'
        noCompress 'lite'
    }
```

The preceding code snippet makes sure that the `tflite` files are not stored in compressed form in the **Android Package Kit** (**APK**).

3. Next, we need to include the already saved `model.tflite` and `labels.txt` files in the **assests** folder, as shown in the following screenshot:

4. Specify the paths to the files inside the `pubspec.yaml` file, as follows:

```
flutter:
uses-material-design: true
//Specify the paths to the respective files
assets:
  - assets/model.tflite
  - assets/labels.txt
```

5. Now, we are all set to start with loading and running our first TensorFlow Lite model on the device. We begin by importing the `tflite.dart` file into `PlantSpeciesRecognition.dart`, as follows:

```
import 'package:tflite/tflite.dart';
```

6. To carry out all the related tasks, we define the `analyzeTFLite()` method. Here, we start by loading the model, passing the `model.tflite` file and the `labels.txt` file as inputs to the `model` and `labels` parameters in `Tflite.loadModel()`.

We store the resulting output in the `res` string variable that will contain the `success` value if the model was loaded successfully, as follows:

```
String res = await Tflite.loadModel(
    model: "assets/model.tflite",
    labels: "assets/labels.txt",
    numThreads: 1 // defaults to 1
);
print('Model Loaded: $res');
```

7. We now run the model on the image using the `Tflite.runModelOnImage()` method and passing the path of the selected image stored inside the device. We store the result in the `recognitions` variable, like this:

```
var recognitions = await Tflite.runModelOnImage(
    path: _image.path
);
setState(() {
    _recognitions = recognitions;
});
```

8. Once the model has run successfully on the image and the results have been stored in the `recognitions` local variable, we create a _recognitions global list and set its state to the value stored in `recognitions` so that the UI can be updated properly with the results.

The whole `analyzeTfLite()` method, after putting everything together, will look like this:

```
Future analyzeTFLite() async {
    String res = await Tflite.loadModel(
        model: "assets/model.tflite",
        labels: "assets/labels.txt",
        numThreads: 1 // defaults to 1
    );
    print('Model Loaded: $res');
    var recognitions = await Tflite.runModelOnImage(
        path: _image.path
    );
    setState(() {
        _recognitions = recognitions;
    });
    print('Recognition Result: $_recognitions');
}
```

Both of the preceding defined methods, `visionAPICall()` and `analyzeTFLite()`, are called from `chooseImageGallery()`, after an image is successfully chosen and stored, depending upon the button clicked by the user, which is decided upon by the value passed in the `PlantSpeciesRecognition` constructor: 0 for the Cloud Vision API, and 1 for TensorFlow Lite.

The modified `chooseImagGallery()` method will look like this:

```
Future chooseImageGallery() async {
    var image = await ImagePicker.pickImage(source:
ImageSource.gallery);
    if (image == null) return;
    setState(() {
      _busy = true;
      _image = image;
    });

    //Deciding on which method should be chosen for image analysis
    if(widget.modelType == 0)
      await visionAPICall();
    else if(widget.modelType == 1)
      await analyzeTFLite();
    setState(() {
      _image = image;
      _busy = false;
    });
}
```

The `await` keyword is mentioned before the method call to make sure all of the operations take place asynchronously. Here, we also set the value of _image to `image` and _busy to `false` to indicate that all the processing has been completed and the UI can now be updated.

Updating the UI with results

In the previous section, *Creating the user interface*, we updated the UI by adding an extra child to `stackChildren`, to show the image selected by the user. Now, we will add another child to the stack to show the result of the image analysis, as follows:

1. First, we will add the results of the Cloud Vision API, as follows:

```
stackChildren.add( Center (
  child: Column(
    children: <Widget>[
```

```
        str != null?
        new Text(str,
            style: TextStyle(
              color: Colors.black,
              fontSize: 20.0,
              background: Paint()
                ..color = Colors.white,
              )
            ): new Text('No Results')
          ],
        )
      )
    );
```

Recall that the JSON response of the request was already parsed, formatted, and stored in the `str` variable. Here, we have used the value of `str` to create a `Text` with a specified color and background. We then added this `Text` as a child to a column and aligned the `Text` to display at the center of the screen. Finally, we wrapped the entire format around `stackChildren.add()`, to add it to the stack of UI elements.

2. Next, we will add the results of TensorFlow Lite, as follows:

```
stackChildren.add(Center(
child: Column(
  children: _recognitions != null
      ? _recognitions.map((res) {
    return Text(
      "${res["label"]}: ${res["confidence"].toStringAsFixed(3)}",
      style: TextStyle(
        color: Colors.black,
        fontSize: 20.0,
        background: Paint()
          ..color = Colors.white,
      ),
    );
  }).toList() : [],
),
));
```

The result of the TensorFlow Lite model stored in the `_recognitions` list is iterated element by element and is mapped to a list specified using `.map()`. Each element of the list is further transformed to a `Text` and is added as a column's child aligned to the center of the screen.

Also, note that either output from the Cloud Vision API or the TensorFlow Lite model needs to be added to the stack. To ensure this, we wrap the preceding code inside an `if-else` block such that the output of the former is added if the value passed in the constructor—that is, `modelChosen`—is 0, and the latter is added if the value is 1.

3. Finally, running the Cloud Vision API on various sets of images would give different outputs. Some of the examples are shown in the following screenshot:

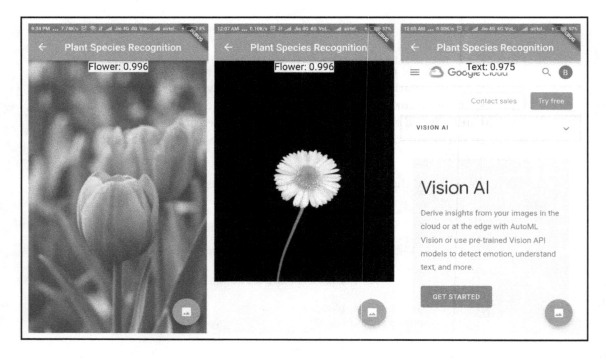

The recognitions differ when the same set of images is used with the TensorFlow Lite model. Some examples are shown in the following screenshot:

In the previous screenshot, we can see that the species of the flowers for which the images are loaded into the gallery are correctly identified.

Summary

In this chapter, we covered how we can use image processing using a popular deep-learning-based API service. We also discussed how we can apply the same with a custom trained model, by extending a previously created base model. While we did not explicitly mention it, the extension of the base model was a part of the process termed **transfer learning** (TL), where models trained on a certain dataset are imported into and used in a completely different scenario, with little or minimal fine-tuning.

Furthermore, the chapter covered why and when TensorFlow Lite is a good candidate for building a model, and how Flutter can be used for applying the same on the device model, which runs offline and is very fast. This chapter sets a milestone, with the introduction of Python and TensorFlow into the project, both of which will be used extensively in the upcoming chapters.

In the next chapter, we'll be covering a very exciting domain of computer science—namely, augmented reality—and see the application of deep learning in the real world.

5
Generating Live Captions from a Camera Feed

As humans, we see a million objects around us every day, in different scenarios. For humans, describing a scene is usually a trivial task: something we do without even taking a noticeable amount of time to think. But it is a huge task for machines to comprehend the elements and scenarios presented to it in visual media such as images or videos. However, for several applications of **artificial intelligence (AI)**, it is useful to have the capability of comprehending such images in the computer system. For example, it would be of immense help to visually impaired people if we could devise machines that could translate their surroundings into audio in real time. Also, there has been a constant effort from researchers to generate captions for images and videos in real time, so as to improve the accessibility of content presented on websites and apps.

This chapter presents a method of using a camera feed for generating natural language captions in real time. In this project, you will create a camera application that uses a customized pre-trained model stored on the device. The model uses a deep **Convolutional Neural Network (CNN)** and **Long Short-Term Memory (LSTM)** for caption generation.

We will cover the following topics in this chapter:

- Designing the project architecture
- Understanding an image caption generator
- Understanding the camera plugin
- Creating a camera application
- Generating image captions from the camera feed
- Creating the material app

Let's begin by discussing the architecture that we will follow for this project.

Designing the project architecture

In this project, we will be building a mobile app, which, when pointed at any scenery, will be able to create captions describing that scenery. Such an app is highly beneficial for people with visual defects, as it can be used both as an assistive technology on the web and as a day-to-day app if paired with a voice interface such as Alexa or Google Home. The app will be calling a hosted API that will produce captions for any given image passed to it. The API returns three best possible captions for the image, and the app then displays them right below the camera view in the app.

From a bird's-eye view, the project architecture can be illustrated by means of the following diagram:

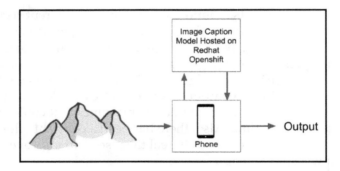

The input will be the camera feed obtained in a smartphone, which is sent to an image caption generation model hosted as a web API. The model is hosted as a Docker container on Red Hat OpenShift. The image caption generation model returns a caption for the image, which is then displayed to the user.

With a clear idea about how we'll be building the app, let's first talk about the problems with image captioning, and how we can solve them.

Understanding an image caption generator

A very popular domain of computer science is that of image processing. It deals with the manipulation of images and the various methods by which we can extract information from them. Another popular domain, **Natural Language Processing** (**NLP**), deals with how we can make machines that can understand and produce meaningful natural languages. Image captioning defines a mixture of the two topics, which attempts to first extract the information of objects appearing in any image and then to generate a caption describing the objects.

The caption should be generated in such a way that it is a meaningful string of words and is expressed in the form of a natural language sentence.

Consider the following image:

The objects that can be detected in the image are as follows: spoon, glass, coffee, and table.

However, do we have answers to the following questions?

1. Does the glass contain the coffee or the spoon, or is it empty?
2. Is the table above or below the glass?
3. Is the spoon above the table or below it?

We realize that, in order to answer the preceding questions, we need to use sentences such as the following:

1. The glass contains coffee.
2. The glass is kept on the table.
3. The spoon is kept on the table.

Hence, instead of simply recognizing the items in the image, if we attempt to create a caption around it, we also need to establish some positional and characteristical relations between the visible items. This will help us arrive at a good caption for the image, which could be something such as **a glass of coffee on a table with a spoon lying beside it**. In image caption generation algorithms, we try to create such captions from images.

However, a single caption may not always be enough to describe the scenery, and we might have to choose between two equally possible captions, as illustrated in the following screenshot:

Photo by Allef Vinicius on Unsplash

How do you describe the image in the preceding screenshot?

You could come up with any of the following captions:

1. Two trees with cloudy sky in the background.
2. A chair and a guitar kept on the ground.

This opens up the question of what, according to a user, is important in any image. While there are recent methods devised to handle such situations, such as the Attention Mechanism method, we will not be discussing these in depth in this chapter.

You can check out a very cool demo of an image caption system created by Microsoft at CaptionBot at `https://captionbot.ai`.

Let's now define the dataset we will be using to create our image captioning model.

Understanding the dataset

As expected, we need a large collection of general-purpose images, along with possible captions listed for them. We have shown in the previous section, *Understanding an image caption generator*, that a single image can have multiple captions without any of them having to be wrong. Hence, in this project, we will be working on the Flickr8k dataset. Besides this, we will also require the GloVE embeddings created by Jeffrey Pennington, Richard Socher, and Christopher D. Manning. In short, GloVE tells us which words are likely to follow after any given word, helping us form meaningful sentences from a set of disjoint words.

You can read more about GloVE embeddings, and the paper describing them, at `https://nlp.stanford.edu/projects/glove/`.

The Flickr8k dataset contains 8,000 samples of images, along with five possible captions for each of the images. There are other datasets available for the task, such as the Flickr30k dataset, with 30,000 samples, or the Microsoft COCO dataset, with 180,000 images. While using larger databases is expected to produce better results, for the sake of being able to train the model on an average machine, we will not be using them. However, in the event of availability of high-grade computing power, you can definitely try building your model around the larger datasets.

You can download the Flickr8k dataset by requesting it in this form provided by the University of Illinois at Urbana-Champaign: `https://forms.illinois.edu/sec/1713398`.

When you download the dataset, you'll be able to see the following folder structure:

```
Flickr8k/
    - dataset
        - images
            - 8091 images
    - text
        - Flickr8k.token.txt
```

```
- Flickr8k.lemma.txt
- Flickr_8k.trainImages.txt
- Flickr_8k.devImages.txt
- Flickr_8k.testImages.txt
- ExpertAnnotations.txt
- CrowdFlowerAnnotations.txt
```

Out of the available text files, the one of interest to us is the `Flickr8k.token.txt`, which contains the raw captions for each image in the `images` folder under the `dataset` directory.

The captions are present in the following format:

```
1007129816_e794419615.jpg#0 A man in an orange hat staring at something .
1007129816_e794419615.jpg#1 A man wears an orange hat and glasses .
1007129816_e794419615.jpg#2 A man with gauges and glasses is wearing a
Blitz hat .
1007129816_e794419615.jpg#3 A man with glasses is wearing a beer can
crocheted hat .
1007129816_e794419615.jpg#4 The man with pierced ears is wearing glasses
and an orange hat .
```

On inspection, we can observe that each row in the preceding sample contains the following parts:

```
Image_Filename#Caption_Number Caption
```

Thus, by going through each row in this file from the images present in the `dataset/images` folder, we can map the captions to each image.

Let's now begin working on the image caption generator code.

Building an image caption generation model

In this section, we will be looking at the code that will help us create a pipeline to convert images thrown at it into captions. We have broken this section down into four parts, as follows:

1. Initializing the caption dataset
2. Preparing the caption dataset
3. Training
4. Testing

Let's begin with project initialization.

Initializing the caption dataset

In the steps presented in this section, we'll be importing the required modules for the project and loading the dataset into the memory. Let's begin with importing the required modules, as follows:

1. Import the necessary libraries as follows:

```
import numpy as np
import pandas as pd

import nltk
from nltk.corpus import stopwords

import re
import string
import pickle

import matplotlib.pyplot as plt

%matplotlib inline
```

   You can see that there are a number of modules and sub-modules we'll be using in this project. They're all important at some point in the operation of the model and so are the helper modules, in essence. We will import more modules specific to building the model in the next step.

2. Import Keras and the sub-modules, as follows:

```
import keras
from keras.layers.merge import add
from keras.preprocessing import image
from keras.utils import to_categorical
from keras.models import Model, load_model
from keras.applications.vgg16 import VGG16
from keras.preprocessing.sequence import pad_sequences
from keras.layers import Input, Dense, Dropout, Embedding, LSTM
from keras.applications.resnet50 import ResNet50, preprocess_input,
decode_predictions
```

We imported the Keras module, along with several other sub-modules and methods, to help us with building the deep learning model quickly. Keras is one of the most popular deep learning libraries available and is usable with several other frameworks besides TensorFlow, such as Theano and PyTorch.

3. Load captions—in this step, we will load all the captions present in the `Flickr8k.token.txt` file into a single `captions` list, like this:

```
caption_file = "./data/Flickr8k/text/Flickr8k.token.txt"

captions = []

with open(caption_file) as f:
    captions = f.readlines()

captions = [x.strip() for x in captions]
```

Once we have loaded all the captions from the file, let's see what they contain, as follows:

```
captions[:5]
```

As expected, and mentioned earlier in the *Understanding the dataset* section, we obtain the following first five rows in the dataset:

```
['1000268201_693b08cb0e.jpg#0\tA child in a pink dress is climbing
up a set of stairs in an entry way .',
 '1000268201_693b08cb0e.jpg#1\tA girl going into a wooden building
.',
 '1000268201_693b08cb0e.jpg#2\tA little girl climbing into a wooden
playhouse .',
 '1000268201_693b08cb0e.jpg#3\tA little girl climbing the stairs to
her playhouse .',
 '1000268201_693b08cb0e.jpg#4\tA little girl in a pink dress going
into a wooden cabin .']
```

Now that we have seen the pattern with which each row is written, we can move ahead with splitting each row such that we can put the data in a data structure, which helps with quicker access and updating than a large list of strings.

Preparing the caption dataset

In the following steps, we will process the loaded captions dataset, and convert it to forms suitable for performing training on it:

1. In this step, we split the image descriptions and store them in a dictionary format for easier use in the future code, as shown in the following code block:

```
descriptions = {}

for x in captions:
    imgid, cap = x.split('\t')
    imgid = imgid.split('.')[0]
    if imgid not in descriptions.keys():
        descriptions[imgid] = []
    descriptions[imgid].append(cap)
```

   In the preceding lines of code, we broke down each line in the file into the parts of image ID and captions for each of those images. We created a dictionary out of it, where the image ID is the dictionary key and each key-value pair contains a list of five captions.

2. Next, we begin with basic string preprocessing in order to proceed with applying natural language techniques on the captions, as follows:

```
for key, caps in descriptions.items():
    for i in range(len(caps)):
        caps[i] = caps[i].lower()
        caps[i] = re.sub("[^a-z]+", " ", caps[i])
```

3. Also, to aid us in allocating the right sizes of memory spaces in the future and to prepare a vocabulary, let's create a list of all the words in the caption texts, like this:

```
allwords = []

for key in descriptions.keys():
    _ = [allwords.append(i) for cap in descriptions[key] for i in
cap.split()]
```

4. Once we've created a list of all the words, we can create a frequency count of the words. In order to do so, we use the `Counter` method of the `collections` module. Some words appear very rarely in the dataset. It is a good idea to remove these words as they're unlikely to appear frequently in the input the user provides and, hence, do not add much value to the caption generation algorithm. We do so with the following code:

```
from collections import Counter

freq = dict(Counter(allwords))
freq = sorted(freq.items(), reverse=True, key=lambda x:x[1])

threshold = 15
freq = [x for x in freq if x[1]>threshold]

print(len(freq))

allwords = [x[0] for x in freq]
```

Let's try to see which words are used most frequently by running the following code:

```
freq[:10]
```

We see the following output:

```
[('a', 62995),
 ('in', 18987),
 ('the', 18420),
 ('on', 10746),
 ('is', 9345),
 ('and', 8863),
 ('dog', 8138),
 ('with', 7765),
 ('man', 7275),
 ('of', 6723)]
```

We can conclude that the stop words make a large proportion of the caption texts. However, since we need them while generating sentences, we will not remove them.

Training

In the following steps, we load the training and test image datasets and perform training on them:

1. Let's now load the separated training and test files into the dataset. They contain the list of image filenames, which are actually the image IDs with file extensions, as can be seen in the following code block:

```
train_file = "./data/Flickr8k/text/Flickr_8k.trainImages.txt"
test_file = "./data/Flickr8k/text/Flickr_8k.testImages.txt"
```

Now, we will be processing the train images list file to extract the image IDs, and leave out the file extension since it is the same in all cases, as shown in the following code snippet:

```
with open(train_file) as f:
    cap_train = f.readlines()

cap_train = [x.strip() for x in cap_train]
```

We do the same with the test images list, as follows:

```
with open(test_file) as f:
    cap_test = f.readlines()

cap_test = [x.strip() for x in cap_test]

train = [row.split(".")[0] for row in cap_train]
test = [row.split(".")[0] for row in cap_test]
```

2. Now, we will create a single string that merges all the five possible captions for each of the images, and store them in a `train_desc`. dictionary. We use `#START#` and `#STOP#` to differentiate between the captions, in order to use these in the future for caption generation, as illustrated in the following code block:

```
train_desc = {}
max_caption_len = -1

for imgid in train:
    train_desc[imgid] = []
    for caption in descriptions[imgid]:
        train_desc[imgid].append("#START# " + caption + " #STOP#")
        max_caption_len = max(max_caption_len,
len(caption.split())+1)
```

3. We'll be using the `ResNet50` pre-trained model from the Keras model repository. We set the input shape to 224 x 224 x 3, where 224 x 244 is the dimension of each image as it will be passed to the model, and 3 is the number of color channels. Note that, unlike the **Modified National Institute of Standards and Technology (MNIST)** dataset, where the dimensions of each image were equal, this is not the case with the Flickr8k dataset. The code can be seen in the following snippet:

```
model = ResNet50(weights="imagenet", input_shape=(224,224,3))
model.summary()
```

Once the model is downloaded or loaded from the cache, the summary of the model will be displayed for each layer. However, we need to retrain the model for our needs, and so we will remove and recreate the last two layers of the model. To do so, we create a new model using the same inputs as in the loaded model, and the output is equivalent to the second-last layer's output, as shown in the following code snippet:

```
model_new = Model(model.input, model.layers[-2].output)
```

4. We'll be needing a function to repeatedly preprocess images, predict the features contained in that image, and form a feature vector from the recognized objects or properties in the image. Hence, we create an `encode_image` function that accepts an image as the input parameter and returns a feature vector representation of the image, by running it through the `ResNet50` retrained model, as follows:

```
def encode_img(img):
    img = image.load_img(img, target_size=(224,224))
    img = image.img_to_array(img)
    img = np.expand_dims(img, axis=0)
    img = preprocess_input(img)
    feature_vector = model_new.predict(img)
    feature_vector = feature_vector.reshape((-1,))
    return feature_vector
```

5. Now, we need to encode all images in the dataset into the feature vectors. To do so, we first need to load all images from the dataset into the memory one by one and apply the `encode_img` function to them. Let's first set the path of the `images` folder, as shown in the following code snippet:

```
img_data = "./data/Flickr8k/dataset/images/"
```

Once done, we iterate over all the images in the folder, using the list of training images created previously, and apply the `encode_img` function to each image. We then store the feature vectors in a dictionary with the image ID as the key, as follows:

```
train_encoded = {}

for ix, imgid in enumerate(train):
    img_path = img_data + "/" + imgid + ".jpg"
    train_encoded[imgid] = encode_img(img_path)
    if ix%100 == 0:
        print(".", end="")
```

We similarly encode all images in the test dataset with the following code:

```
test_encoded = {}

for i, imgid in enumerate(test):
    img_path = img_data + "/" + imgid + ".jpg"
    test_encoded[imgid] = encode_img(img_path)
    if i%100 == 0:
        print(".", end="")
```

6. In the next few steps, we will need to match the loaded GloVe embeddings to the list of words we have in our project. To do so, we will certainly have to find the index of any given word or to find the word at any given index. To facilitate this, we'll create two dictionaries from all the words we found in the captions dataset, mapping them to and from their indices, as shown in the following code snippet:

```
word_index_map = {}
index_word_map = {}

for i,word in enumerate(allwords):
    word_index_map[word] = i+1
    index_word_map[i+1] = word
```

We'll also create two additional key-value pairs in both dictionaries with the `"#START#"` and `"#STOP#"` words, as follows:

```
index_word_map[len(index_word_map)] = "#START#"
word_index_map["#START#"] = len(index_word_map)

index_word_map[len(index_word_map)] = "#STOP#"
word_index_map["#STOP#"] = len(index_word_map)
```

7. Let's now load the GloVe embeddings into the project, like this:

```
f = open("./data/glove/glove.6B.50d.txt", encoding='utf8')
```

With the find `open`, we read the embeddings into a dictionary where each word is the key, as follows:

```
embeddings = {}

for line in f:
    words = line.split()
    word_embeddings = np.array(words[1:], dtype='float')
    embeddings[words[0]] = word_embeddings
```

Once we are done reading the `embeddings` file, we will close it for better memory management, as follows:

```
f.close()
```

8. Let's now create the embedding matrix between all the words in the captions we have found in the dataset and the GloVe embeddings, as shown in the following code block:

```
embedding_matrix = np.zeros((len(word_index_map) + 1, 50))
for word, index in word_index_map.items():
    embedding_vector = embeddings.get(word)

    if embedding_vector is not None:
        embedding_matrix[index] = embedding_vector
```

Notice that the maximum number of embeddings we store is 50, which is very ample for generating long, meaningful strings.

9. Next, we will be creating another model that will specifically work on generating the captions for unseen images after obtaining feature vectors from the previous steps. To do so, we create an `Input` layer with the shape of the feature vector as the input, as shown in the following code block:

```
in_img_feats = Input(shape=(2048,))
in_img_1 = Dropout(0.3)(in_img_feats)
in_img_2 = Dense(256, activation='relu')(in_img_1)
```

Once done, we also need to take an input of the words in the captions in the entire training dataset, in the form of an LSTM such that given any word, we are able to predict the next 50 words. We do it with the following code:

```
in_caps = Input(shape=(max_caption_len,))
in_cap_1 = Embedding(input_dim=len(word_index_map) + 1,
output_dim=50, mask_zero=True)(in_caps)
in_cap_2 = Dropout(0.3)(in_cap_1)
in_cap_3 = LSTM(256)(in_cap_2)
```

Finally, we need to add a decoder layer that takes in the image features and the words in the form of LSTM and outputs the next possible word in the generation of the caption, like this:

```
decoder_1 = add([in_img_2, in_cap_3])
decoder_2 = Dense(256, activation='relu')(decoder_1)
outputs = Dense(len(word_index_map) + 1,
activation='softmax')(decoder_2)
```

Let's now get a summary of this model, after duly adding the input and output layers, by running the following code:

```
model = Model(inputs=[in_img_feats, in_caps], outputs=outputs)
model.summary()
```

We get the following output, describing the model layers:

Layer (type)	Output Shape	Param #	Connected to
input_3 (InputLayer)	(None, 37)	0	
input_2 (InputLayer)	(None, 2048)	0	
embedding_1 (Embedding)	(None, 37, 50)	74800	input_3[0][0]
dropout_1 (Dropout)	(None, 2048)	0	input_2[0][0]
dropout_2 (Dropout)	(None, 37, 50)	0	embedding_1[0][0]
dense_1 (Dense)	(None, 256)	524544	dropout_1[0][0]
lstm_1 (LSTM)	(None, 256)	314368	dropout_2[0][0]
add_18 (Add)	(None, 256)	0	dense_1[0][0] lstm_1[0][0]
dense_4 (Dense)	(None, 256)	65792	add_18[0][0]
dense_5 (Dense)	(None, 1496)	384472	dense_4[0][0]

```
Total params: 1,363,976
Trainable params: 1,289,176
Non-trainable params: 74,800
```

Next, let's now set the weights of the model before training it.

10. We will be plugging in the `embedding_matrix` we created earlier between the words in the GloVe embeddings and the words available in the captions of our dataset, as shown in the following code block:

```
model.layers[2].set_weights([embedding_matrix])
model.layers[2].trainable = False
```

With this, we are ready to compile the model, as follows:

```
model.compile(loss='categorical_crossentropy', optimizer='adam')
```

11. Since the dataset is huge, we would not want to load all the images into the dataset simultaneously while training. In order to facilitate memory-efficient training of the model, we use a generator function, as follows:

```
def data_generator(train_descs, train_encoded, word_index_map,
max_caption_len, batch_size):
    X1, X2, y = [], [], []
    n = 0
    while True:
        for key, desc_list in train_descs.items():
            n += 1
            photo = train_encoded[key]
            for desc in desc_list:
                seq = [word_index_map[word] for word in
desc.split() if word in word_index_map]
                for i in range(1, len(seq)):
                    xi = seq[0:i]
                    yi = seq[i]
                    xi = pad_sequences([xi],
maxlen=max_caption_len, value=0, padding='post')[0]
                    yi = to_categorical([yi],
num_classes=len(word_index_map) + 1)[0]
                    X1.append(photo)
                    X2.append(xi)
                    y.append(yi)
                if n==batch_size:
                    yield [[np.array(X1), np.array(X2)],
np.array(y)]
                    X1, X2, y = [], [], []
                    n = 0
```

12. We're now ready to train the model. Before we do so, we must set some of the hyperparameters of the model, as shown in the following code snippet:

```
batch_size = 3
steps = len(train_desc)//batch_size
```

Once we've set the hyperparameters, we can begin training with the following lines of code:

```
generator = data_generator(train_desc, train_encoded,
word_index_map, max_caption_len, batch_size)
model.fit_generator(generator, epochs=1, steps_per_epoch=steps,
verbose=1)
model.save('./model_weights/model.h5')
```

Testing

Now, in the following steps, we will create functions to predict captions based on the model trained in the previous steps, and test the captioning on a sample image:

1. We're finally at the stage where we can use our model to generate the captions of the images. We create a function that takes in the images and uses the `model.predict` method to come up with one word at each step until `#STOP#` is encountered in the predictions. It stops there and outputs the generated caption, as follows:

```
def predict_caption(img):
    in_text = "#START#"
    for i in range(max_caption_len):
        sequence = [word_index_map[w] for w in in_text.split() if w
in word_index_map]
        sequence = pad_sequences([sequence],
maxlen=max_caption_len, padding='post')
        pred = model.predict([img, sequence])
        pred = pred.argmax()
        word = index_word_map[pred]
        in_text += (' ' + word)
        if word == "#STOP#":
            break
    caption = in_text.split()[1:-1]
    return ' '.join(caption)
```

2. Let's test the generation model on some of the images in the test dataset, as follows:

```
img_name = list(test_encoded.keys())[np.random.randint(0, 1000)]
img = test_encoded[img_name].reshape((1, 2048))

im = plt.imread(img_data + img_name + '.jpg')
caption = predict_caption(img)

print(caption)
plt.imshow(im)
plt.axis('off')
plt.show()
```

Say we input the image shown in the following screenshot to the algorithm:

We get the following generated caption for the image shown in the preceding screenshot: **a brown dog is running through the grass**. While the caption is not very accurate, missing out entirely on the second animal in the picture, it does well enough to determine that a brown dog is running in the grass.

However, our trained model is very inaccurate and hence is unsuitable for use on production or usage beyond experimentation. You may have noticed that we set the number of epochs in the training to 1, which is a very low value. This was done in order to allow the training of this program to complete within a reasonable time for you to follow along with this book!

In the next section, we will look at how we can deploy an image caption generation model as an API and use it to generate live camera-feed captions.

Creating a simple click-deploy image caption generation model

While the image caption generation model we developed in the previous section, *Testing*, looks good enough, it is not very good. Hence, in this section, we will be showing you a way to click-deploy a production-ready model as a Docker image, hosted on Red Hat OpenShift and created by the amazing machine learning experts at IBM.

This is a very common practice to use microservices for such small and dedicated actions that are performed on any website and, hence, we will be treating this image caption service as a microservice.

The image we will be using is the *MAX Image Caption Generator* model developed by IBM. It is based on the `im2txt` model's code, hosted on GitHub as an openly available TensorFlow implementation of the *Show and Tell: Lessons learned from the 2015 MSCOCO Image Captioning Challenge* paper by Oriol Vinyals, Alexander Toshev, Samy Bengio, and Dumitru Erhan.

The model used in the image is trained on the much larger Microsoft COCO dataset that contains more than 200,000 instances of labeled images, and over 300,000 instances of images in total. The dataset contains images containing more than 1.5 million distinct objects, and is one of the largest and most popular datasets for building object detection and image labeling models. However, due to its sheer size, it is tough to train the model on a low-end device. Hence, we will be using the already available Docker image instead of attempting to train our model on it. However, the method described in the previous sections of the project chapter is very similar to the method used by the code present in the Docker image, and, with ample available resources, you can definitely try to train and improve the accuracy of the model.

 You can check out all the details about this Docker image project at the following link: `https://developer.ibm.com/exchanges/models/all/max-image-caption-generator/`

While there are other methods available to deploy this image that you can read about on the project page of this Docker image, we will be showing you the deployment on Red Hat OpenShift, to quickly enable you to test the model simply by making a few clicks.

Let's see how we can deploy this image, as follows:

1. Create a Red Hat OpenShift account. To do so, point your browser to `https://www.openshift.com/` and click on **FREE TRIAL**.

2. Choose to try out **RedHat OpenShift Online**, as shown in the following screenshot:

3. In the next screen, choose to **Sign up for Openshift Online**. Then, click on **Register** on the top right of the page to find the **Registration** page.

4. Fill in all the necessary details, and submit the form. You will be asked for email verification, upon completion of which you will be taken to the subscription **Confirmation** page, which will ask you to confirm the details of your free subscription of the platform, as shown in the following screenshot:

Note that the preceding subscription details are subject to change at any time and might reflect other values, regions, or duration of the subscription.

5. Once you confirm your subscription, you will have to wait for a few minutes before your system resources are provisioned. Once the provisioning is complete, you should be able to see the button that will take you to the management console, as shown in the following screenshot:

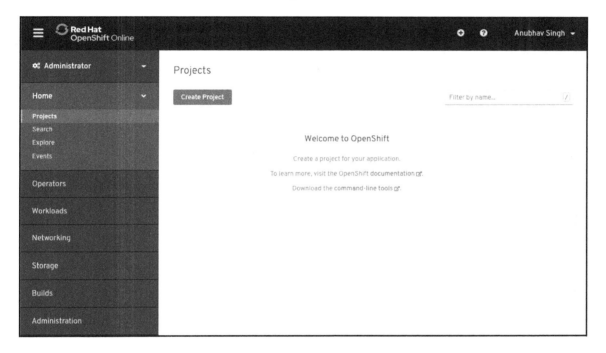

On the left of the management console shown in the preceding screenshot, you can find the various menu options, and on the center of the current page, you will be prompted to create a new project.

6. Click on **Create Project** and fill the project name in the dialog box that appears. Make sure that the project you create has a unique name. Once the project is created, you will be presented with a dashboard showing the monitoring of all the available resources and their usage.

On the left menu, select **Developer** to switch to the **Developer** view of the console, as shown in the following screenshot:

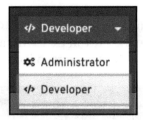

7. You should now be able to see the **Developer** view of the console, along with the updated left menu. Here, click on **Topology** to get the following deployment options:

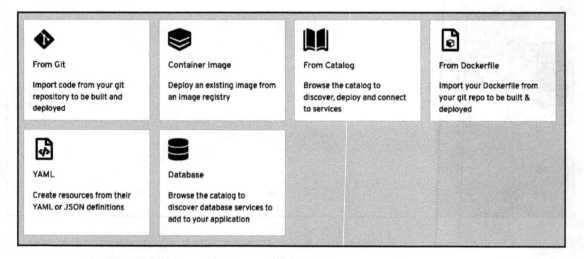

8. Click on **Container Image** in the screen displayed to you with the deployment options so as to bring up the form for container image deployment.

Here, fill in the image name as `codait/max-image-caption-generator` and click on the **Search** icon. The remainder of the fields are automatically fetched, and you'll be displayed the information pertaining to the image, as shown in the following screenshot:

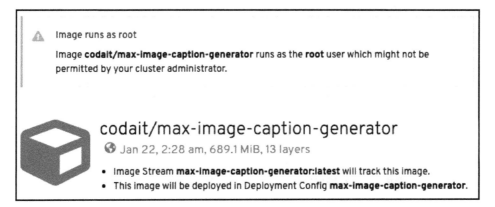

9. In the next screen that appears with the deployment details, click on the deployed image option at the center of the screen, as shown in the following screenshot:

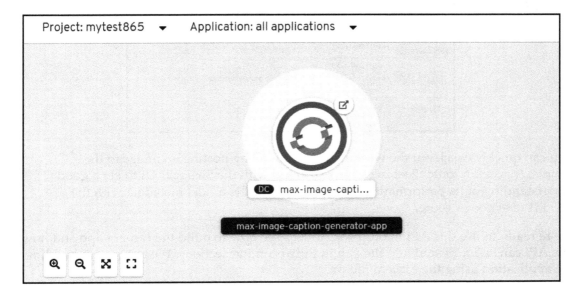

10. Then, scroll down the information panel that appears up on the right of the screen, and find the **Routes** information, which will resemble the following screenshot:

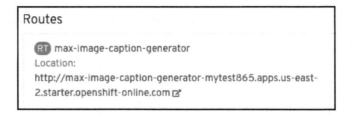

Click on this route, and you'll be presented with the following Swagger UI for the API that you have successfully deployed:

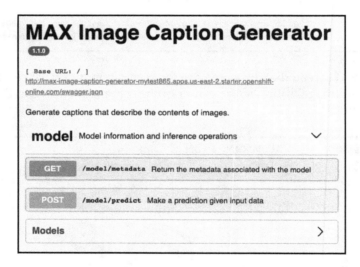

You can quickly check out the working of the model by posting an image to the /model/predict route. Feel free to play around with the Swagger UI to get a good understanding of its performance. You can also find the model metadata with the /model/metadata route.

We're ready to use this API in our project. Let's see how to build the camera app and how this API can be integrated into the app in the upcoming sections. We begin with building the application using the camera plugin.

Understanding the camera plugin

The Camera plugin, available as a `camera` dependency, allows us to access the device's camera freely. It provides support for both Android and iOS devices. The plugin is open sourced and is hosted on GitHub so that anyone can freely access the code, fix errors, and suggest enhancements to the current version.

The plugin can be used to display the live camera preview on a widget, capture images, and store them locally on a device. It can also be used to record a video. Further more, it has the capability to access the image stream.

The Camera plugin can be added to any application with the following three simple steps:

1. Installing the package
2. Adding methods for persistent storage and proper execution
3. Coding

Let's now discuss each of these steps in detail.

Installing the camera plugin

To use the camera plugin in the application, we need to add `camera` as a dependency in the `pubspec.yaml` file. This can be done as follows:

```
camera: 0.5.7+3
```

Finally, run `flutter pub get` to add the dependency to the application.

Adding methods for persistent storage and proper execution

For iOS devices, we also need to specify a space to store configuration data that can be easily accessed by the system. iOS devices determine the icons to be displayed, document types supported by the application, and other behaviors, with the help of `Info.plist` files. You need to modify the `Info.plist` file present in `ios/Runner/Info.plist` in this step.

This can be done by adding the following text:

```
<key>NSCameraUsageDescription</key>
<string>Can I use the camera please?</string>
<key>NSMicrophoneUsageDescription</key>
<string>Can I use the mic please?</string>
```

For Android devices, the minimum **software development kit (SDK)** version required for the plugin to execute properly is 21. Hence, change the minimum Android SDK version to 21 (or higher), stored in the `android/app/build.gradle` file, as follows:

```
minSdkVersion 21
```

After installing the dependencies and making the required changes, let's now start to code the application.

Coding

After installing the plugin and making the required modifications, it can now be used to access the camera, click pictures, and record videos.

The most important steps involved are as follows:

1. Import the plugin by running the following code:

```
import 'package:camera/camera.dart';
```

2. Detect available cameras by running the following code:

```
List<CameraDescription> cameras = await availableCameras();
```

3. Initialize the camera control instance as follows:

```
CameraController controller = CameraController(cameras[0],
ResolutionPreset.medium);
    controller.initialize().then((_) {
      if (!mounted) {
        return;
      }
      setState(() {});
    });
```

4. Dispose of the controller instance by running the following code:

```
controller?.dispose();
```

Now that we have a basic knowledge of the camera plugin, let us build the live camera preview for the application.

Creating a camera application

We will now start to build the mobile application to generate captions for objects at which the camera is pointed. It will consist of a camera preview to capture images and a text view to display the captions returned by the model.

The application can be broadly divided into two parts, as follows:

1. Building the camera preview
2. Integrating the model to fetch the captions

In the following section, we will talk about building a basic camera preview.

Building the camera preview

We will now build the camera preview for the application. We start by creating a new file, `generate_live_caption.dart`, with a `GenerateLiveCaption` stateful widget.

Let us look at the following steps to create a live camera preview:

1. To add a live camera preview, we will be using the `camera` plugin. We begin by adding the dependency to the `pubspec.yaml` file, as follows:

```
camera: ^0.5.7
```

Next, we need to add the dependency to the project by running `flutter pub get`.

2. We now create a new file, `generate_live_captions.dart`, containing a `GenerateLiveCaptions` stateful widget. All of the code described in the further steps will be included in the `_GenerateLiveCaptionState` class.

3. Import the `camera` library. We import it to `generate_live_captions.dart`, as follows:

```
import 'package:camera/camera.dart';
```

4. We now need to detect all the cameras available on the device. Define the `detectCameras()` function for the same, like this:

```
Future<void> detectCameras() async{
    cameras = await availableCameras();
}
```

`cameras` is a global list containing all the available cameras, and is declared inside `GenerateLiveCaptionState`, as follows:

```
List<CameraDescription> cameras;
```

5. We now create an instance of `CameraController`, using the `initializeController()` method, like this:

```
void initializeController() {
    controller = CameraController(cameras[0],
ResolutionPreset.medium);
        controller.initialize().then((_) {
            if (!mounted) {
                return;
            }
            setState(() {});
        });
    }
```

In the application, we will be using the rear camera of the device, so we create the `CameraController` instance using `camera[0]` and specify the resolution to be medium, using `ResolutionPreset.medium`. Next, we initialize the controller, using `controller.initialize()`.

6. To display the camera feed on the screen of the application, we define a `buildCameraPreview()` method, as follows:

```
Widget _buildCameraPreview() {
    var size = MediaQuery.of(context).size.width;
        return Container(
            child: Column(
                children: <Widget>[
                    Container(
                        width: size,
                        height: size,
```

```
                   child: CameraPreview(controller),
             ),
       ]
    )
  );
}
```

In the preceding method, we use `MediaQuery.of(context).size.width` to get the width of the container and store it in a `size` variable. Next, we create a column of widgets, where the first element is a `Container`. The child of the `Container` is simply a `CameraPreview`, to show the camera feed on the screen of the application.

7. Now, we override `initState` so that all the cameras are detected as soon as `GenerateLiveCaption` is initialized, as follows:

```
@override
void initState() {
  super.initState();
  detectCameras().then((_){
    initializeController();
  });
}
```

In the preceding code snippet, we simply make a call to `detectCameras()` to first detect all the available cameras and then call `initializeController()` to initialize `CameraController` with the rear camera.

8. To generate captions from the camera feed, we will take pictures from the camera feed and store them in the device locally. These clicked pictures will be later retrieved from the image files to generate captions. Hence, we need a mechanism to read and write files. We make use of the `path_provider` plugin here by adding to the following dependency in the `pubspec.yaml` file:

```
path_provider: ^1.4.5
```

Next, we install the package by running `flutter pub get` in the terminal.

9. To use the `path_provider` plugin in the application, we need to import it in `generate_live_caption.dart` by adding the `import` statement at the top of the file, like this:

```
import 'package:path_provider/path_provider.dart';
```

10. To save the image files to disk, we also need to import the `dart:io` library, as follows:

```
import 'dart:io';
```

11. Now, let us define a method, `captureImages()`, to capture images from the camera feed and store them in the device. These stored image files will be used later to generate captions. The method is defined as follows:

```
capturePictures() async {
    String timestamp =
DateTime.now().millisecondsSinceEpoch.toString();
    final Directory extDir = await
getApplicationDocumentsDirectory();
    final String dirPath =
'${extDir.path}/Pictures/generate_caption_images';
    await Directory(dirPath).create(recursive: true);
    final String filePath = '$dirPath/${timestamp}.jpg';
    controller.takePicture(filePath).then((_){
      File imgFile = File(filePath);
      });
  }
```

In the preceding code snippet, we first find out the current time in milliseconds using `DateTime.now().millisecondsSinceEpoch()`, and then convert it to string and store it in the variable timestamp. The timestamp will be used to provide unique names to the image files we will be storing further. Next, we get the path to the directory that can be used to store the images using `getApplicationDocumentsDirectory()`, and store it in `extDir` of the `Directory` type. Now, we create a proper directory path by appending the external directory with `'/Pictures/generate_caption_images'`. Then, we create the final `filePath` by combining the directory path with the current timestamp and giving it a `.jpg` format. The `filePath` for all the clicked images will always be unique since the timestamp will always have different values. Finally, we capture the image by calling `takePicture()`, using the current camera controller instance, and passing in the `filePath`. We store the image file created in `imgFile` that will be used later to generate proper captions.

12. As discussed earlier, to generate captions from a live camera feed, we capture images at periodic intervals. To get this to work, we modify `initializeController()` and add a timer, as follows :

```
void initializeController() {
    controller = CameraController(cameras[0],
```

```
ResolutionPreset.medium);
    controller.initialize().then((_) {
        if (!mounted) {
            return;
        }
        setState(() {});
        const interval = const Duration(seconds:5);
        new Timer.periodic(interval, (Timer t) =>
capturePictures());
    });
}
```

Inside `initializeController()`, once the camera controller is properly initialized and mounted, we create a duration of 5 seconds using the `Duration()` class, and store it in the interval. Now, we create a periodic timer using `Timer.periodic` and give it an interval of 5 seconds. The callback specified here is `capturePictures()`. It will be invoked repeatedly in the specified interval.

At this point, we have created a live camera feed that is displayed on the screen and is able to capture images at intervals of 5 seconds. In the next section, we will integrate the model to generate captions for all the captured images.

Generating image captions from the camera feed

Now that we have a clear idea about the image caption generator and have an application with a camera feed, we are ready to generate captions for the images from the camera feed. The logic to be followed is very simple. Images are captured from the live camera feed at a specific time interval and are stored in the device's local storage. Next, the stored pictures are retrieved and an `HTTP POST` request is created for the hosted model, passing in the retrieved image to fetch the generated captions, parsing the response, and displaying it on the screen.

Let's now look at the detailed steps, as follows:

1. We will first add an `http` dependency to the `pubspec.yaml` file to make `http` requests, as follows:

   ```
   http: ^0.12.0
   ```

Install the dependency to the project using `flutter pub get`.

2. To use the `http` package in the application, we need to import it in `generate_live_caption.dart`, like this:

```
import 'package:http/http.dart' as http;
```

3. Now, we define a method, `fetchResponse()`, that takes in an image file and creates a post to the hosted model, using the image as follows:

```
Future<Map<String, dynamic>> fetchResponse(File image) async {
    final mimeTypeData =
        lookupMimeType(image.path, headerBytes: [0xFF,
0xD8]).split('/');
    final imageUploadRequest = http.MultipartRequest(
        'POST',
        Uri.parse(
"http://max-image-caption-generator-mytest865.apps.us-east-2.starte
r.openshift-online.com/model/predict"));
    final file = await http.MultipartFile.fromPath('image',
image.path,
        contentType: MediaType(mimeTypeData[0], mimeTypeData[1]));
    imageUploadRequest.fields['ext'] = mimeTypeData[1];
    imageUploadRequest.files.add(file);
    try {
      final streamedResponse = await imageUploadRequest.send();
      final response = await
http.Response.fromStream(streamedResponse);
      final Map<String, dynamic> responseData =
json.decode(response.body);
      parseResponse(responseData);
      return responseData;

    } catch (e) {
      print(e);
      return null;
    }
  }
```

In the preceding method, we first find the mime type of the selected file by looking at the header bytes of the file. Then, we initialize a multipart request, as expected by the hosted API. We attach the file passed to the function as the `image` post parameter. We explicitly pass the extension of the image with the request body since `image_picker` has some bugs due to which it mixes up image extensions with filenames such as `filenamejpeg`, which creates problems at the server side to manage or verify the file extension. The response is in JSON format and, therefore, we need to decode it using `json.decode()`, passing in the body of the response using `res.body`. We now parse the response by making a call to `parseResponse()`, defined in the next step. Additionally, we use `catchError()` to detect and print any error that might have occurred while executing the `POST` request.

4. After successfully executing the `POST` request and getting the response from the model with the generated captions for the image that was passed, we parse the response inside the `parseResponse()` method, as follows:

```
void parseResponse(var response) {
    String resString = "";
    var predictions = response['predictions'];
    for(var prediction in predictions) {
      var caption = prediction['caption'];
      var probability = prediction['probability'];
      resString = resString + '${caption}: ${probability}\n\n';
    }
    setState(() {
      resultText = resString;
    });
  }
```

In the preceding method, we first store the list of all predictions present in `response['predictions']` and store it in the `prediction` variable. Now, we iterate through each of the predictions inside the `for each` loop, using the `prediction` variable. For every prediction, we take out the caption and probability stored in `prediction['caption']` and `prediction['probability']`, respectively. We append them to a `resString` string variable that will contain all the predicted captions along with the probability. Finally, we set the state of `resultText` to the value stored in `resString`. `resultText` is a global string variable here that will be used in the next steps to display the predicted captions.

5. Now, we modify `capturePictures()` so that the HTTP post request is made every time a new image is captured, as follows:

```
capturePictures() async {
    . . . . .
    controller.takePicture(filePath).then((_){
      File imgFile = File(filePath);
      fetchResponse(imgFile);
      });
}
```

In the preceding code snippet, we add a call to `fetchResponse()`, passing in the image file.

6. Now, let's modify `buildCameraPreview()` to display all the predictions, as follows:

```
Widget buildCameraPreview() {
    . . . . .
    return Container(
      child: Column(
        children: <Widget>[
          Container(
            . . . . .
            child: CameraPreview(controller),
          ),
          Text(resultText),
        ]
      )
    );
}
```

In the preceding code snippet, we simply add a `Text` with `result.Text`. `result.Text` is a global string variable that will contain all the predictions as described in *Step 5* and is declared as follows:

```
String resultText = "Fetching Response..";
```

7. Finally, we override the `build()` method to create the final scaffold for the application, as follows:

```
@override
  Widget build(BuildContext context) {
    return Scaffold(
      appBar: AppBar(title: Text('Generate Image Caption'),),
      body:
(controller.value.isInitialized)?buildCameraPreview():new
```

```
      Container(),
            );
      }
```

In the preceding code snippet, we return a scaffold with an `appBar` having the title `Generate Image Caption`. The body is initially set to an empty container. Once the camera controller is initialized, the body is updated to display the camera feed along with the predicted captions.

8. Finally, we dispose of the camera controller as follows:

```
@override
  void dispose() {
    controller?.dispose();
    super.dispose();
  }
```

Now, we have successfully created a mechanism to display a live camera feed on the screen. The live camera feed is captured at intervals of 5 seconds and is sent as an input to the model. The predicted captions for all the captured images are then displayed on the screen.

In the next section, let's now create the final material app to bring everything together.

Creating the material app

After making all the segments work properly, let's create the final material app. Inside the `main.dart` file, we create a `StatelessWidget` and override the `build()` method, as follows:

```
class MyApp extends StatelessWidget {
@override
  Widget build(BuildContext context) {
    return MaterialApp(
      title: 'Flutter Demo',
      theme: ThemeData(
        primarySwatch: Colors.blue,
      ),
      home: GenerateLiveCaption()
    );
  }
}
```

Finally, we execute the code as follows:

```
void main() => runApp(MyApp());
```

You should be able to have an app screen as shown in the following screenshot:

Notice the captions displayed in the image, as follows:

- **a laptop computer sitting on top of a desk**.
- **an open laptop computer sitting on top of a desk**.
- **an open laptop computer sitting on top of a wooden desk**.

These captions are fairly accurate in their descriptions. However, they may not perform very well at times due to the unavailability of relevant pictures in the training datasets.

Summary

In this chapter, we saw how we can create an app that produces captions in real time for a camera feed using deep CNNs and LSTMs. We also saw how we can quickly deploy some machine learning/deep learning models present in the form of Docker images to Red Hat OpenShift and easily obtain them in the form of callable APIs. This is very crucial from the perspective of an application developer as, when working with a team of machine learning developers, they will often provide you with Docker images of models to work with, such that you are not required to perform any code or configuration on the system. Such applications can be put to several uses, such as creating assistive technology for blind people, generating transcripts of events happening at that moment, or—say—having a live tutor for children to help them identify the objects in their environment. We covered how you can apply the Flutter Camera plugin and perform deep learning on the frames.

In the next chapter, we will look at how we can develop a deep learning model for performing application security.

6
Building an Artificial Intelligence Authentication System

Authentication is one of the most prominent features of any application, regardless of it being a native mobile software or a website, and has been an actively growing field since the onset of the need to protect data, and the need for privacy in relation to sensitive data, that is being shared on the internet. In this chapter, we will begin with a simple Firebase-based login to an application, and then improvise step by step to include an artificial intelligence (AI)-based authentication confidence metric, and ReCaptcha by Google. All these authentication methods use deep learning at their core and present a state-of-the-art method of implementing security in mobile apps.

In this chapter, we will cover the following topics:

- A simple login application
- Adding Firebase authentication
- Understanding anomaly detection for authentication
- A custom model for authenticating users
- Implementing ReCaptcha for spam protection
- Deploying the model in Flutter

Technical requirements

For a mobile application, Visual Studio Code with Flutter and the Dart plugin plus of Firebase Console are required

GitHub URL: `https://github.com/PacktPublishing/Mobile-Deep-Learning-Projects/tree/master/Chapter6`

A simple login application

We will first create a simple authentication application that uses Firebase authentication to authenticate users before allowing them to enter the main screen. The application will allow the user to enter their email and password to create an account and then enable them to sign in subsequently using this email and password.

The following screenshot shows the complete flow of the application:

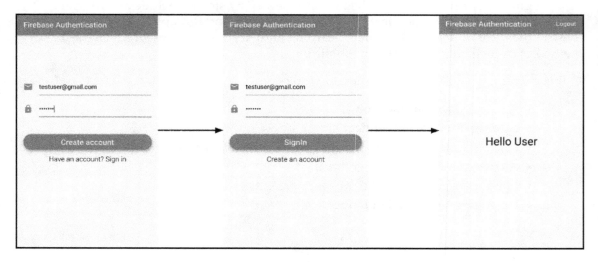

The widget tree of the application is as follows:

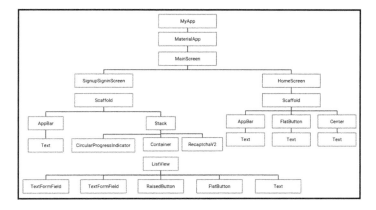

Let's now discuss the implementation of each of the widgets in detail.

Creating the UI

Let's start by creating the login screen for the application. The **user interface** (**UI**) will consist of two **TextFormField** to take in the user's email ID and password, **RaisedButton** to sign up/in, and **FlatButton** to switch between sign-up and sign-in operations.

The following screenshot labels the widget that will be used for the first screen of the application:

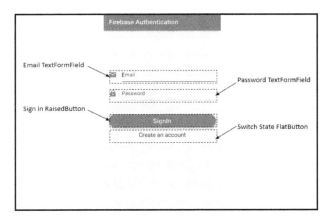

Let's now create the UI of the application as follows:

1. We begin by creating a new dart file called `signup_signin_screen.dart`. This file contains a stateful widget – `SignupSigninScreen`.

2. The topmost widget in the first screen is `TextField`, for taking in the user's mail ID. The `_createUserMailInput()` method helps us to build the widget:

```
Widget _createUserMailInput() {
  return Padding(
    padding: const EdgeInsets.fromLTRB(0.0, 100.0, 0.0, 0.0),
    child: new TextFormField(
      maxLines: 1,
      keyboardType: TextInputType.emailAddress,
      autofocus: false,
      decoration: new InputDecoration(
        hintText: 'Email',
        icon: new Icon(
          Icons.mail,
          color: Colors.grey,
        )),
      validator: (value) => value.isEmpty ? 'Email can\'t be
empty' : null,
      onSaved: (value) => _usermail = value.trim(),
    ),
  );
}
```

First of all, we provided padding to the widget using `EdgeInsets.fromLTRB()`. This helps us to create offsets in each of the four cardinal directions, namely, left, top, right, and bottom, with different values. Next, we created `TextFormField` with `maxLines` (the maximum number of lines for the input) that have a value of 1 as the child, which takes in the email address of the user. Also, we specified the type of keyboard that will be used inside the property – `keyboardType`, depending on the input type, which is `TextInputType.emailAddress`. We then set `autoFocus` to `false`. Then, we used `InputDecoration` inside the decoration property to provide `hintText` "Email" and an icon, `Icons.mail`. To make sure that the user does not attempt to sign in without entering an email address or a password, we add a validator. This shows a warning, **"Email can't be empty"**, when a login attempt is made with empty fields. Finally, we trimmed the value entered by using `trim()` to remove all the trailing spaces, and then stored the entered value inside the `_usermail` string variable.

3. Similar to `TextField` in *Step 2*, we define the next method, `_createPasswordInput()`, to create a `TextFormField()` for entering the password:

```
Widget _createPasswordInput() {
  return Padding(
    padding: const EdgeInsets.fromLTRB(0.0, 15.0, 0.0, 0.0),
    child: new TextFormField(
      maxLines: 1,
      obscureText: true,
      autofocus: false,
      decoration: new InputDecoration(
          hintText: 'Password',
          icon: new Icon(
            Icons.lock,
            color: Colors.grey,
          )),
      validator: (value) => value.isEmpty ? 'Password can\'t be
empty' : null,
      onSaved: (value) => _userpassword = value.trim(),
    ),
  );
}
```

We start by providing padding in all four cardinal directions using `EdgeInsets.fromLTRB()` to give an offset of `15.0` at the top. Next, we create a `TextFormField` with `maxLines` as 1, and set `obscureText` to `true` and `autofocus` to `false`. `obscureText` is used to hide the text that is being typed. We use `InputDecoration` to provide the `hintText` password and a gray-colored icon, `Icons.lock`. To make sure that the text field isn't left empty, a validator is used that gives a warning, `Password can't be empty`, when a null value is passed, that is, the user attempts to sign in/up without entering a password. Finally, `trim()` is used to remove all trailing spaces and store the password in a `_userpassword` string variable.

4. Next, we declare the `FormMode` enumeration outside `_SignupSigninScreenState` that operates between two modes, `SIGNIN` and `SIGNUP`, as seen in the following code snippet:

```
enum FormMode { SIGNIN, SIGNUP }
```

We will use this enumeration for the button that would let the user both sign in and sign up. It will help us easily switch between the two modes. Enumeration is a set of identifiers that is used for denoting constant values.

An enumerated type is declared using the enum keyword. Each of the identifiers declared inside enum represents an integer value; for example, the first identifier has the value 0, and the second identifier has the value 1. By default, the value of the first identifier is 0.

5. Let's define a `_createSigninButton()` method that returns the button widget to let the user sign up and sign in:

```
Widget _createSigninButton() {
  return new Padding(
      padding: EdgeInsets.fromLTRB(0.0, 45.0, 0.0, 0.0),
      child: SizedBox(
        height: 40.0,
        child: new RaisedButton(
          elevation: 5.0,
          shape: new RoundedRectangleBorder(borderRadius: new
BorderRadius.circular(30.0)),
          color: Colors.blue,
          child: _formMode == FormMode.SIGNIN
            ? new Text('SignIn',
                style: new TextStyle(fontSize: 20.0, color:
Colors.white))
            : new Text('Create account',
                style: new TextStyle(fontSize: 20.0, color:
Colors.white)),
          onPressed: _signinSignup,
        ),
      ));
  }
```

We start with Padding, giving the button offset of 45.0 at the top and adding SizedBox with a height of 40.0 as the child that also has RaisedButton as its child. The raised button is given a rounded rectangular shape using RoundedRectangleBorder() with a border-radius of 30.0 and a color blue. The text of the button that is added as the child depends on the current value of _formMode. If the value of _formMode (an instance of the FormMode enumeration) is FormMode.SIGNIN, the button shows SignIn, otherwise Create account. The _signinSignup method will be called when the button is pressed and is described in the later sections.

6. Now, we add the fourth button to the screen to let the user switch between the SIGNIN and SIGNUP form modes. We define the _createSigninSwitchButton() method that returns FlatButton as follows:

```
Widget _createSigninSwitchButton() {
  return new FlatButton(
    child: _formMode == FormMode.SIGNIN
      ? new Text('Create an account',
          style: new TextStyle(fontSize: 18.0, fontWeight:
FontWeight.w300))
      : new Text('Have an account? Sign in',
          style:
              new TextStyle(fontSize: 18.0, fontWeight:
FontWeight.w300)),
    onPressed: _formMode == FormMode.SIGNIN
      ? _switchFormToSignUp
      : _switchFormToSignin,
  );
}
```

If the current value of _formMode is SIGNIN and the button is pressed, it should change to SIGNUP and it should display Create an account. Otherwise, if _formMode has SIGNUP as its current value and the button is pressed, the value should be switched to SIGNIN denoted by the text Have an account? Sign in. This logic of toggling between texts is added while creating the Text child of the RaisedButton using a ternary operator. A very similar logic is used for the onPressed property, which again checks the value of _formMode to switch between modes and update the value of _formMode using the _switchFormToSignUp and _switchFormToSignin methods. We will define the, _switchFormToSignUp and _switchFormToSignin methods in *Steps 7* and *8*.

7. Now, we define _switchFormToSignUp() as follows:

```
void _switchFormToSignUp() {
  _formKey.currentState.reset();
  setState(() {
    _formMode = FormMode.SIGNUP;
  });
}
```

This method resets the value of _formMode and updates it to FormMode.SIGNUP. Changing the value inside setState() helps to notify the framework that the internal state of the object has changed and that the UI may require an update.

8. We define _switchFormToSignin() in a very similar manner to _switchFormToSignUp():

```
void _switchFormToSignin() {
  _formKey.currentState.reset();
  setState(() {
    _formMode = FormMode.SIGNIN;
  });
}
```

This method resets the value of _formMode and updates it to FormMode.SIGNIN. Changing the value inside setState() helps to notify the framework that the internal state of the object has changed and that the UI may require an update.

9. Now, let's bring all the screen widgets, Email TextField, Password TextFied, SignIn Button, and FlatButton, to switch between sign up and sign in inside a single container. For this, we define a method, createBody(), as follows:

```
Widget _createBody(){
  return new Container(
      padding: EdgeInsets.all(16.0),
      child: new Form(
        key: _formKey,
        child: new ListView(
          shrinkWrap: true,
          children: <Widget>[
            _createUserMailInput(),
            _createPasswordInput(),
            _createSigninButton(),
            _createSigninSwitchButton(),
            _createErrorMessage(),
          ],
        ),
      )
    );
}
```

This method returns a new `Container` with `Form` as a child and provides it with padding of `16.0`. The form uses _formKey as its key and adds `ListView` as its child. The elements of the `ListView` are the widgets that we had created in the preceding methods to add `TextFormFields` and `Buttons`. `shrinkWrap` is set to `true` to ensure that `ListView` occupies only the necessary space and does not attempt to expand and fill the whole screen

> The `Form` class is used to group and validate multiple `FormFields` together. Here, we are using `Form` to wrap two `TextFormFields`, one `RaisedButton`, and one `FlatButton` together.

10. One important thing to note here is that since authenticating, the user will ultimately be a network operation, it might take some time to make the network request. Adding a progress bar here prevents the deadlock of the UI while the network operation is in progress. We declare a `boolean` flag _loading , which is set to `true` when the network operation starts. Now, we define a _createCircularProgress() method as follows:

```
Widget _createCircularProgress(){
  if (_loading) {
    return Center(child: CircularProgressIndicator());
  } return Container(height: 0.0, width: 0.0,);
}
```

The method returns `CircularProgressIndicator()` only if _loading is `true` and a network operation is in progress.

11. Finally, let's add all the widgets inside the `build()` method:

```
@override
Widget build(BuildContext context) {
  return new Scaffold(
      appBar: new AppBar(
        title: new Text('Firebase Authentication'),
      ),
      body: Stack(
        children: <Widget>[
          _createBody(),
          _createCircularProgress(),
        ],
      ));
}
```

From inside `build()`, we return a scaffold after adding the `AppBar` variable that contains the title of the application. The body of the scaffold contains a stack with children as the widgets returned by the, `_createBody()` and `_createCircularProgress()` function calls.

We are now ready with the primary UI structure of our application.

 The entire code of `SignupSigninScreen` can be found at `https://github.com/PacktPublishing/-Mobile-Deep-Learning-Projects/blob/master/Chapter6/firebase_authentication/lib/signup_login_screen.dart`.

In the next section, we will look at the steps involved in adding Firebase authentication to the application.

Adding Firebase authentication

As discussed earlier, in the *Simple login application* section, we will be using the user's email and password for authentication integrated through Firebase.

 To create and configure a Firebase project on Firebase Console, refer to the *Appendix*.

The following steps discuss in detail about how to set up the project on Firebase Console:

1. We begin by selecting the project on Firebase Console:

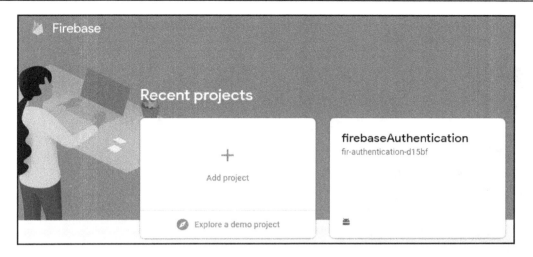

2. Next, we will click on the **Authentication** option from the **Develop** menu:

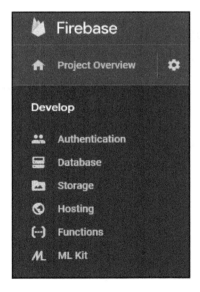

This will take us to the authentication screen.

3. Migrate to the sign-in tab and enable the **Email/Password** option under **Sign-in providers**:

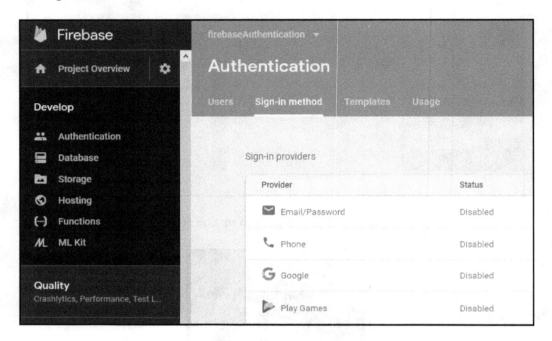

This is all that is required to set up Firebase Console.

Next, we will integrate Firebase in the code. This is done as follows:

1. Migrate to the project in your Flutter SDK and add `firebase-auth` to the app level `build.gradle` file:

```
implementation 'com.google.firebase:firebase-auth:18.1.0'
```

2. To get `FirebaseAuthentication` working in the application, we will be using a `firebase_auth` plugin here. Add the plugin dependency inside dependencies in the `pubspec.yaml` file:

```
firebase_auth: 0.14.0+4
```

Be sure to run `flutter pub get` to install the dependency.

Now, let's write some code to provide the Firebase authentication functionality inside the application.

Creating auth.dart

Now, we will create a Dart file, `auth.dart`. This file will act as a centralized point to access the authentication methods provided by the `firebase_auth` plugin:

1. First, import the `firebase_auth` plugin:

```
import 'package:firebase_auth/firebase_auth.dart';
```

2. Now, create an abstract class, `BaseAuth`, which lists all the authentication methods and acts a middle layer between the UI components and the authentication methods:

```
abstract class BaseAuth {
  Future<String> signIn(String email, String password);
  Future<String> signUp(String email, String password);
  Future<String> getCurrentUser();
  Future<void> signOut();
}
```

As the name of the methods suggests, we will be using four primary features of authentication:

- `signIn()`: To sign in an already existing user using an email and password
- `signUp()`: To create an account for a new user using an email and password
- `getCurrentUser()`: To get the current signed-in user
- `signOut()`: To sign out a signed-in user

 One important thing to note here is that since this is a network operation, all the methods operate asynchronously and return a `Future` value once execution is complete.

3. Create an `Auth` class that implements `BaseAuth`:

```
class Auth implements BaseAuth {
    //. . . . .
}
```

In the next steps, we will define all the methods declared in `BaseAuth`.

4. Create an instance of `FirebaseAuth`:

```
final FirebaseAuth _firebaseAuth = FirebaseAuth.instance;
```

5. The `signIn()` method is implemented as follows:

```
Future<String> signIn(String email, String password) async {
    AuthResult result = await
_firebaseAuth.signInWithEmailAndPassword(email: email, password:
password);
    FirebaseUser user = result.user;
    return user.uid;
}
```

This method takes in a user's email and password and calls
`signInWithEmailAndPassword()`, passing in the email and password to sign in
an already existing user. Once the sign-in operation is complete, an `AuthResult`
instance is returned. We store it in `result` and also use `result.user`, which
returns `FirebaseUser`. It can be used to get the information relating to the user,
such as their `uid`, `phoneNumber`, and `photoUrl`. Here, we return `user.uid`,
which is a unique identification for each of the existing users. As stated
previously, since this is a network operation, it runs asynchronously and
returns `Future` once execution is complete.

6. Next, we will define the `signUp()` method to add new users:

```
Future<String> signUp(String email, String password) async {
    AuthResult result = await
_firebaseAuth.createUserWithEmailAndPassword(email: email,
password: password);
    FirebaseUser user = result.user;
    return user.uid;
}
```

The preceding method takes in an email and password that was used during signup and passes in the value in its call to `createUserWithEmailAndPassword`.
Similar to the one defined in the previous step, this call also returns
an `AuthResult` object, which is further used to extract `FirebaseUser`. Finally,
the `signUp` method returns the `uid` of the newly created user.

7. Now, we will define `getCurrentUser()`:

```
Future<String> getCurrentUser() async {
  FirebaseUser user = await _firebaseAuth.currentUser();
  return user.uid;
}
```

In the function defined previously, we extract the information of the currently signed-in user using `_firebaseAuth.currentUser()`. This method returns the complete information wrapped up in a `FirebaseUser` object. We store this in the `user` variable. Finally, we return the `uid` of the user by using `user.uid`.

8. Next, we execute `signOut()`:

```
Future<void> signOut() async {
  return _firebaseAuth.signOut();
}
```

This function simply calls `signOut()` on the current `FirebaseAuth` instance and signs out the signed-in user.

At this point, we are done with all the basic coding for the implementation of Firebase authentication.

 The entire code inside `auth.dart` can be viewed at `https://github.com/PacktPublishing/-Mobile-Deep-Learning-Projects/blob/master/Chapter6/firebase_authentication/lib/auth.dart`.

Let's now see how we can bring authentication into effect inside the application.

Adding authentication in SignupSigninScreen

In this section, we will add Firebase authentication inside `SignupSigninScreen`.

We define a `_signinSignup()` method in the `signup_signin_screen.dart` file. The method is called when the sign-in button is pressed. The body of the method appears as follows:

```
void _signinSignup() async {
  setState(() {
    _loading = true;
  });
  String userId = "";
```

```
        if (_formMode == FormMode.SIGNIN) {
          userId = await widget.auth.signIn(_usermail, _userpassword);
        } else {
          userId = await widget.auth.signUp(_usermail, _userpassword);
        }
        setState(() {
          _loading = false;
        });
        if (userId.length > 0 && userId != null && _formMode ==
    FormMode.SIGNIN) {
            widget.onSignedIn();
        }
    }
```

In the preceding method, we begin by setting the value of _loading to true so that the progress bars shows on the screen until the sign-in process is complete. Next, we create a userId string that will store the value of userId once the sign-in/up operation is complete. Now, we check the current value of _formMode. If it is equal to FormMode.SIGNIN, the user wanted to sign in to an already existing account. Hence, we call the signIn() method defined inside the Auth class using its instance that passed into the constructor of SignupSigninScreen.

This is discussed in more detail in later sections. Otherwise, if the value of _formMode is equal to FormMode.SIGNUP, the signUp() method of the Auth class is called, passing in the user's mail and password to create a new account. The userId variable is used to store the user's ID once signing in/up has been completed successfully. Once the entire process is complete, _loading is set to false to remove the circular progress indicator from the screen. Also, if userId has a valid value while the user was signing in to an existing account, onSignedIn() is called, which directs the user to the home screen of the application.

This method also passed into the constructor of SignupSigninScreen and is discussed in the upcoming sections. Finally, we wrap the whole body inside a try-catch block so that any exception occurring during sign-in can be caught without crashing the app and can be displayed on the screen.

Creating the main screen

We would also need to determine the authentication status, that is, whether the user was signed in when the application was launched and direct them to the home screen if already signed in. If the user wasn't signed in, `SignInSignupScreen` should appear first and, after completing the process, the home screen is launched. To implement this, we create a stateful widget, `MainScreen`, inside a new dart file, `main_screen.dart`, and perform the following steps:

1. We will begin by defining the enumeration, `AuthStatus`, which denotes the current authentication status of the user, which can either be signed in or not signed in:

   ```
   enum AuthStatus {
     NOT_SIGNED_IN,
     SIGNED_IN,
   }
   ```

2. Now, we create a variable of the `enum` type to store the current authentication status whose initial value is set to `NOT_SIGNED_IN`:

   ```
   AuthStatus authStatus = AuthStatus.NOT_SIGNED_IN;
   ```

3. As soon as the widget is initialized, we establish whether the user was logged in by overriding the `initState()` method:

   ```
   @override
   void initState() {
     super.initState();
     widget.auth.getCurrentUser().then((user) {
       setState(() {
         if (user != null) {
           _userId = user;
         }
         authStatus =
             user == null ? AuthStatus.NOT_SIGNED_IN :
   AuthStatus.SIGNED_IN;
       });
     });
   }
   ```

getCurrentUser() of the Auth class is called using the instance of the class that was passed in the constructor. If the value returned by the method is not null, this means that a user is already logged in. Therefore, the value of the _userId string variable is set to the returned value. Also, authStatus is set to AuthStatus.SIGNED_IN. Otherwise, if the value returned is null, this means that no user was signed in, and so the value of authStatus is set to AuthStatus.NOT_SIGNED_IN.

4. Now, we will define two other methods, onSignIn() and onSignOut(), to ensure that the authentication status is stored correctly in the variable and the user interface is updated accordingly:

```
void _onSignedIn() {
   widget.auth.getCurrentUser().then((user){
     setState(() {
       _userId = user;
     });
   });
   setState(() {
     authStatus = AuthStatus.SIGNED_IN;
   });
 }
 void _onSignedOut() {
   setState(() {
     authStatus = AuthStatus.NOT_SIGNED_IN;
     _userId = "";
   });
 }
```

The _onSignedIn() method checks whether a user was already signed in and sets authStatus to AuthStatus.SIGNED_IN.. The _onSignedOut() method checks whether the user was signed out and sets authStatus to AuthStatus.SIGNED_OUT.

5. Finally, we override the `build` method to direct the user to the correct screen:

```
@override
Widget build(BuildContext context) {
  if(authStatus == AuthStatus.SIGNED_OUT) {
    return new SignupSigninScreen(
      auth: widget.auth,
      onSignedIn: _onSignedIn,
    );
  } else {
    return new HomeScreen(
      userId: _userId,
      auth: widget.auth,
      onSignedOut: _onSignedOut,
    );
  }
}
```

If `authStatus` is `AuthStatus.SIGNED_OUT`, `SignupSigninScreen` is returned, passing the `auth` instance and the `_onSignedIn()` method. Otherwise, `HomeScreen` is returned directly, passing in the `userId` of the signed-in user, the `Auth` instance class, and the `_onSignedOut()` method.

 The entire code for `main_screen.dart` can be viewed here: https://github.com/PacktPublishing/-Mobile-Deep-Learning-Projects/blob/master/Chapter6/firebase_authentication/lib/main_screen.dart

In the next section, we will add a very simple home screen for the application.

Creating the home screen

Since we are more interested in the authentication part here, the home screen, that is, the screen where the user is directed to after a successful sign-in, should be pretty simple. It will just contain some text and an option to log out. As we have done for all the previous screens and widgets, we begin by creating a `home_screen.dart` file and a stateful `HomeScreen` widget.

The home screen will appear as follows:

The entire code here resides inside the overridden `build()` method:

```
@override
Widget build(BuildContext context) {
    return new Scaffold(
        appBar: new AppBar(
            title: new Text('Firebase Authentication'),
            actions: <Widget>[
                new FlatButton(
                    child: new Text('Logout',
                    style: new TextStyle(fontSize: 16.0, color:
Colors.white)),
                    onPressed: _signOut
                )
            ],
        ),
        body: Center(child: new Text('Hello User',
        style: new TextStyle(fontSize: 32.0))
        ),
    );
}
```

We return a `Scaffold` here, which contains an `AppBar` with the title `Text Firebase Authentication` and a list of widgets for the `actions` property. `actions` is used to add a list of widgets to the app bar alongside the title of the application. Here, it just contains a `FlatButton`, `Logout`, that calls `_signOut` when pressed.

The `_signOut()` method appears as follows:

```
_signOut() async {
  try {
    await widget.auth.signOut();
    widget.onSignedOut();
  } catch (e) {
    print(e);
  }
}
```

The method primarily makes a call to the `signOut()` method defined in the `Auth` class to sign the user out from the application. Recall the `_onSignedOut()` method of `MainScreen` that was passed in to `HomeScreen`. The method is used here as `widget.onSignedOut()` to change `authStatus` to `SIGNED_OUT` when the user signs out. Also, it is wrapped inside a `try-catch` block to catch and print any exception that might have occurred here.

 The entire code of `home_screen.dart` can be viewed here: `https://github.com/PacktPublishing/-Mobile-Deep-Learning-Projects/blob/master/Chapter6/firebase_authentication/lib/main.dart`

At this point, the major components of the application are ready, so let's now create the final material app.

Creating main.dart

Inside `main.dart`, we create `Stateless Widget`, `App`, and override the `build()` method as follows:

```
@override
Widget build(BuildContext context) {
  return new MaterialApp(
      title: 'Firebase Authentication',
      debugShowCheckedModeBanner: false,
      theme: new ThemeData(
        primarySwatch: Colors.blue,
      ),
      home: new MainScreen(auth: new Auth()));
}
```

The method returns `MaterialApp`, providing a title, a theme, and from home screen.

The `main.dart` file can be viewed here: `https://github.com/PacktPublishing/-Mobile-Deep-Learning-Projects/blob/master/Chapter6/firebase_authentication/lib/main.dart`

Understanding anomaly detection for authentication

Anomaly detection is a much-studied branch of machine learning. The term is simplistic in its meaning. Basically, it is a collection of methods for detecting anomalies. Imagine a bag of apples. To identify and pick out the bad apples would be an act of anomaly detection.

Anomaly detection is performed in several ways:

- By identifying data samples in the dataset that are very different from the rest of the samples by using minimum-maximum ranges of columns
- By plotting the data as a line graph and identifying sudden spikes in the graph
- By plotting the data around a Gaussian curve and marking the points lying on the extreme ends as outliers (anomalies)

Some of the commonly used methods are support vector machines, Bayesian networks, and k-nearest neighbors. We will focus on anomaly detection in relation to security in this section.

Imagine you generally log in to your account on your app from your home. It would be very suspicious if you suddenly logged in to your account from a location thousands of miles away or, in another instance, you had never used public computers previously to log in to your account, but suddenly one day you do just that. Yet another suspicious case could be the fact that you took 10-20 attempts at the password, getting the password wrong every time before suddenly logging in successfully. All these cases are possibilities of behavior when your account may be compromised. Hence, it is important to incorporate a system that is able to determine your **regular** behavior and classify the **anomalous** behavior. In other words, the attempts to compromise your account should be marked as anomalies even when the hacker has the correct password.

This brings us to an interesting point, that is, determining the regular behavior of the user. How do we do this? What constitutes regular behavior? Is it specific to each user or a general concept? The answer to the questions is that it is very user-specific. However, there are aspects of behavior that can be the same for all users. An app may have multiple screens from where it could initiate the login. A single user may prefer one or two of the methods. This would lead to user-specific behavior that is regular to that user. However, if a login is attempted from a screen that is not marked as a login screen by the developers, it is certainly an anomaly, irrespective of which user tries it.

In our app, we will integrate one such system. To do so, we will be making a log of all login attempts made by a number of users of our app over an extended period of time. We will specifically be noting the screens from which they attempt a login and what sort of data they pass to the system. Once we have collected a lot of these samples, we are able to determine the confidence of the system regarding authentication in terms of any action performed by the user. If, at any point, the system feels that the behavior exhibited by the user differs widely from their customary behavior, this user will be unauthenticated and asked to verify their account details.

Let's begin by creating a predictive model to determine whether the user authentication is regular or anomalous.

A custom model for authenticating users

We will break this section down into two major sub-sections:

- Building a model for an authentication validity check
- Hosting the custom authentication validation model

Let's begin with the first section.

Building a model for an authentication validity check

In this section, we will build the model that determines whether any user is performing a regular or an anomalous login:

1. We begin by importing the requisite modules, as shown here:

```
import sys
import os
```

```
import json
import pandas
import numpy
from keras.models import Sequential
from keras.layers import LSTM, Dense, Dropout
from keras.layers.embeddings import Embedding
from keras.preprocessing import sequence
from keras.preprocessing.text import Tokenizer
from collections import OrderedDict
```

2. Now, we will import the dataset into the project. The dataset can be found at `https://github.com/PacktPublishing/Mobile-Deep-Learning-Projects/blob/master/Chapter6/Model/data/data.csv`:

```
csv_file = 'data.csv'

dataframe = pandas.read_csv(csv_file, engine='python',
quotechar='|', header=None)
count_frame = dataframe.groupby([1]).count()
print(count_frame)
total_req = count_frame[0][0] + count_frame[0][1]
num_malicious = count_frame[0][1]

print("Malicious request logs in dataset:
{:0.2f}%".format(float(num_malicious) / total_req * 100))
```

The preceding block of code loads the CSV dataset into the project. It also prints some stats pertaining to the data, as shown here:

```
              0
1
0   13413
1   13360
Malicious request logs in dataset: 49.90%
```

3. The data that we've loaded in the previous step is in an as yet unusable format for performing deep learning. In this step, we split it apart into the feature columns and the label column, as shown here:

```
X = dataset[:,0]
Y = dataset[:,1]
```

4. Next, we will drop some of the columns contained in the dataset since we do not require all of them to build a simple model:

```
for index, item in enumerate(X):
    reqJson = json.loads(item, object_pairs_hook=OrderedDict)
```

```
del reqJson['timestamp']
del reqJson['headers']
del reqJson['source']
del reqJson['route']
del reqJson['responsePayload']
X[index] = json.dumps(reqJson, separators=(',', ':'))
```

5. Next, we will perform tokenization on the remaining request body. Tokenizing is the method used to break large blocks of text into smaller ones, such as paragraphs into sentences and sentences into words. We do this as follows:

```
tokenizer = Tokenizer(filters='\t\n', char_level=True)
tokenizer.fit_on_texts(X)
```

6. After tokenization, we convert the text in the request body into word vectors, as shown in the next step. We split the dataset and DataFrame labels into two parts, 75%-25%, for training and testing:

```
num_words = len(tokenizer.word_index)+1
X = tokenizer.texts_to_sequences(X)

max_log_length = 1024
train_size = int(len(dataset) * .75)

X_processed = sequence.pad_sequences(X, maxlen=max_log_length)
X_train, X_test = X_processed[0:train_size],
X_processed[train_size:len(X_processed)]
Y_train, Y_test = Y[0:train_size], Y[train_size:len(Y)]
```

7. Next, we create a **long short-term memory (LSTM)**-based **recurrent neural network (RNN)**, which will learn to recognize **regular** user behavior. The word embeddings are added to the layers to help maintain the relationship between word vectors and the words:

```
model = Sequential()
model.add(Embedding(num_words, 32, input_length=max_log_length))
model.add(Dropout(0.5))
model.add(LSTM(64, recurrent_dropout=0.5))
model.add(Dropout(0.5))
model.add(Dense(1, activation='sigmoid'))
```

Our output is a single neuron that holds either a 0 in the case of a normal login or 1 if the login is anomalous.

8. Now, we compile the model with accuracy as the metric, while the loss is calculated as the binary cross-entropy:

```
model.compile(loss='binary_crossentropy', optimizer='adam',
metrics=['accuracy'])
print(model.summary())
```

9. Now, we are ready to proceed with the training of the model:

```
model.fit(X_train, Y_train, validation_split=0.25, epochs=3,
batch_size=128)
```

10. We will quickly check the accuracy achieved by the model. The current model achieves an accuracy of over 96%:

```
score, acc = model.evaluate(X_test, Y_test, verbose=1,
batch_size=128)
print("Model Accuracy: {:0.2f}%".format(acc * 100))
```

The output of the preceding code block is shown in the following screenshot:

```
In [14]: score, acc = model.evaluate(X_test, Y_test, verbose=1, batch_size=128)
         6694/6694 [==============================] - 24s 4ms/step

In [15]: print("Model Accuracy: {:0.2f}%".format(acc * 100))
         Model Accuracy: 96.47%
```

11. Now, we save the model weights and the model definition. We'll be loading these into the API script later to validate the authentication of users:

```
model.save_weights('lstm-weights.h5')
model.save('lstm-model.h5')
```

We can now proceed toward hosting the authentication model as an API, which we will demonstrate in the next section.

Hosting the custom authentication validation model

In this section, we will create an API that is used to authenticate users when they submit their login request to the model. The request headers will be parsed as a string and the model will use it to predict whether the login is valid:

1. We begin by importing the modules needed to create the API server:

```
from sklearn.externals import joblib
from flask import Flask, request, jsonify
from string import digits

import sys
import os
import json
import pandas
import numpy
import optparse
from keras.models import Sequential, load_model
from keras.preprocessing import sequence
from keras.preprocessing.text import Tokenizer
from collections import OrderedDict
```

2. Now, we instantiate a **Flask** app object. We also load the saved model definition and model weights from the previous section, *Building a model for an authentication validity check*. Then, we recompile the model and use the _make_predict_function( ) method to create its predict method, as shown in the following steps:

```
app = Flask(__name__)

model = load_model('lstm-model.h5')
model.load_weights('lstm-weights.h5')
model.compile(loss = 'binary_crossentropy', optimizer = 'adam',
metrics = ['accuracy'])
model._make_predict_function()
```

3. We then create a `remove_digits()` function, which is used to strip all digits from the input provided to it. This will be used to clean the request body text before putting it into the model:

```
def remove_digits(s: str) -> str:
    remove_digits = str.maketrans('', '', digits)
    res = s.translate(remove_digits)
    return res
```

4. Next, we will create a `/login` route in the API server. This route is handled by the `login()` method and responds to GET and POST request methods. As we did with the training input, we drop non-essential components of the request headers. This ensures that the model will make predictions on data similar to what it was trained on:

```
@app.route('/login', methods=['GET, POST'])
def login():
    req = dict(request.headers)
    item = {}
    item["method"] = str(request.method)
    item["query"] = str(request.query_string)
    item["path"] = str(request.path)
    item["statusCode"] = 200
    item["requestPayload"] = []

    ## MORE CODE BELOW THIS LINE

    ## MORE CODE ABOVE THIS LINE

    response = {'result': float(prediction[0][0])}
    return jsonify(response)
```

5. Now, we will add code to the `login()` method that will tokenize the request body and pass it to the model to perform prediction regarding the validity of the login request, as shown here:

```
@app.route('/login', methods=['GET, POST'])
def login():
    ...
    ## MORE CODE BELOW THIS LINE
    X = numpy.array([json.dumps(item)])
    log_entry = "store"

    tokenizer = Tokenizer(filters='\t\n', char_level=True)
    tokenizer.fit_on_texts(X)
    seq = tokenizer.texts_to_sequences([log_entry])
    max_log_length = 1024
```

```
        log_entry_processed = sequence.pad_sequences(seq,
    maxlen=max_log_length)

        prediction = model.predict(log_entry_processed)
        ## MORE CODE ABOVE THIS LINE
        ...
```

Finally, the app returns its confidence of the user being authenticated in the form of a JSON string.

6. Finally, we use the `run()` method of `app` to start the server script:

```
    if __name__ == '__main__':
        app.run(host='0.0.0.0', port=8000)
```

7. Save this file as `main.py`. To begin server execution, open a new terminal and use the following command:

```
    python main.py
```

The server listens to all incoming IPs of the system it runs on. This is made possible by running it on the 0.0.0.0 IP. This is required if we wish to deploy the script on a cloud-based server later. Not specifying the 0.0.0.0 host would make it listen to 127.0.0.1 by default, which is not suitable for deployment on public servers. You can read more about the difference between these addresses here: `https://xprilion.com/difference-between-localhost-127.0.0.1-and-0.0.0.0/`

In the next section, we will see how we can integrate ReCaptcha into the application we've built so far in this project. After that, we will integrate the API we've built in this section into the app.

Implementing ReCaptcha for spam protection

To add another layer of security to Firebase authentication, we will use ReCaptcha. This is a test supported by Google that helps us to protect data from automated bots for the purpose of spam and abuse. The test is simple and can be easily solved by humans, but obstructs bots and malicious users.

To read more about ReCaptcha and its uses, visit `https://support.google.com/recaptcha/?hl=en`.

ReCAPTCHA v2

In this section, we will be integrating ReCaptcha Version 2 into our application. In this version, the user is presented with a simple checkbox. If the tick turns green, the user has been verified.

Additionally, the user can also be presented with a challenge to distinguish between a human and a bot. This challenge can easily be solved by humans; all they need to do is select a bunch of images according to the instructions. A traditional flow for authentication using ReCaptcha appears as follows:

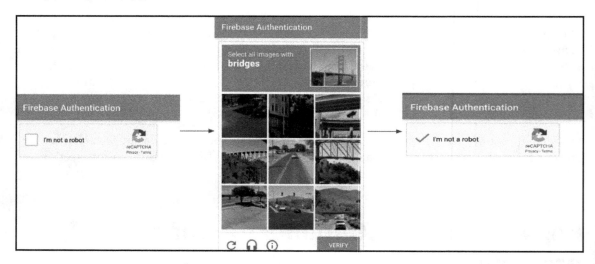

Once the user is able to verify their identity, they can log in successfully.

Obtaining the API key

To use ReCaptcha inside our application, we will need to register the application in the `reCAPTCHA` admin console and get the site key and secret key. To this end, visit `https://www.google.com/recaptcha/admin` and register the application. You will need to navigate to the **Register a new site** section, as shown in the following screenshot:

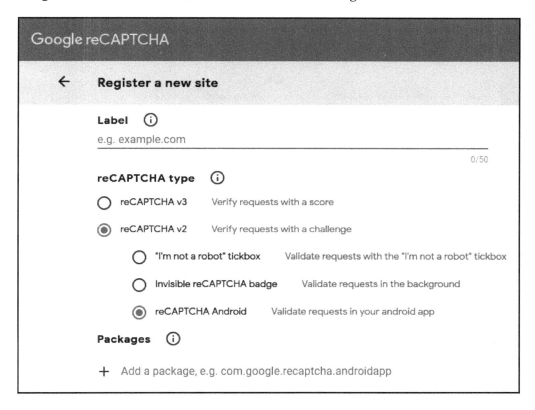

We can obtain the API key by following two simple steps:

1. Start by providing a domain name. Here, we will be choosing **reCAPTCHA Android** under **reCAPTCHA v2**.
2. After selecting the Android version, add the package name of the project. Once all the information is filled in correctly, click on **Register**.

This will direct you to the screen that displays the site key and secret key, as demonstrated in the following screenshot:

Copy and save **Site key** and **Secret key** to a secure place. We will be using these while coding the application.

Code integration

To include ReCaptcha v2 in our application, we will be using the Flutter package, `flutter_recaptcha_v2`. Add the `flutter_recaptcha_v2:0.1.0` dependency to the `pubspec.yaml` file, followed by running `flutter packages get` in the terminal to get the required dependency. The following steps discuss the integration in detail:

1. We will be adding the code to `signup_signin_screen.dart`. Start by importing the dependency:

   ```
   import 'package:flutter_recaptcha_v2/flutter_recaptcha_v2.dart';
   ```

2. Next, create a `RecaptchaV2Controller` instance:

   ```
   RecaptchaV2Controller recaptchaV2Controller =
   RecaptchaV2Controller();
   ```

3. The **reCAPTCHA** checkbox will be added as a widget. To start with, let's define a
   `_createRecaptcha()` method that returns the widget:

```
Widget _createRecaptcha() {
  return RecaptchaV2(
    apiKey: "Your Site Key here",
    apiSecret: "Your API Key here",
    controller: recaptchaV2Controller,
    onVerifiedError: (err){
      print(err);
    },
    onVerifiedSuccessfully: (success) {
      setState(() {
      if (success) {
        _signinSignup();
      } else {
        print('Failed to verify');
      }
      });
    },
  );
}
```

In the preceding method, we simply use the `RecaptchaV2()`
constructor, specifying the values for the specific properties. Add the site key and
secret key that you saved earlier while registering inside the `apiKey` and
`apiSecret` properties. We use the instance of the `recaptcha`
controller, `recaptchaV2Controller`, that we created earlier for the property
controller. If the user is verified successfully, the `_signinSignup()` method is
called to enable the user to sign in. If an error occurs during verification, we print
the error.

4. Now, since `reCaptcha` should appear while the user is attempting to sign in, we
   modify the `onPressed` property of the sign-in raised button inside
   `createSigninButton()` to `recaptchaV2Controller`:

```
Widget _createSigninButton() {
    . . . . . . .
    return new Padding(
        . . . . . . . .
        child: new RaisedButton(
            . . . . . .
            //Modify the onPressed property
            onPressed: recaptchaV2Controller.show
        )
    )
```

```
      }

5. Finally, we add _createRecaptcha() to the main body stack inside build():

      @override
      Widget build(BuildContext context) {
        . . . . . . .
        return new Scaffold(
          . . . . . . .
          body: Stack(
            children: <Widget>[
              _createBody(),
              _createCircularProgress(),

              //Add reCAPTCHA Widget
              _createRecaptcha()
                ],
        ));
      }
```

That's everything! Now we have another level of security above Firebase authentication to protect the application's data from automated bots. Let's now look at how we can integrate our custom model to detect malicious users.

Deploying the model in Flutter

At this point, we have our Firebase authentication application running along with ReCaptcha protection. Now, let's add the final layer of security that won't allow any malicious users to enter the application.

We already know that the model is hosted at the endpoint: http://34.67.126.237:8000/login. We will simply make an API call from within the application, passing in the email and password provided by the user, and get the result value from the model. The value will assist us in judging whether the login was malicious by using a threshold result value.

If the value is less than 0.20, the login will be considered malicious and the following message will be shown on the screen:

Let's now look at the steps to deploy the model in the Flutter application:

1. First of all, since we are fetching data and will be using network calls, that is, HTTP requests, we need to add an `http` dependency to the `pubspec.yaml` file, and import it as follows:

```
import 'package:http/http.dart' as http;
```

2. Start by adding the following function declaration in the `BaseAuth` abstract class defined inside `auth.dart`:

```
Future<double> isValidUser(String email, String password);
```

3. Now, let's define the `isValidUser()` function in the `Auth` class:

```
Future<double> isValidUser(String email, String password) async{
    final response = await http.Client()
.get('http://34.67.160.232:8000/login?user=$email&password=$password');
    var jsonResponse = json.decode(response.body);
```

```
        var val = '${jsonResponse["result"]}';
        double result = double.parse(val);
        return result;
    }
```

This function takes in a user's email and password as parameters and appends them to the request URL so that the output is generated for a specific user. The `get request` response is stored in the variable response. Since the response is in JSON format, we decode it using `json.decode()` and store the decoded response in another variable response. Now, we access the value of the result in `jsonResponse` using '`${jsonResponse["result"]}`', cast it into a double type integer using `double.parse()`, and store it in a result. Finally, we return the value of the result.

4. To activate malicious detection inside the code, we make a call to the `isValidUser()` method from `SigninSignupScreen`. This method is called when a user with an existing account chooses to sign in from inside the `if-else` block:

```
if (_formMode == FormMode.SIGNIN) {

    var val = await widget.auth.isValidUser(_usermail,
_userpassword);

    . . . .
    } else {
    . . . .
    }
```

The value returned by `isValidUser` is stored in the `val` variable.

5. If the value is less than 0.20, this denotes that the login activity was malicious. Hence, we throw an exception and `catch` it inside the catch block and display the error message on the screen. This can be done by creating a custom exception class, `MalicousUserException`, that returns an error message whenever it is instantiated:

```
class MaliciousUserException implements Exception {
  String message() => 'Malicious login! Please try later.';
}
```

6. We will now add an `if` block after the call to `isValidUser()` to check whether an exception needs to be thrown:

```
var val = await widget.auth.isValidUser(_usermail, _userpassword);
//Add the if block
if(val < 0.20) {
    throw new MaliciousUserException();
}
```

7. The exception is now caught inside the `catch` block and the user is not allowed to proceed with signing in. Additionally, we set `_loading` to `false` to denote that no further network operation is required:

```
catch(MaliciousUserException) {
        setState(() {
          _loading = false;
            _errorMessage = 'Malicious user detected. Please try
again later.';
        });
```

That's everything! The Flutter application that we created earlier based on Firebase authentication can now find malicious users with an intelligent model running in the background.

Summary

In this chapter, we saw how we can build a cross-platform app using Flutter with an authentication system powered by Firebase, while incorporating the benefits of deep learning. We then understood how hacking attempts can be classified as anomalies in general user behavior, and created a model to sort these anomalies out to prevent malicious users from logging in. Finally, we used ReCaptcha by Google to remove spammy use of the app, and hence make it more resilient in relation to automated spam or scripted hacking attacks.

In the next chapter, we will explore a very interesting project – transcript generation of music using deep learning on mobile apps.

7
Speech/Multimedia Processing - Generating Music Using AI

Given the increasing number of applications of **artificial intelligence** (**AI**), the idea of using AI with music has been around for a long time and is much researched. Since music is a series of notes, it is a classic example of a time series dataset. Time series datasets have proven very useful recently in a number of forecast areas – stock markets, weather patterns, sales patterns, and other time-based datasets. **Recurrent neural networks** (**RNNs**) are one of the most models for working with time series datasets. A popular enhancement made to RNNs is called **long short-term memory** (**LSTM**) neurons. We'll be using LSTMs in this chapter to work with the music notes.

Multimedia processing, too, isn't a new topic. Earlier in this project series, we covered image processing in detail in multiple chapters. In this chapter, we will discuss and go beyond image processing and provide an example of deep learning with audio. We will train a Keras model to generate music samples, a new one every time. We will then use this model with a Flutter app to deploy through an audio player on Android and iOS devices.

In this chapter, we will cover the following topics:

- Designing the project's architecture
- Understanding multimedia processing
- Developing RNN-based models for music generation
- Deploying an audio generation API on Android and iOS

Let's begin with an overview of this project's architecture.

Designing the project's architecture

This project has a slightly different architecture to a regular deep learning project deployed as an app. We will have two different sets of samples of music. The first set of samples will be used to train an LSTM model that can generate music. The other set of samples will be used as a random input to the LSTM model, which will output the generated music samples. The LSTM-based model that we'll be developing and using later will be deployed on **Google Cloud Platform (GCP)**. You can, however, deploy it on AWS or any other hosting of your choice.

The interaction between the different components that will be used in this project have been summarized in the following diagram:

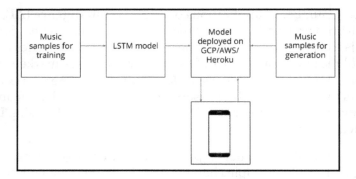

The mobile application asks the model deployed on the server to generate a new music sample. The model uses a random music sample as input to generate a new music sample by passing it through the pretrained model. The new music sample is then fetched by the mobile device and played to the user.

You may compare this architecture to the ones we have covered previously, in which there would be a single set of samples of the data that would be used for training, and then the model would be deployed either on the cloud or locally, and used to make predictions.

We could also change this project architecture to deploy the model locally in the presence of midi file handling libraries written for the Dart language. However, as of the time of writing, there are no such stable libraries compatible with the requirements of the Python midi file library we've used while developing the model.

Let's begin by learning what multimedia processing means, and how we can use OpenCV to process multimedia files.

Understanding multimedia processing

Multimedia is a collective term for nearly all forms of content that are visual, auditory, or both. The term **multimedia processing** in itself is very vague. A more precise way of discussing this term would be to break it down into two fundamental parts—visual or auditory. Hence, we will be discussing multimedia processing in the terms it is composed of—image processing and audio processing. A mixture of these terms gives rise to video processing, which is just another form of multimedia.

In the following sections, we will begin by discussing them in their separate forms.

Image processing

Image processing, or computer vision, is one of the most researched branches of AI to date. It has grown rapidly over the last few decades and has been instrumental in the advancements of several technologies, including the following:

- Image filters and editors
- Facial recognition
- Digital cartography
- Autonomous vehicles

We discussed the basics of image processing in an earlier project. In this project, we will discuss a very popular library for performing image processing—OpenCV. OpenCV is short for *Open Source Computer Vision*. It was developed by Intel and taken forward by Willow Garage and Itseez (which was later acquired by Intel). It is, without doubt, the foremost choice of the majority of developers worldwide for performing image processing due to its compatibility with all major machine learning frameworks, such as TensorFlow, PyTorch, and Caffe. In addition to this, OpenCV works with several languages, such as C++, Java, and Python.

To install OpenCV on your Python environment, you can use the following command:

```
pip install opencv-contrib-python
```

The preceding command installs the main OpenCV module along with the contrib module. You can find more modules to choose from here: https://docs.opencv.org/master/. For more installation instructions, if the preceding link does not meet your requirements, you can follow the official documentation here: https://docs.opencv.org/master/df/d65/tutorial_table_of_content_introduction.html.

Let's walk you through a very simple example of how to perform image processing with OpenCV. Create a new Jupyter notebook and begin with the following steps:

1. To import OpenCV into the notebook, use the following line of code:

```
import cv2
```

2. Let's also import matplotlib into the notebook, because Jupyter Notebook crashes if you try to use the native OpenCV image-showing function:

```
from matplotlib import pyplot as plt
%matplotlib inline
```

3. Let's create a substitute function for the OpenCV's native image-showing function using matplotlib to facilitate the displaying of images in the notebook:

```
def showim(image):
    image = cv2.cvtColor(image, cv2.COLOR_BGR2RGB)
    plt.imshow(image)
    plt.show()
```

Notice that we convert the color scheme of the image from **Blue Green Red (BGR)** to **RGB (Red Green Blue)**. This is due to the fact that OpenCV, by default, uses the BGR color scheme. However, matplotlib uses the RGB scheme while displaying the pictures, and without this conversion, our image would appear oddly colored.

4. Now, let's read an image into the Jupyter notebook. Once done, we will be able to see our loaded image:

```
image = cv2.imread("Image.jpeg")
showim(image)
```

The output of the preceding code depends on the image that you choose to load into the notebook:

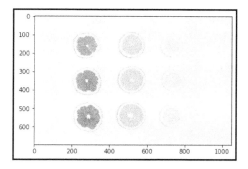

In our example, we've loaded an image of citrus fruit slices, an amazing photo taken by Isaac Quesada on Unsplash.

You can find the preceding image at `https://unsplash.com/photos/6mw7bn9k9jw`.

5. Let's make a simple manipulation of the preceding image by converting it to a grayscale image. To do so, we simply use the conversion method as we did in the `showim()` function we declared:

```
gray_image = cv2.cvtColor(image, cv2.COLOR_BGR2GRAY)
showim(gray_image)
```

This produces the following output:

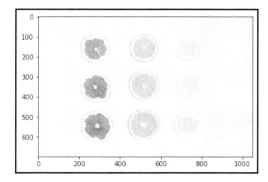

6. Let's now execute another common manipulation, image blurring. Blurring is often employed in image processing in order to remove unnecessary (at that moment) detailing of information in the image. We use the Gaussian Blur filter, which is one of the most common algorithms for creating a blur on the image:

```
blurred_image = cv2.GaussianBlur(image, (7, 7), 0)
showim(blurred_image)
```

This produces the following output:

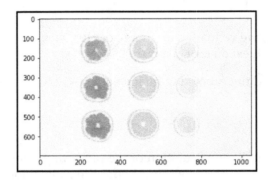

Notice that the preceding image is less sharp than the original image. However, it would easily serve the purpose of someone willing to count the number of objects in this image.

7. In order to locate objects in an image, we first need to mark the edges in the image. To do so, we can use the `Canny()` method, which is one among other options available in OpenCV for finding edges in an image:

```
canny = cv2.Canny(blurred_image, 10, 50)
showim(canny)
```

This produces the following output:

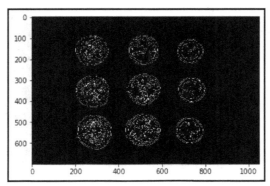

Notice the high number of edges found in the preceding image. While this displays the detailing of the image, it wouldn't help if we were trying to count the edges try to determine the number of objects in the image.

8. Let's try to count the number of distinct items in the image generated in the previous step:

```
contours, hierarchy= cv2.findContours(canny, cv2.RETR_EXTERNAL,
cv2.CHAIN_APPROX_SIMPLE)
print("Number of objects found = ", len(contours))
```

The preceding code will produce the following output:

```
Number of objects found = 18
```

However, we know that there are not 18 objects in the preceding image. There are just 9. Hence, we'll play around with the value of the threshold in the `canny` method while finding edges.

9. Let's increase the threshold of edge finding in the canny method. This makes it harder for edges to get detected, and hence keeps only the most noticeable edges visible:

```
canny = cv2.Canny(blurred_image, 50, 150)
showim(canny)
```

This produces the following output:

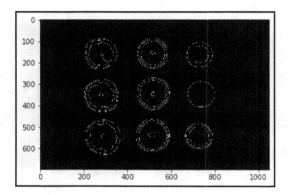

Notice the sharp reduction in the edges discovered within the body of the citrus fruit, leaving only their outline prominently visible. We would expect this to yield fewer objects when counted.

10. Let's we run the following block again:

```
contours, hierarchy= cv2.findContours(canny, cv2.RETR_EXTERNAL,
cv2.CHAIN_APPROX_SIMPLE)
print("Number of objects found = ", len(contours))
```

This produces the following output:

```
Number of objects found = 9
```

This is the expected value. However, it is only in special circumstances that this value is as accurate.

11. Finally, let's try to outline the objects that we have detected. We do so by drawing the contours identified in the previous step of the findContours() method:

```
_ = cv2.drawContours(image, contours, -1, (0,255,0), 10)
showim(image)
```

This produces the following output:

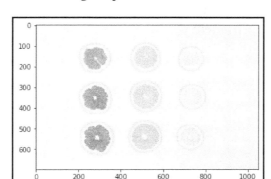

Notice that we have pretty accurately identified the nine slices of fruit in the original image we took. We could extend this example further to find certain types of object in any image.

 To find out more about OpenCV and find some ready examples to learn from, visit the following repository: `https://github.com/ayulockin/ myopenCVExperiments`.

Let's now learn how to process audio files.

Audio processing

We have seen how images are processed and information can be extracted out of them. In this section, we'll be covering the processing of audio files. Audio, or sound, is something that engulfs the environment around you. On many occasions, you'll be able to predict correctly the area or environment merely from an audio clip of that area, without actually seeing any visual hints. Audio in vocal form or speech is a form of communication between people. Audio in the form of well-arranged rhythmic patterns is called music and can be produced by using musical instruments.

Some popular formats of audio files are as follows:

- **MP3**: A very popular format used widely for sharing music files.
- **AAC**: An improvement over the MP3 format, AAC is mostly used by Apple devices.

- **WAV**: Created by Microsoft and IBM, this format is lossless compression and might be very large even for small audio files.
- **MIDI**: Musical Instrument Digital Interface files do not actually contain audio. They contain notes of musical instruments, and hence are small and easy to work with.

Audio processing is a requirement in the growth of the following technologies:

- Speech processing for voice-based interfaces or assistants
- Voice generation for virtual assistants
- Music generation
- Caption generation
- Recommendation for similar music

A very popular tool for audio processing is Magenta, from the TensorFlow team.

 You can visit the Magenta home page at `https://magenta.tensorflow.org/`. This tool allows for rapid generation of audio and transcription of audio files.

Let's explore Magenta briefly.

Magenta

Magenta was developed as part of the research undertaken by the Google Brain team also involved in TensorFlow. It was developed as a tool that would allow artists to enhance their music or art generation pipelines with the help of deep learning and reinforcement learning algorithms. Here is Magenta's logo:

Let's start with the following steps:

1. To install Magenta on your system, you can use the pip repository for Python:

   ```
   pip install magenta
   ```

2. If you are missing any dependencies, you can install them using the following command:

   ```
   !apt-get update -qq && apt-get install -qq libfluidsynth1 fluid-
   soundfont-gm build-essential libasound2-dev libjack-dev

   !pip install -qU pyfluidsynth pretty_midi
   ```

3. To import Magenta into your project, you can use the following command:

   ```
   import magenta
   ```

   Or, by popular convention, to load just the music part of Magenta, you can use the following command:

   ```
   import magenta.music as mm
   ```

   You will find a lot of samples online using the preceding import.

Let's create some music quickly. We'll be creating some drum roll sounds and then save the same to a MIDI file:

1. We'll first need to create a NoteSequence object. In Magenta, all music is stored in the format of note sequences, which is similar to how MIDI stores music:

   ```
   from magenta.protobuf import music_pb2

   drums = music_pb2.NoteSequence()
   ```

2. Once the NoteSequence object has been created, it is empty, so we need to add some notes to it:

   ```
   drums.notes.add(pitch=36, start_time=0, end_time=0.125,
   is_drum=True, instrument=10, velocity=80)
   drums.notes.add(pitch=38, start_time=0, end_time=0.125,
   is_drum=True, instrument=10, velocity=80)
   drums.notes.add(pitch=42, start_time=0, end_time=0.125,
   is_drum=True, instrument=10, velocity=80)
   drums.notes.add(pitch=46, start_time=0, end_time=0.125,
   is_drum=True, instrument=10, velocity=80)
   .
   ```

```
    .
    .
    .
drums.notes.add(pitch=42, start_time=0.75, end_time=0.875,
is_drum=True, instrument=10, velocity=80)
drums.notes.add(pitch=45, start_time=0.75, end_time=0.875,
is_drum=True, instrument=10, velocity=80)
```

Notice in the preceding code that each note has a pitch and velocity. This is again similar to the MIDI files.

3. Let's now add a tempo to the notes and set the total time for the music to play:

```
drums.total_time = 1.375

drums.tempos.add(qpm=60)
```

With this done, we're now ready to export the MIDI file.

4. We first need to convert the Magenta `NoteSequence` object to the MIDI file:

```
mm.sequence_proto_to_midi_file(drums, 'drums_sample_output.mid')
```

The preceding code first converts the note sequence to MIDI and then writes them to the `drums_sample_output.mid` file on the disk. You can now play the `midi` file with any suitable music player.

Moving ahead, let's explore how we can process videos.

Video processing

Video processing is another important part of multimedia processing. Often, we require to make sense of what's happening inside moving scenarios. For instance, if we're making a self-driving vehicle, it would need to process a lot of video in real time to be able to drive smoothly. Another instance of this can be a device that converts sign language to text in order to help interact with speech-impaired people. Further, video processing is required to create movies and motion effects.

We shall again be exploring OpenCV in this section. However, we'll be demonstrating how to use a live camera feed with OpenCV to detect faces.

Create a new Python script and perform the following steps:

1. First, we need to make the necessary imports to the script. This will be straightforward, as we only require the OpenCV module:

```
import cv2
```

2. Now, let's load a Haar cascade model into the script. A Haar cascade is an algorithm that is used to detect objects in any given image. Since the video is nothing but a stream of images, we'll be breaking it down into a series of frames and detect faces in them:

```
faceCascade =
cv2.CascadeClassifier("haarcascade_frontalface_default.xml")
```

You will have to grab the `haarcascade_frontalface_default.xml` file from this location: `https://github.com/opencv/opencv/blob/master/data/haarcascades/haarcascade_frontalface_default.xml`.

Haar cascades are a class of classifier algorithms that use cascading functions to perform classification. They were introduced by Paul Viola and Michael Jones, in their attempt to build an object detection algorithm that was fast enough to run on low-end devices. Cascading functions pool results from several smaller classifiers.

Haar cascade files are usually found in the format of **Extensible Markup Language** (**XML**) and usually perform one specific function, such as face detection, body posture detection, object detection, and others. You can read more about Haar cascades here: `http://www.willberger.org/cascade-haar-explained/`.

3. We'll now have to instantiate the camera for video capture. We can use the default laptop camera for this purpose:

```
video_capture = cv2.VideoCapture(0)
```

4. Let's now capture the frames from the video and display them:

```
while True:
    # Capture frames
    ret, frame = video_capture.read()

    ### We'll add code below in future steps

    ### We'll add code above in future steps
```

```
# Display the resulting frame
cv2.imshow('Webcam Capture', frame)

if cv2.waitKey(1) & 0xFF == ord('q'):
    break
```

This would allow you to show the live video feed on your screen. Before we run this, we need to release the camera and close the windows properly.

5. To shut down the live capture properly, use the following commands:

```
video_capture.release()
cv2.destroyAllWindows()
```

Now, let's give your script a test run.

You should get a window containing the live capture of your face (if you're not shy) visible on it.

6. Let's add face detection to this video feed. Since the Haar cascade for face detection works better with grayscale images, we will first convert each frame to gray and then perform the face detection on it. We need to add this code to the while loop, as shown in the following code:

```
### We'll add code below in future steps

gray = cv2.cvtColor(frame, cv2.COLOR_BGR2GRAY)

faces = faceCascade.detectMultiScale(
    gray,
    scaleFactor=1.1,
    minNeighbors=5,
    minSize=(30, 30),
    flags=cv2.CASCADE_SCALE_IMAGE
)

### We'll add code above in future steps
```

With this, we have detected the faces, so let's mark them on the video feed!

7. We'll simply use the rectangle drawing function of OpenCV to mark the faces on the screen:

```
minNeighbors=5,
    minSize=(30, 30),
    flags=cv2.CASCADE_SCALE_IMAGE
)
```

```
for (x, y, w, h) in faces:
    cv2.rectangle(frame, (x, y), (x+w, y+h), (0, 255, 0), 2)

### We'll add code above in future steps
```

Let's now again try to run the script.

Go to the terminal and use the following command to run the script:

```
python filename.py
```

Here, the filename is the name of your script file when you save it.

You should get an output similar to the following screenshot:

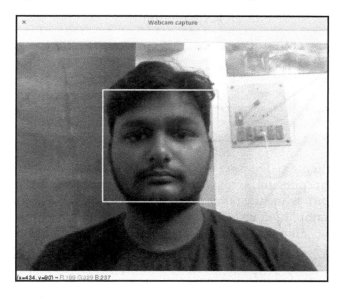

To quit the live webcam capture, use the *Q* key on your keyboard (we have set this in the preceding code).

We have studied an overview of the three major forms of multimedia processing. Let's now move ahead and build our LSTM-based model for generating audio.

Developing RNN-based models for music generation

In this section, we'll be developing a music generation model. We'll be using RNNs for that, and using the LSTM neuron model for the same. An RNN is different from a simple **artificial neural network** (**ANN**) in a very significant way—it allows the reuse of input between layers.

While, in an ANN, we expect input values that enter the neural network to move forward and then produce error-based feedback to be incorporated into the network weights, RNNs make the input come back to the previous layers in loops several times.

The following diagram represents an RNN neuron:

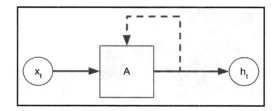

From the preceding diagram, we can see that the input after passing through the activation function in the neuron splits into two parts. One part moves forward in the network toward the next layer or output, while the other part is fed back into the network. In a time series dataset, where each sample can be labeled relative to the time of a given sample at **t**, we might expand the preceding diagram as shown here:

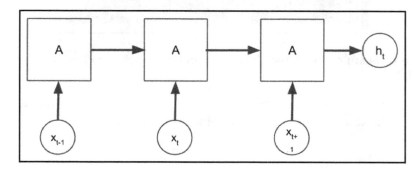

However, due to repeated exposure of the values through the activation functions, an RNN tends toward **gradient vanishing** in which the values of the RNN gradually turn negligibly small (or large in the case of gradient explosion). To avoid this, the LSTM units were introduced, which allowed the retaining of information for a longer period by storing it in the units. Each LSTM unit is composed of three gates and a memory cell. The three gates—the input, output, and forget gates—are responsible for deciding what values are stored in the memory cell.

Thus, the LSTM units become independent from the update frequency of the rest of the RNN, and each cell has its own time of remembering the values that it holds. This mimics nature more closely in terms of us forgetting some random pieces of information much later compared to other pieces.

> You can find a detailed and easy to understand explanation of RNNs and LSTMs at the following link: `https://skymind.ai/wiki/lstm`.

Before we begin building the model for our project, we need to set up the project directory, as shown in the following code:

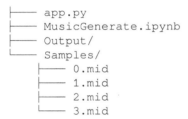

```
├── app.py
├── MusicGenerate.ipynb
├── Output/
└── Samples/
    ├── 0.mid
    ├── 1.mid
    ├── 2.mid
    └── 3.mid
```

Notice that we have downloaded four samples of MIDI files in the `Samples` folder. We then created the `MusicGenerate.ipynb` Jupyter notebook for working on. In the next few steps, we'll be working solely on this Jupyter notebook. The `app.py` script is currently empty and, in the future, we'll use it to host the model.

Let's now begin by creating the LSTM-based model for generating music.

Creating the LSTM-based model

In this section, we'll be working on the `MusicGenerate.ipynb` notebook inside the Jupyter notebook environment:

1. We'll require quite a few module imports in this notebook. Use the following code to import them:

```
import mido
from mido import MidiFile, MidiTrack, Message
from tensorflow.keras.layers import LSTM, Dense, Activation,
Dropout, Flatten
from tensorflow.keras.preprocessing import sequence
from tensorflow.keras.models import Sequential
from tensorflow.keras.optimizers import Adam
from sklearn.preprocessing import MinMaxScaler
import numpy as np
```

We've used the `mido` library. If you do not have it installed on your system, you can use the following command to install it:

```
pip install mido
```

Notice in the preceding code that we have also imported the Keras module and subparts. The TensorFlow version used in this project is 2.0. In order to install the same on your system or to upgrade the current TensorFlow installation, you can use the following commands:

```
pip install --upgrade pip
```

```
pip install --upgrade tensorflow
```

Now, we'll move on to reading the sample files.

2. To read a MIDI file into the project notebook, use the following code:

```
notes = []
for msg in MidiFile('Samples/0.mid') :
    try:
        if not msg.is_meta and msg.channel in [0, 1, 2, 3] and
msg.type == 'note_on':
            data = msg.bytes()
            notes.append(data[1])
    except:
        pass
```

This loads all the opening notes of channel 0, 1, 2, and 3 in the `notes` list.

 To understand more about notes, messages, and channels, use the following documentation: `https://mido.readthedocs.io/en/latest/messages.html`

3. Since the notes are in a varying range that is larger than the 0–1 range, we'll scale them to fit a common range, using the following code:

```
scaler = MinMaxScaler(feature_range=(0,1))
scaler.fit(np.array(notes).reshape(-1,1))
notes = list(scaler.transform(np.array(notes).reshape(-1,1)))
```

4. What we essentially have is a list of notes arranged over time. We need to convert this to a time series dataset format. To do so, we use the following code to convert the list:

```
notes = [list(note) for note in notes]

X = []
y = []

n_prev = 20
for i in range(len(notes)-n_prev):
    X.append(notes[i:i+n_prev])
    y.append(notes[i+n_prev])
```

We have converted it to a collection where each sample has the future 20 notes along with it and, toward the end of the dataset, the past 20. This works in the following way—if we have 5 samples, say M_1, M_2, M_3, M_4, and M_5, then we arrange them in, let's say, pairings of 2 (analogous to our 20) as shown here:

- M_1 M_2
- M_2 M_3
- M_3 M_4 and so on

5. We shall now create the LSTM model using Keras, as shown in the following code:

```
model = Sequential()
model.add(LSTM(256, input_shape=(n_prev, 1),
return_sequences=True))
model.add(Dropout(0.3))
model.add(LSTM(128, input_shape=(n_prev, 1),
```

```
                  return_sequences=True))
model.add(Dropout(0.3))
model.add(LSTM(256, input_shape=(n_prev, 1),
                  return_sequences=False))
model.add(Dropout(0.3))
model.add(Dense(1))
model.add(Activation('linear'))
optimizer = Adam(lr=0.001)
model.compile(loss='mse', optimizer=optimizer)
```

Feel free to play around with the hyperparameters of this LSTM model.

6. Finally, we'll fit our training sample to the model and save the model file:

```
model.fit(np.array(X), np.array(y), 32, 25, verbose=1)
model.save("model.h5")
```

This would create the `model.h5` file in our project directory. We'll be using this file with other samples of music to generate a new piece randomly every time the user makes a generation request from the app.

Now, let's deploy this model using a Flask server.

Deploying a model using Flask

For this part of the project, you may use your local system or deploy the script in `app.py` elsewhere. We will be editing this file to create a Flask server that generates music and allows the MIDI files that are generated to be downloaded.

Some of the code in this file will be similar to the Jupyter notebook, since the audio samples will always require a similar treatment every time they're loaded and used with the model we've generated:

1. We use the following code to make the required module imports to this script:

```
import mido
from mido import MidiFile, MidiTrack, Message
from tensorflow.keras.models import load_model
from sklearn.preprocessing import MinMaxScaler
import numpy as np
import random
import time
from flask import send_file
import os
```

```
from flask import Flask, jsonify

app = Flask(__name__)
```

Notice that the last four imports we've made are different from what we imported previously in the Jupyter notebook. Also, we do not need to import the several Keras components into this script since we'll be loading from an already prepared model.

In the last line of code in the previous code block, we've instantiated a Flask object named app.

2. In this step, we'll be creating the first part of a function that would generate new music samples when the /generate route is called on the API:

```
@app.route('/generate', methods=['GET'])
def generate():

    songnum = random.randint(0, 3)

    ### More code below this
```

3. Once we've randomly decided which sample file to use during the music generation, we need to make it undergo similar transformations as with the training sample in the Jupyter notebook:

```
def generate():
    .
    .

    .
    notes = []

    for msg in MidiFile('Samples/%s.mid' % (songnum)):
        try:
            if not msg.is_meta and msg.channel in [0, 1, 2, 3] and
msg.type == 'note_on':
                data = msg.bytes()
                notes.append(data[1])
        except:
            pass

    scaler = MinMaxScaler(feature_range=(0, 1))
    scaler.fit(np.array(notes).reshape(-1, 1))
    notes = list(scaler.transform(np.array(notes).reshape(-1, 1)))

    ### More code below this
```

In the preceding code block, we loaded the sample file and extracted its notes from the same channels we used during training.

4. We will now scale the notes similarly as we did during training:

```
def generate():
    .
    .
    .
    notes = [list(note) for note in notes]

    X = []
    y = []

    n_prev = 20
    for i in range(len(notes) - n_prev):
        X.append(notes[i:i + n_prev])
        y.append(notes[i + n_prev])

    ### More code below this
```

We also transform this list of notes to a shape suitable for input into the model, exactly as we did with the input during training.

5. Next, we'll have the following code to load the Keras model and create a new list of notes from the model:

```
def generate():
    .
    .
    .
    model = load_model("model.h5")

    xlen = len(X)

    start = random.randint(0, 100)

    stop = start + 200

    prediction = model.predict(np.array(X[start:stop]))
    prediction = np.squeeze(prediction)
    prediction =
np.squeeze(scaler.inverse_transform(prediction.reshape(-1, 1)))
    prediction = [int(i) for i in prediction]

    ### More code below this
```

6. Now, we can convert this list of notes to a MIDI sequence using the following code:

```
def generate():
    .
    .
    .
    mid = MidiFile()
    track = MidiTrack()
    t = 0
    for note in prediction:
        vol = random.randint(50, 70)
        note = np.asarray([147, note, vol])
        bytes = note.astype(int)
        msg = Message.from_bytes(bytes[0:3])
        t += 1
        msg.time = t
        track.append(msg)
    mid.tracks.append(track)

    ### More code below this
```

7. We're now ready to save the file to disk. It contains randomly generated music from the model:

```
def generate():
    .
    .
    .
    epoch_time = int(time.time())

    outputfile = 'output_%s.mid' % (epoch_time)
    mid.save("Output/" + outputfile)

    response = {'result': outputfile}

    return jsonify(response)
```

Thus, the /generate API returns the name of the generated file in a JSON format. We can then download and play this file.

8. To download the files to the client, we need to use the following code:

```
@app.route('/download/<fname>', methods=['GET'])
def download(fname):
    return send_file("Output/"+fname, mimetype="audio/midi",
as_attachment=True)
```

Notice that the preceding function works on the `/download/filename` route where the filename is supplied by the client based on the output of the previous generation API call. The file downloaded has a MIME type of audio/midi, which tells the client that it is a MIDI file.

9. Finally, we can add the code that will execute this server:

```
if __name__ == '__main__':
    app.run(host="0.0.0.0", port=8000)
```

This done, we can use the following command in the terminal to run the server:

```
python app.py
```

You'll get some debug information from the console if there are any warnings produced in the code. With this done, we're ready to move toward building the Flutter app client for our API in the next section.

Deploying an audio generation API on Android and iOS

After successfully creating and deploying the model, let's now begin by building the mobile application. The application will be used to fetch and play music generated by the model created earlier.

It will have three buttons:

- **Generate Music**: To generate a new audio file
- **Play**: To play the newly generated file
- **Stop**: To stop the music that is playing

Also, it will have some text at the bottom to show the current status of the application.

The application will appear as follows:

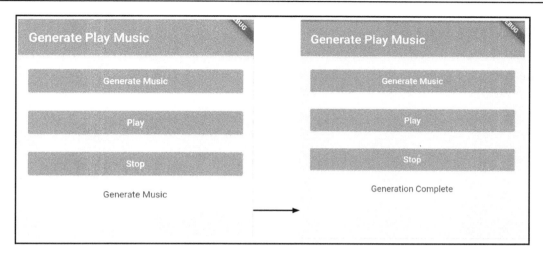

The widget tree of the application would look as follows:

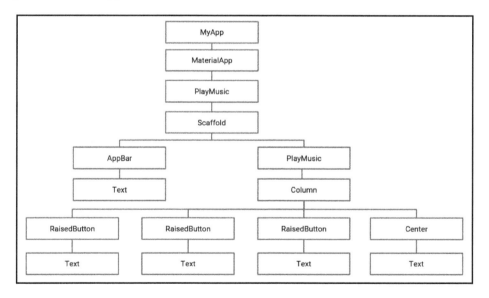

Let's now start building the UI of the application.

Creating the UI

We start by creating a new Dart file, `play_music.dart`, and a stateful widget, `PlayMusic`. In this file, we will create the three buttons, as stated earlier, to perform the basic functions. The following steps describe how to create the UI:

1. Define a `buildGenerateButton()` method to create the `RaisedButton` variable that will be used to generate new music files:

```
Widget buildGenerateButton() {
  return Padding(
    padding: EdgeInsets.only(left: 16, right: 16, top: 16),
    child: RaisedButton(
      child: Text("Generate Music"),
      color: Colors.blue,
      textColor: Colors.white,
    ),
  );
}
```

In the function defined previously, we create a `RaisedButton` with `Generate Music` text added as a child. The `Colors.blue` value of the `color` property is used to give the button a blue color. Also, we modify `textColor` to `Colors.white` so that the text inside the button is white in color. The button is given left, right, and top padding using `EdgeInsets.only()`. In a later section, we will add the `onPressed` property to the button to fetch new music files from the hosted model every time the button is pressed.

2. Define a `buildPlayButton()` method to play the newly generated audio file:

```
Widget buildPlayButton() {
  return Padding(
    padding: EdgeInsets.only(left: 16, right: 16, top: 16),
    child: RaisedButton(
      child: Text("Play"),
      onPressed: () {
        play();
      },
      color: Colors.blue,
      textColor: Colors.white,
    ),
  );
}
```

In the function defined previously, we create a `RaisedButton` with `"Play"` text added as a child. The `Colors.blue` value of the `color` property is used to give the button a blue color. Also,we modify `textColor` to `Colors.white` so that the text inside the button is white in color. The button is given left, right, and top padding using `EdgeInsets.only()`. In a later section, we will add the `onPressed` property to the button to play the newly generated music file every time the button is pressed.

3. Define a `buildStopButton()` method to stop the audio that is playing currently:

```
Widget buildStopButton() {
  return Padding(
    padding: EdgeInsets.only(left: 16, right: 16, top: 16),
    child: RaisedButton(
      child: Text("Stop"),
      onPressed: (){
        stop();
      },
      color: Colors.blue,
      textColor: Colors.white,
    )
  );
}
```

In the function defined previously, we create a `RaisedButton` with `"Stop"` text added as a child. The `Colors.blue` value of the `color` property is used to give the button a blue color. Also, we modify `textColor` to `Colors.white` so that the text inside the button is white in color. The button is given left, right, and top padding using `EdgeInsets.only()`. In a later section, we will add the `onPressed` property to the button to stop the currently playing audio when the button is pressed.

4. Override the `build()` method inside `PlayMusicState` to create a `Column` of the buttons created previously:

```
@override
Widget build(BuildContext context) {
  return Scaffold(
    appBar: AppBar(
      title: Text("Generate Play Music"),
    ),
    body: Column(
      crossAxisAlignment: CrossAxisAlignment.stretch,
      children: <Widget>[
```

```
            buildGenerateButton(),
            buildPlayButton(),
            buildStopButton(),
        ],
    )
  );
}
```

In the preceding code snippet, we return a `Scaffold`. It contains an `AppBar` with **Generate Play Music** as the `title`. The body of the `Scaffold` is a `Column`. The children of the column are the buttons that we had created in the previous step. The buttons are added to the column by making calls to the respective methods. Additionally, the `crossAxisAlignment` property is set to `CrossAxisAlignment.stretch` so that the buttons occupy the total width of the parent container, that is, the column.

At this point, the app looks as follows:

In the next section, we will add a mechanism to play audio files in the application.

Adding Audio Player

After creating the UI of the application, we will now add Audio Player to the application to play audio files. We will make use of the `audioplayer` plugin to add Audio Player as follows:

1. We start by adding the dependency to the `pubspec.yaml` file:

   ```
   audioplayers: 0.13.2
   ```

   Now, get the packages by running `flutter pub get`.

2. Next, we import the plugin in `play_music.dart`.

   ```
   import 'package:audioplayers/audioplayers.dart';
   ```

3. Then, create an instance of `AudioPlayer` inside `PlayMusicState`:

   ```
   AudioPlayer audioPlayer = AudioPlayer();
   ```

4. Now, let's define a `play()` method to play a remotely available audio file as follows:

   ```
   play() async {
      var url =
   'http://34.70.80.18:8000/download/output_1573917221.mid';
      int result = await audioPlayer.play(url);
      if (result == 1) {
        print('Success');
        }
    }
   ```

   Initially, we will use a sample audio file stored in the `url` variable. The audio file is played using `audioPlayer.play()` by passing in the value in `url`. Also, the result is stored in a result variable whose value will be 1 if the audio file is accessed and played successfully from the `url` variable.

5. Let's now add the `onPressed` property to the play button built inside `buildPlayButton` so that the audio file is played whenever the button is pressed:

   ```
   Widget buildPlayButton() {
      return Padding(
        padding: EdgeInsets.only(left: 16, right: 16, top: 16),
        child: RaisedButton(
         ....
   ```

```
    onPressed: () {
      play();
    },
    ....
    ),
  );
}
```

In the preceding code snippet, we add the `onPressed` property and call the `play()` method so that the audio file is played whenever the button is pressed.

6. We will now define `stop()` to stop the music that is already playing:

```
void stop() {
   audioPlayer.stop();
}
```

Inside the `stop()` method, we simply call `audioPlayer.stop()` to stop the music that is already playing.

7. Finally, we add the `onPressed` property for the stop button built inside `buildStopButton()`:

```
Widget buildStopButton() {
  return Padding(
    padding: EdgeInsets.only(left: 16, right: 16, top: 16),
    child: RaisedButton(
      ....
    onPressed: (){
      stop();
    },
    ....
  )
 );
}
```

In the preceding code snippet, we add a call to `stop()` inside `onPressed` so that the audio is stopped as soon as the stop button is pressed.

Let's now start to deploy the model with the Flutter application.

Deploying the model

After successfully adding a basic play and stop functionality to the application, let's now access the hosted model to generate, fetch, and play a new audio file every time. The following steps discuss in detail how we can access the model inside the application:

1. First of all, we define the `fetchResponse()` method to generate and fetch new audio files:

```
void fetchResponse() async {
   final response =
     await http.get('http://35.225.134.65:8000/generate');
   if (response.statusCode == 200) {
     var v = json.decode(response.body);
     fileName = v["result"] ;
   } else {
     throw Exception('Failed to load');
   }
}
```

We begin by fetching the response from the API using `http.get()` and passing in the URL where the model is hosted. The response from the `get()` method is stored in the `response` variable. When the `get()` operation is complete, we check the status code using `response.statusCode`. If the value of the status is `200`, the fetch was successful. Next, we convert the body of the response from raw JSON to `Map<String,dynamic>` using `json.decode()` so that the key-value pairs contained in the response body can be accessed easily. We access the value for the new audio file using `v["result"]` and store it inside the global `fileName` variable. If the `responseCode` was not `200`, we simply throw an error.

2. Let's now define `load()` to make proper calls to `fetchResponse()`:

```
void load() {
   fetchResponse();
}
```

In the preceding code lines, we simply define a `load()` method that is used to call `fetchResponse()` to fetch the value for the newly generated audio file.

3. We will now modify the `onPressed` property inside `buildGenerateButton()` to generate new audio files every time:

```
Widget buildGenerateButton() {
   return Padding(
      ....
```

```
      child: RaisedButton(
        ....
        onPressed: () {
          load();
        },
        ....
      ),
    );
  }
```

According to the functionality of the application, whenever the generate button is pressed, a new audio file should be generated. This directly means that whenever the generate button is pressed, we need to make a call to the API to get the name of the newly generated audio file. Therefore, we modify `buildGenerateButton()` to add the `onPressed` property so that whenever the button is pressed, it makes a call to `load()`, which subsequently calls `fetchResponse()` and stores the name of the new audio file in the output.

4. An audio file that is hosted has two parts, a `baseUrl` and a `fileName`. `baseUrl` remains the same for all the calls. Therefore, we declare a global string variable storing `baseUrl`:

```
String baseUrl = 'http://34.70.80.18:8000/download/';
```

Recall that we have already stored the name of the new audio file inside `fileName` in *step 1*.

5. Now, let's modify `play()` to play the newly generated files:

```
play() async {
   var url = baseUrl + fileName;
   AudioPlayer.logEnabled = true;
   int result = await audioPlayer.play(url);
   if (result == 1) {
     print('Success');
     }
}
```

In the preceding code snippet, we modify the `play()` method defined earlier. We create a new URL by appending `baseUrl` and `fileName` so that the value inside `url` always corresponds to the newly generated audio file. We pass the value of the URL while making a call to `audioPlayer.play()`. This ensures that every time the play button is pressed, the most recently generated audio file is played.

6. Also, we add a `Text` widget to reflect the file-generating status:

```
Widget buildLoadingText() {
  return Center(
    child: Padding(
      padding: EdgeInsets.only(top: 16),
      child: Text(loadText)
    )
  );
}
```

In the function defined previously, we create a simple `Text` widget to reflect the fact that the fetch operation is in operation and when it is complete. The `Text` widget is given top padding and is aligned to the `Center`. The `loadText` value is used to create the widget.

The variable is declared globally with an initial value of `'Generate Music'`:

```
String loadText = 'Generate Music';
```

7. Update the `build()` method to add the new `Text` widget:

```
@override
 Widget build(BuildContext context) {
   return Scaffold(
     ....
   body: Column(
     ....
     children: <Widget>[
       buildGenerateButton(),
       ....
       buildLoadingText()
     ],
   )
 );
}
```

Now, we update the `build()` method to add the newly created `Text` widget. The widget is simply added as a child of the `Column` created earlier.

8. We need to change the text when the user wants to generate a new text file and while the fetch operation is in progress:

```
void load() {
    setState(() {
    loadText = 'Generating...';
    });
    fetchResponse();
}
```

In the preceding code snippet, the `loadText` value is set to `'Generating...'` to reflect the fact that the `get()` operation is in progress.

9. Finally, we update the text when the fetch is complete:

```
void fetchResponse() async {
    final response =
        await
http.get('http://35.225.134.65:8000/generate').whenComplete((){
        setState(() {
          loadText = 'Generation Complete';
        });
    });
    ....
}
```

Once the fetch is complete, we update the value of `loadText` to `'Generation Complete'`. This signifies that the application is now ready to play the newly generated file.

 The entire code for `play_music.dart` can be viewed here: https:// github.com/PacktPublishing/Mobile-Deep-Learning-Projects/blob/ master/Chapter7/flutter_generate_music/lib/play_music.dart.

After making all the segments of the application work properly, let's now finally put everything together by creating the final material app.

Creating the final material app

Let's now create the `main.dart` file. The file contains a stateless widget, `MyApp`. We override the `build()` method and set `PlayMusic` as its child:

```
@override
Widget build(BuildContext context) {
  return MaterialApp(
    title: 'Flutter Demo',
    theme: ThemeData(
      primarySwatch: Colors.blue,
    ),
    home: PlayMusic(),
  );
}
```

Inside the overridden `build()` method, we simply create the `MaterialApp` with home as `PlayMusic()`.

 The entire project can be viewed here: `https://github.com/ PacktPublishing/Mobile-Deep-Learning-Projects/tree/master/ Chapter7/flutter_generate_music`.

Summary

In this chapter, we covered the study of multimedia processing by breaking it into the core components of image, audio, and video processing, and discussed some of the most common tools for working on them. We saw how easy it becomes for us to perform image or video processing using OpenCV. Also, we saw a quick example of generating drum music using Magenta. In the later part of this chapter, we covered how LSTMs work with time series data, and built an API that could generate instrumental music from sample files provided. Finally, we used this API with a Flutter app, which is cross-platform and can be deployed on Android, iOS, and the web simultaneously.

In the next chapter, we will be looking at how we can use **deep reinforcement learning (DRL)** to create agents that can play board games such as chess.

8
Reinforced Neural Network-Based Chess Engine

Games have been provided with an entire section of their own on several online application stores and on almost every software store as well. The importance and craze of games cannot be overlooked, which is why developers all over the world keep trying to come up with better and more engrossing games.

In the world of popular board games, chess is one of the most competitive and complex games that is played all over the world. There have been several attempts to come out with strong automated programs for playing chess and competing against humans. This chapter will discuss the approach that's used by the developers at DeepMind who created Alpha Zero, a self-learning algorithm that taught itself to play chess so that it could beat the then best chess AI on the market, Stockfish 8, with a one-sided score in just 24 hours of training.

In this chapter, we will introduce the concepts that you need to understand in order to build such a deep reinforcement learning algorithm and then build a sample project. Note that this project will require that you have good knowledge of Python and machine learning.

We will cover the following topics in this chapter:

- Introduction to reinforcement learning
- Reinforcement learning in mobile games
- Exploring Google's DeepMind
- Alpha Zero-like AI for Connect 4
- Underlying project architecture
- Developing a GCP-hosted REST API for the chess engine
- Creating a simple chess UI on Android
- Integrating the chess engine API with a UI

Let's begin by discussing the usage and popularity of reinforcement learning agents in mobile games.

Introduction to reinforcement learning

In the last few years, reinforcement learning has emerged to be a prominent field of study among machine learning researchers. It has been increasingly used to build agents that learn to perform better in any given environment, in search of a better reward to the actions they have performed. This, in a nutshell, brings us to the definition of reinforcement learning – in the field of artificial intelligence, this is when an algorithm aims to create virtual **agents** that perform **actions** at any given **state** within an **environment** to achieve the best possible **reward** after the sequence of actions has been performed.

Let's try to give this definition more structure by defining the variables associated with a common reinforcement learning algorithm:

- **Agent:** A virtual entity that performs actions. It is the entity that replaces the designated user of the game/software.
- **Action (a):** The possible actions that the agent can perform.
- **Environment (e):** A set of scenarios available in the software/game.
- **State (S):** A collection of all scenarios, along with the configurations available in them.
- **Reward (R):** A value that's returned for any action that's performed by the agent, which the agent then tries to maximize.
- **Policy (π):** The strategy that the agent uses to determine which actions have to be performed next.
- **Value (V):** R is a short-term per-action reward, whereas value is the total reward expected at the end of a set of actions. Vπ(s) defines the expected total reward by following policy π under the state, S.

The flow of this algorithm can be seen in the following diagram:

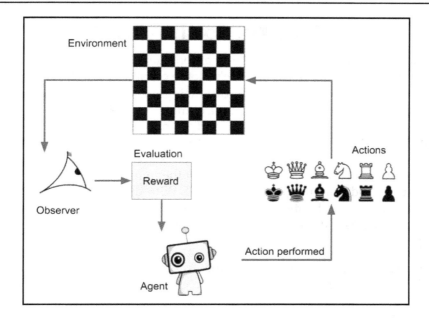

While we didn't mention the observer in the preceding list of definitions, it is a necessity to have an observer or evaluator in order to produce rewards. Sometimes, the observer itself could be a complex piece of software, but often, this is a simple evaluation function or metric.

To get a more detailed idea of reinforcement learning, you can read the Wikipedia article at https://en.wikipedia.org/wiki/Reinforcement_learning. For a quick sample of a reinforcement learning agent in action, read the following DataCamp article: https://www.datacamp.com/community/tutorials/introduction-reinforcement-learning

In the next section, we will learn how reinforcement learning found its place in mobile games.

Reinforcement learning in mobile games

Reinforcement learning has gained popularity among developers who wish to build game-playing AIs for various reasons – to simply check the capabilities of the AI, to build a training agent that helps professionals improve their game, and so on. From a researcher's point of view, games offer the best testing environment for reinforcement learning agents that can make decisions based on experience and learn to survive/achieve in any given environment. This is due to the fact that games can be designed with simple and precise rules, where the reaction of the environment to a certain action can be accurately predicted. This makes it easier to evaluate the performance of the reinforcement learning agents, and thereby facilitate a good training ground for the AI. With the breakthroughs in game-playing AIs taken into consideration, it has also been voiced that we're moving faster toward a general-purpose AI than what was expected. But how do reinforcement learning concepts map to games?

Let's consider a simple game, such as tic-tac-toe. Alternatively, if you're feeling quirky, just Google *Tic-Tac-Toe* and you'll be presented with a game right in your search results!

Consider you're playing Tic-Tac-Toe against the computer. The computer here is the agent. What is the environment, in this case? You guessed correctly – the Tic-Tac-Toe board, along with the set of rules that govern the game in the environment. The already placed markers on the Tic-Tac-Toe board make the state the environment is in. The X or the O that the agent can put on the board are the actions they can perform, where a loss, a win, or a tie or advancing toward a loss, win, or a tie is the reward given back to the agent after they perform any action. The strategy that's followed by the agent to win the game is the policy it follows.

Hence, from this example, it is conclusive that reinforcement learning agents are highly suitable for building AI that learns to play any game. This has led to a number of developers coming up with game-playing AIs for several popular games besides chess, such as Go, checkers, Counter-Strike, and others. Even games such as Chrome Dino have found developers attempting to play them using AI.

In the next section, we will provide a brief overview of Google's DeepMind, one of the most popular companies in the field of game-playing AI makers.

Exploring Google's DeepMind

DeepMind is probably one of the most prominent names that comes up when you talk about the growth of self-learning artificial intelligence, owing to their groundbreaking research and achievements in the field. Acquired by Google in 2014, DeepMind is currently a wholly-owned subsidiary of Alphabet since the restructuring of Google in 2015. The most notable works of DeepMind include AlphaGo and its successor, Alpha Zero. Let's discuss these projects in greater depth and try to understand what makes them so important in the present day.

AlphaGo

In 2015, AlphaGo became the first piece of computer software to defeat a professional Go player, Lee Sedol, on a 19x19 board. The breakthrough was documented and released as a documentary movie. The impact of the victory over Lee Sedol was so great that the Korea Baduk Association granted an honorary 9-dan certificate, which essentially means a Go player whose skill of the game borders on divinity. This was the first time ever in the history of Go that an honorary 9-dan certificate had been provided, so the certificate that was provided to AlphaGo was numbered 001. Its ELO rating then was 3,739.

The successor to AlphaGo – the AlphaGo Master – later defeated the then reigning world champion of the game, Ke Jie, in a three-match game. In recognition of the feat, it was awarded the 9-dan certification from the Chinese Weiqi Association. This piece of software achieved an ELO rating of 4,858 at the time.

However, both pieces of software were overpowered by their successor, AlphaGo Zero, which, in 3 days of self-taught learning, was able to defeat AlphaGo with a 100:0 game score and AlphaGo Master with an 89:11 game score after 21 days of training. After 40 days, it had exceeded the skill of all previous Go AIs, with an ELO rating of 5,185.

AlphaGo was based upon the Monte Carlo tree search algorithm and employed deep learning performed over generated and human player game logs. The initial training for the model was made from human games. Then, the computer would play against itself and try to improve its game. The tree search would be capped to a set depth to avoid huge computational overheads in which the computer would try to reach all possible moves to get to the end of the game before making any move.

In summary, the following process was followed:

1. Initially, the model would be trained on human game logs.
2. Once trained on a baseline, the computer would play against itself using the model it trained on in the previous step and used a capped Monte Carlo tree search to ensure that moves were made without stalling the software for a long time. Logs were generated for these games.
3. Training was then performed on the generated games, which improved the overall model.

Now, let's discuss Alpha Zero.

Alpha Zero

A successor to AlphaGo Zero, Alpha Zero was an attempt at generalizing the algorithm so that it could be used to play other board games as well. Alpha Zero was trained to play chess, shogi (a Japanese game similar to chess), and Go and achieved performance on par with the existing AIs of the respective games. After 34 hours of training, Alpha Zero for Go was able to defeat AlphaGo Zero, which was trained over 3 days, with a score of 60:40. This led to an ELO rating of 4,430.

Alpha Zero was able to defeat Stockfish 8, the 2016 winner of the TCEC contest, after about 9 hours of training. Thus, it remains the most powerful chess AI so far, though some claim that the latest version of Stockfish will be able to defeat it.

The major differences between AlphaGo Zero and the Alpha Zero variant are as follows:

- **Possibility of a tie**: While in Go, one player is guaranteed to win, the same is not true for chess. Hence, Alpha Zero was modified so that tied games were allowed.
- **Symmetry**: AlphaGo Zero took advantage of the symmetric nature of the board. However, with chess not being an asymmetric game, Alpha Zero had to be modified to work accordingly.
- **Hardcoded hyperparameter search**: Alpha Zero had hardcoded rules for hyperparameter searches.
- The neural network keeps on updating in the case of Alpha Zero.

At this point, you might be wondering, "What is the Monte Carlo tree search?". Let's try to answer that question!

Monte Carlo tree search

When we talk about games such as chess, Go, or Tic-Tac-Toe, which are games of strategy based upon the current scenario, we're talking about a huge number of possible scenarios and actions that can be performed in them at any given point. While, for smaller games such as tic-tac-toe, the number of possible states and actions is within the reach of modern-day computers to calculate, more complex games such as chess and Go exponentially increase in terms of how many possible states of the game can be made.

The Monte Carlo tree search attempts to find the right series of actions required to win any game or to achieve a better reward in a given environment. The reason it is called a **tree search** is due to the fact that it creates a tree of all the possible states in the game, with all the possible moves in it by creating a branch to each state, which are represented as the nodes in the tree.

Let's consider the following simple game example. Say you are playing a game that asks you to guess a three-digit number, where each guess has an associated reward with it. The possible range of digits is 1 to 5, and the number of times you can guess is three. If you make an exact guess, which would be to correctly guess the number at any given position, you'll be rewarded with a score of 5. However, if you make a wrong guess, a score is provided in a linear decrement on both sides of the correct number.

For instance, if the number to be guessed was 2, the following reward scores are possible:

- If you guess 1, the score is 4
- If you guess 2, the score is 5
- If you guess 3, the score is 4
- If you guess 4, the score is 3
- If you guess 5, the score is 2

Hence, the optimal total score in the game is 15, that is, 5 points for each correct guess. Given that, at each step, you can choose between any of the five options, the total number of possible states in the game is 5 * 5 * 5 = 125, with just one state giving the optimal score.

Let's try to depict the preceding game in a tree. Say the number you're trying to guess is 413. In the first step, you'd have the following tree:

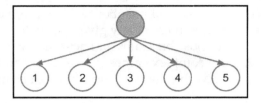

Upon making your choice, you'd be presented with the reward, and again you'd have five options to choose from – in other words, five branches in each node to traverse. In optimal gameplay, the following tree would be obtained:

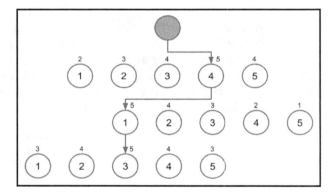

Now, let's consider the fact that the game of Go has a total of 3^{361} possible states. It becomes impractical to try and compute each possibility before the AI makes a move. This is where the Monte Carlo tree search, combined with the Upper Confidence Bound algorithm, gains an advantage over other methods since it can be terminated to any search depth, and can yield results that tend toward an optimal score. Thus, it is not required for the algorithm to traverse down each branch of the tree. The tree search algorithm, once it realizes that any particular branch is performing poorly, can stop going down on that path and focus on the better performing paths. Also, it can terminate any path early on and return the expected reward at that point, making it possible to adjust the time taken by the AI to make any move.

In more definite terms, the Monte Carlo tree search follows these steps:

1. **Selection**: The best rewarding branch is selected from the current node of the tree. For instance, in the preceding gameplay tree, choosing any branch other than 4 would yield a lower score, so 4 is selected.

2. **Expanding**: Once the best rewarding node has been selected, the tree under that node is expanded further, creating nodes with all possible options (branches) available at that node. This can be understood as laying out the future moves of the AI from any point in the game.

3. **Simulating**: Now, since it is not known beforehand which future option that was created during the expanding phase is the most rewarding, we simulate the game with each option one by one using reinforcement learning and create a reward score for each node. Note that, when combined with the Upper Confidence Bound algorithm, it is not important to compute the game up until its termination. A computation of rewards for any *n* steps is also a good way to proceed.

4. **Update**: Finally, the reward scores of the nodes and the parent nodes are updated. Though it is not possible to go back in the game, and since the value of any node has decreased, the AI will not follow that path if a better alternative is found at that stage in future games, thereby improving its gameplay over several iterations.

Next, we'll build a system that works like Alpha Zero and attempts to learn to play the Connect 4 game, which is more complex than the game of Tic-Tac-Toe and yet big enough for us to explain the idea of how a similar chess engine can be built.

Alpha Zero-like AI for Connect 4

Before we begin working on the AI that plays Connect4, let's briefly understand the game and its dynamics. Connect 4, also sometimes known as Four in a row, Four in a line, Four up, and so on, is one of the most popular board games among children all over the world. We can also understand it as a more advanced version of the Tic-Tac-Toe game, where you have to place three markers of the same type either horizontally, vertically, or diagonally. The board is generally a 6x7 grid, and two players play with a marker each.

The rules of Connect 4 can vary, so let's lay down some concrete rules for the version of the rules that our AI will learn to play:

- The game is simulated as being played on a vertical board that has seven hollow columns and six rows. Each column has an opening on top of the board, which is where pieces can be dropped in. Pieces that have been put into the board can be viewed.
- Both players have 21 pieces shaped like coins of a different color.
- Placing a coin on the board constitutes a move.

- Pieces drop from the opening on top to the last row or pile up on the last piece in that column.
- The first player to connect any four of their coins in any direction so that there are no gaps or coins of the other player between them wins.

Now, let's break down the problem of building a Connect 4 playing, self-learning AI into subproblems:

1. First, we'll need to create a virtual representation of the board.
2. Next, we'll have to create functions that allow moves according to the game's rules.
3. Then, in order to save states of the game, we'll need a state managing system in place.
4. Next, we'll have to facilitate gameplay, wherein the users will be prompted to make moves and announce game termination.
5. After that, we'll have to create a script that can generate sample gameplays for the system to learn from.
6. Then, we'll have to create training functions to train the system.
7. Next, we'll need a **Monte Carlo tree search** (**MCTS**) implementation.
8. Finally, we'll need an implementation of a neural network.
9. Besides the preceding concrete steps, we will also need to create a number of driver scripts for the system to make it more usable.

Let's move sequentially over the preceding points, covering each part of the system one step at a time. However, first, we'll quickly go through the directory structure and the files present in this project, which are also available in this book's GitHub repository: `https://github.com/PacktPublishing/Mobile-Deep-Learning-Projects/tree/master/Chapter8/connect4`. Let's take a look:

- `command/`:
    - `__init__.py`: This file makes it possible for us to use this folder as a module.
    - `arena.py`: This file takes and parses the commands that are used to run the game.
    - `generate.py`: This file takes and parses commands for the self-play move generation system.
    - `newmodel.py`: This file is used for creating a new blank model for the agent.

- `train.py`: This file is used for training the reinforcement learning-based neural network on how to play the game.
- `util/`:
  - `__init__.py`: This file makes it possible for us to use this folder as a module.
  - `arena.py`: This file creates and maintains records of the matches that have been played between the players and allows us to switch between whose turn it is.
  - `compat.py`: This file is a handy utility for making the program compatible with both Python 2 and Python 3. You may skip this file if you're sure of the version you're developing on and expect to run on.
  - `generate.py`: This file plays out a number of games with random moves combined with the MCTS move to generate a log of the games that can be used for training purposes. The file stores the winner of each game, along with the moves that were made by the players.
  - `internal.py`: This file creates a virtual representation of the board and defines the functions associated with the board, such as putting pieces on the board, finding a winner, or simply creating new boards.
  - `keras_model.py`: This file defines the model that acts as the brain of the agent. We will discuss this file in greater depth later in this project.
  - `mcts.py`: This file provides the MCTS class, which is essentially an implementation of the Monte Carlo tree search.
  - `nn.py`: This file provides the NN class, which is an implementation of a neural network, along with the functions associated with the neural network, such as Fit, predict, save, and others.
  - `player.py`: This file provides classes for two types of players – the MCTS player and the human player. The MCTS player is the agent we will be training to play the game.
  - `state.py`: This is a wrapper around the `internal.py` file that provides a class for accessing the board and board-related functions.
  - `trainer.py`: This allows us to train the model. This is different from the one provided in `nn.py` since it is more focused on covering the training process in terms of the game, while the one in `nn.py` is mostly a wrapper around this function.

Next, we'll dive into exploring some of the important parts of each of these files, while following the steps we laid down previously to build the AI.

Creating a virtual representation of the board

How would you represent a Connect 4 board? There are two commonly used methods for representing the Connect 4 board, along with the game state. Let's take a look:

- **Long, human-readable form**: In this form, the rows and columns of the board are displayed on the x and y axes and the markers of both the players are displayed as x and o, respectively (or any other suitable characters). This may look as follows:

```
 |1 2 3 4 5 6 7
--+--------------
1|. . . . . . .
2|. . . . . . .
3|. . . . . . .
4|. . . o x .
5|x o x . o o .
6|o x x o x x o
```

This form is, however, a bit lengthy and not very computationally friendly.

- **Computationally efficient form**: In this form, we store the board as a 2D NumPy array:

```
array([[1, 1, 0, 0, 0, 0, 0],
       [0, 0, 0, 0, 0, 0, 0],
       [0, 0, 0, 0, 0, 0, 0],
       [0, 0, 0, 0, 0, 0, 0],
       [0, 0, 0, 0, 1, 0, 0],
       [0, 0, 0, 0, 0, 0, 0]], dtype=int8)
```

This array is created in such a manner that when it is flattened into a 1D array, the board positions are sequentially arranged as if the array was actually a 1D array. The first two positions are numbered 0 and 1, respectively, whereas the third one, which is in the 5th row and 5th column, is numbered 32. This condition can be understood easily by mapping the matrix in the previous code block with the table given in the following diagram:

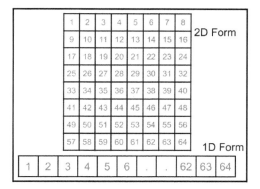

Such a form is suitable for putting into computation, but not suitable for the player to view during gameplay, as it would be tough to decipher for the player.

- Once we've decided on how to represent the board and its pieces, we can start writing the code for this in the `util/internal.py` file, as shown here:

```
BOARD_SIZE_W = 7
BOARD_SIZE_H = 6
KEY_SIZE = BOARD_SIZE_W * BOARD_SIZE_H
```

The preceding lines set the constants for the board, which, in this case, are the number of rows and columns on the board. We also calculate the number of keys or positions on the board by multiplying them.

- Now, let's prepare the code that generates the winning positions on the board, as shown here:

```
LIST4 = []
LIST4 += [[(y, x), (y + 1, x + 1), (y + 2, x + 2), (y + 3, x + 3)]
for y in range(BOARD_SIZE_H - 3) for x in range(BOARD_SIZE_W - 3)]
LIST4 += [[(y, x + 3), (y + 1, x + 2), (y + 2, x + 1), (y + 3, x)]
for y in range(BOARD_SIZE_H - 3) for x in range(BOARD_SIZE_W - 3)]
LIST4 += [[(y, x), (y, x + 1), (y, x + 2), (y, x + 3)] for y in
range(BOARD_SIZE_H) for x in range(BOARD_SIZE_W - 3)]
NO_HORIZONTAL = len(LIST4)
LIST4 += [[(y, x), (y + 1, x), (y + 2, x), (y + 3, x)] for y in
range(BOARD_SIZE_H - 3) for x in range(BOARD_SIZE_W)]
```

The `LIST4` variable stores the possible combinations that can be achieved if any player wins the game.

We will not discuss the entirety of the code in this file; however, the following functions and what they do are important to know:

- `get_start_board()`: This function returns an empty 2D array representation of the board in the form of a NumPy array.
- `clone_board(board)`: This function is used to clone the entire NumPy array of the board element-wise.
- `get_action(board)`: This function returns the positions in the array that have been modified by the players.
- `action_to_string(action)`: This function converts the internal numeric representation of the actions performed by the players into a string that can be displayed to the user in a human-comprehensible form; for example, `place_at(board, pos,`.
- `player)`: Performs the action of placing a piece on the board for any given player. It also updates the board.
- `def get_winner(board)`: This function determines whether the game at the current state of the board has a winner. If yes, then it returns the winning player's identifier, which will be 1 or -1.
- `def to_string(board)`: This function converts the NumPy array representation of the board into a string, which is in a human-readable format.

Next, we'll take a look at how we've programmed the AI to make and accept only valid moves according to the rules of the game.

Allowing moves according to the game's rules

To establish the validity of the moves made by the players, be it man or machine, we need to have a mechanism in place that continuously either only generates valid moves, in the case of the machine, or keeps validating any human player input. Let's get started:

1. One such instance can be found in the `_selfplay(self, state, args)` function in the `util/generator.py` file, as shown in the following code:

```
turn = 0
hard_random_turn = args['hard_random'] if 'hard_random' in args
else 0
soft_random_turn = (args['soft_random'] if 'soft_random' in args
else 30) + hard_random_turn
history = []
```

First, we set the toggle for moves to 0, indicating that no moves have been made at the start of the game. We also take in the amount of hard and soft random turns a user wants in their AI's self-generated games. Then, we set the history of the moves made to blank.

2. Now, we can begin generating the moves for the AI, as shown here:

```
while state.getWinner() == None:
    if turn < hard_random_turn:
        # random action
        action_list = state.getAction()
        index = np.random.choice(len(action_list))
        (action, key) = action_list[index]
```

The preceding code says that until there is no winner of the game, moves have to be generated. In the preceding case, we can see that whenever the probability of making a hard random turn is true, the AI chooses a completely random position to place its piece in.

3. By adding an `else` block to the preceding `if` statement, we're telling the AI that whenever it requires a soft turn, it can check for any random positions to place its piece in, but only within the domain of moves proposed by the MCTS algorithm, as shown here:

```
else:
    action_list = self.mcts.getActionInfo(state,
args['simulation'])
    if turn < soft_random_turn:
        # random action by visited count
        visited = [1.0 * a.visited for a in action_list]
        sum_visited = sum(visited)
        assert(sum_visited > 0)
        p = [v / sum_visited for v in visited]
        index = np.random.choice(len(action_list), p = p)
    else:
        # select most visited count
        index = np.argmax([a.visited for a in action_list])
```

Note that if neither a hard turn nor a soft turn is taking place, the agent makes the most commonly made move at that point of the game, which is expected to take it toward victory.

Thus, in the case of the non-human player, the agent is only able to choose between a set of populated valid moves at any given stage. This is not true for a human player, who, according to their creativity, has the possibility of trying to make an invalid move. Hence, the moves need to be validated when the human player makes them.

4. The method of validating human player moves can be found in the `getNextAction(self, state)` function in the `util/player.py` file, as shown here:

```
action = state.getAction()
available_x = []
for i in range(len(action)):
    a, k = action[i]
    x = a % util.BOARD_SIZE_W + 1
    y = a // util.BOARD_SIZE_W + 1
    print('{} - {},{}'.format(x, x, y))
    available_x.append(x)
```

5. First, we now calculate the possible legal moves for the human player and display them to the user. Then, we prompt the user to enter a move until they make a valid move, as shown here:

```
while True:
    try:
        x = int(compat_input('enter x: '))
        if x in available_x:
            for i in range(len(action)):
                if available_x[i] == x:
                    select = i
                    break
            break
    except ValueError:
        pass
```

Thus, we validate the moves made by the user against a populated set of valid moves. We could also choose to display an error to the user.

Next, we'll look at the state management system of the program, which you must have noticed being used throughout the code we've been looking at so far.

The state management system

The state management system of the game is one of the most important parts of the entire program since it controls all the gameplay, along with facilitating gameplay during the self-learning process of the AI. It makes sure that the players have a board presented to them and are making valid moves. It also stores several state-related variables, which are useful for the game to progress. Let's take a look:

1. Let's discuss the most important features and functions within the `State` class, which is provided in the `util/state.py` file:

   ```
   import .internal as util
   ```

   This class uses the variables and functions defined in the `util/internal.py` file with the name of `util`.

2. `__init__(self, prototype = None)`: This class, when initiated, either carries forward an existing state or creates a new one. The definition of this function is as follows:

   ```
   def __init__(self, prototype = None):
       if prototype == None:
           self.board = util.get_start_board()
           self.currentPlayer = 1
           self.winner = None
       else:
           self.board = util.clone_board(prototype.board)
           self.currentPlayer = prototype.currentPlayer
           self.winner = prototype.winner
   ```

   Here, you can see that this class can be initiated with an existing state of the game and passed as the parameter to the constructor of the class; otherwise, the class creates a new game state.

3. `getRepresentativeString(self)`: This function returns a well-formed string representation of the game state that can be read by the human player. Its definition is as follows:

   ```
   def getRepresentativeString(self):
           return ('x|' if self.currentPlayer > 0 else 'o|') +
   util.to_oneline(self.board)
   ```

A number of other important methods in the state class are as follows:

- `getCurrentPlayer(self)`: This method returns the current player of the game; that is, the player who is supposed to make the move.
- `getWinner(self)`: This method returns the identifier of the winner of the game, if the game has ended.
- `getAction(self)`: This method checks whether the game has ended. If it hasn't, it returns a set of next possible moves at any given state.
- `getNextState(self, action)`: This method returns the next state of the game; that is, it performs a switch from one state to another after placing the currently moving piece on the board and evaluating whether the game has ended.
- `getNnInput(self)`: This method returns the moves performed by the players so far in the game, with a different marker for each player's moves.

Now, let's look at how we can facilitate the gameplay for the program.

Facilitating gameplay

The file that's responsible for governing the facilitation of gameplay in the program is the `util/arena.py` file.

It defines the following two methods within the `Arena` class:

```
def fight(self, state, p1, p2, count):
    stats = [0, 0, 0]
    for i in range(count):
        print('==== EPS #{} ===='.format(i + 1))
        winner = self._fight(state, p1, p2)
        stats[winner + 1] += 1
        print('stats', stats[::-1])
        winner = self._fight(state, p2, p1)
        stats[winner * -1 + 1] += 1
        print('stats', stats[::-1])
```

The preceding `fight()` function manages the stats of victories/losses or ties for the players. It ensures that in each round, two games are played, where each player gets to play first only once.

The other `_fight()` function that was defined in this class is as follows:

```
def _fight(self, state, p1, p2):
    while state.getWinner() == None:
        print(state)
        if state.getCurrentPlayer() > 0:
            action = p1.getNextAction(state)
        else:
            action = p2.getNextAction(state)
        state = state.getNextState(action)
    print(state)
    return state.getWinner()
```

This function takes care of switching the players on the board until a winner is found.

Now, let's look at how we can generate random gameplays for the agent to self-learn on.

Generating sample gameplays

So far, we've talked about the `util/gameplay.py` file to demonstrate the code in the file that pertains to move-making rules – specifically, the self-play function of the file. Now, we'll take a look at how these self-plays can run in iteration to generate a complete gameplay log. Let's get started:

1. Consider the code of the `generate()` method of the `Generator` class provided by this file:

```
def generate(self, state, nn, cb, args):
    self.mcts = MCTS(nn)

    iterator = range(args['selfplay'])
    if args['progress']:
        from tqdm import tqdm
        iterator = tqdm(iterator, ncols = 50)

    # self play
    for pi in iterator:
        result = self._selfplay(state, args)
        if cb != None:
            cb(result)
```

Essentially, this function takes care of running the `_selfplay()` function of the class and makes a decision regarding what has to be done once a self-play has been completed. In most cases, you will be saving the output to a file, which would then be used for training.

2. This has been defined in the `command/generate.py` file. This script can be run as a command with the following signature:

```
usage: run.py generate [-h]
                    [--model, default='latest.h5', help='model filename']
                    [--number, default=1000000, help='number of generated
states']
                    [--simulation, default=100, help='number of
simulations per move']
                    [--hard, default=0, help='number of random moves']
                    [--soft, default=1000, help='number of random moves
that depends on visited node count']
                    [--progress, help='show progress bar']
                    [--gpu, help='gpu memory fraction']
                    [--file, help='save to a file']
                    [--network, help='save to remote server']
```

3. A sample invocation of this command is as follows:

```
python run.py generate --model model.h5 --simulation 100 -n 5000 --
file selfplay.txt --progress
```

Now, let's take a look at the functions we have in place to train the model once the self-play logs have been generated.

System training

To train the agent, we need to create the `util/trainer.py` file, which provides the `train()` function. Let's take a look:

1. The signature is as follows:

```
train(state, nn, filename, args = {})
```

The function accepts a `State` class, a neural network class, and other arguments. It also accepts a filename, which is the path of the file containing the generated gameplays. After training, we have the option of saving the output to another model file, as provided in the `train()` function of the `command/train.py` file.

2. This command has the following signature:

    ```
    usage: run.py train [-h]
                        [--progress, help='show progress bar']
                        [--epoch EPOCH, help='training epochs']
                        [--batch BATCH, help='batch size']
                        [--block BLOCK, help='block size']
                        [--gpu GPU, help='gpu memory fraction']
                        history, help='history file'
                        input, help='input model file name'
                        output, help='output model file name'
    ```

    The history argument is the file that stores the generated gameplays. The input file is the currently saved model file, whereas the output file is the file where the freshly trained model would be saved to.

3. A sample invocation of this command is as follows:

    ```
    python run.py train selfplay.txt model.h5 newmodel.h5 --epoch 3 --
    progress
    ```

Now that we've got a training system in place, we need to create MCTS and neural network implementations.

Monte Carlo tree search implementation

A comprehensive MCTS algorithm implementation is present in the `util/mcts.py` file. This file provides the MCTS class, which has the following important functions:

-   `getMostVisitedAction`: This function returns the action that is most visited when a state is passed to it.
-   `getActionInfo`: This function returns the state information after any action has been performed.
-   `_simulation`: This function performs a single game simulation and returns information about the game that was played during the simulation.

Finally, we need to create a neural network implementation.

Implementing the neural network

In this final section, we shall understand the neural network we have created for the agent to train with. We'll explore the `util/nn.py` file, which provides the NN class, along with the following important methods:

- `__init__(self, filename)`: This function creates a new model using the `util/keras_model.py` functions if none exist on the disk. Otherwise, it loads the model file into the program.
- The model defined in the `util/keras_model.py` file is a residual CNN, which, in combination with MCTS and UCT, performs like a deep reinforcement learning neural network. The model formed has the following configurations:

```
input_dim: (2, util.BOARD_SIZE_H, util.BOARD_SIZE_W),
policy_dim: util.KEY_SIZE,
res_layer_num: 5,
cnn_filter_num: 64,
cnn_filter_size: 5,
l2_reg: 1e-4,
learning_rate: 0.003,
momentum: 0.9
```

By default, the model has five residual convolutional layer blocks. We defined the `BOARD_SIZE_H`, `BOARD_SIZE_W`, and `KEY_SIZE` constants in the `util/internal.py` file previously:

- `save(self, filename)`: This function saves the model to the filename provided.
- `predict(self, x)`: Provided a board state, along with the moves already made, this function outputs a single move that can be made next.
- `fit(self, x, policy, value, batch_size = 256, epochs = 1)`: This function takes care of fitting new samples to the model and updating the weights.

Besides these preceding scripts, we also need a few driver scripts in place. You can look them up in this project's repository to understand their usage.

To run the completed project, you'll need to perform the following steps:

1. Create a new model using the following command:

```
python run.py newmodel model.h5
```

   This will create a new model and print out its summary.

2. Generate a sample gameplay log:

```
python run.py generate --model model.h5 --simulation 100 -n 5000 --
file selfplay.txt --progress
```

The preceding line generates 5,000 sample gameplays with a depth of 100 for MCTS during the simulation.

3. Train the model:

```
python run.py train selfplay.txt model.h5 newmodel.h5 --epoch 3 --
progress
```

The preceding command trains the model on the gameplay files for three epochs and saves the trained model as `newmodel.h5`.

4. Play against the AI:

```
python run.py arena human mcts,newmodel.h5,100
```

The preceding command begins a game against the AI. Here, you'll be presented with a board and gameplay options within the terminal, as shown here:

Now that we have successfully created an Alpha Zero-based program for learning to play a board game, we are ready to extrapolate the idea to a chess AI. However, before we do so, we will briefly lay out the project architecture.

Underlying project architecture

To create a chess engine, hosted on GCP as a REST API, we will be following the general project architecture:

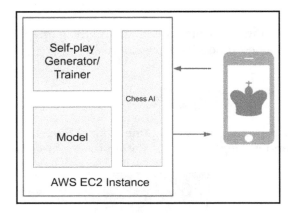

While the preceding diagram presents a very simplified overview of the project, it could be used for much more complex systems that can produce better self-learning chess engines.

The model hosted on GCP will be put inside an EC2 VM instance and will be wrapped in a Flask-based REST API.

Developing a GCP-hosted REST API for the chess engine

Now that we have seen how we will be moving ahead with this project, we also need to discuss how we're going to map the game of Connect 4 to chess and deploy a chess RL engine as an API.

You can find the files we've created for this chess engine at `https://github.com/PacktPublishing/Mobile-Deep-Learning-Projects/tree/master/Chapter8/chess`. Let's quickly understand some of the most important files before we map these files with those in the Connect 4 project:

- `src/chess_zero/agent/`:
    - `player_chess.py`: This file describes the `ChessPlayer` class, which holds information about the players playing the game at any point in time. It provides wrappers for the methods associated with searching for new moves using the Monte Carlo tree search, changing the player state, and other functions required during gameplay for each user.
    - `model_chess.py`: This file describes the residual CNN used in this system.
- `src/chess_zero/config/`:
    - `mini.py`: This file defines the configuration that the chess engine learns or plays with. You will need to tweak these parameters here at times to bring down the size of the batches or virtual RAM consumption during training on a low-end computer.
- `src/chess_zero/env/`:
    - `chess_env.py`: This file describes the setup of the chessboard, the gameplay rules, and the functions required to perform the game operations. It also contains methods for checking the state of the game and validating moves.
- `src/chess_zero/worker/`:
    - `evaluate.py`: This file is responsible for playing games against the current best model and the next-generation model. If the next-generation model performs better over 100 games, it replaces the previous model.
    - `optimize.py`: This file loads the current best model and performs more supervised learning-based training on it.
    - `self.py`: The engine plays against itself and learns new gameplay.
    - `sl.py`: An acronym for supervised learning, this file takes the PGN files of games from other players as input and performs supervised learning on them.

- `src/chess_zero/play_game/`:
    - `uci.py`: This file provides a **Universal Chess Interface (UCI)** standard environment for playing against the engine.
    - `flask_server.py`: The file creates a Flask server that communicates with the engine using the UCI notation of chess gameplay.

Now that we know what each file does, let's establish the mapping of these files with the files in the Connect 4 game.

Recall the steps we laid down while we were discussing the Connect 4 AI? Let's see whether the project for chess also follows the same steps:

1. Create a virtual representation of the board. This is done in the `src/chess_zero/env/chess_env.py` file.
2. Create functions that allow moves to be made according to the game's rules. This is also done in the `src/chess_zero/env/chess_env.py` file.
3. **A state managing system in place**: This functionality is maintained over a number of files, such as `src/chess_zero/agent/player_chess.py` and `src/chess_zero/env/chess_env.py`.
4. **Facilitate gameplay**: This is done by the `src/chess_zero/play_game/uci.py` file.
5. Create a script that can generate sample gameplays for the system to learn from. While this system doesn't explicitly store the generated gameplay as files on the disk, the task is performed by `src/chess_zero/worker/self_play.py`.
6. Create training functions to train the system. These training functions are located at `src/chess_zero/worker/sl.py` and `src/chess_zero/worker/self.py`.
7. Now, we'll need an MCTS implementation. The MCTS implementation of this project can be found within the move search method of the file at `src/chess_zero/agent/player_chess.py`.
8. **An implementation of a neural network**: The project's neural network is defined in `src/chess_zero/agent/model_chess.py`.

In addition to the preceding mappings, we need to discuss the Universal Chess Interface and the Flask server script, both of which are required for gameplay and API deployment.

Understanding the Universal Chess Interface

The file present at `/src/chess_zero/play_game/uci.py` creates a universal chess interface for the engine. But what is UCI exactly?

The UCI is a communication standard that was introduced by Rudolf Huber and Stefan Meyer-Kahlen, which allows gameplay with chess engines from any console environment. The standard uses a small set of commands to invoke chess engines to search and output the best moves for any given position of the board.

The communication through the UCI happens with standard input/output and is platform-agnostic. The commands that are available within the UCI script in our program are as follows:

- `uci`: This prints the details of the running engine.
- `isready`: This enquires whether the engine is ready to be played against.
- `ucinewgame`: This starts a new game with the engine.
- `position [fen | startpos] moves`: This sets the position of the board. If the user is starting from a non-starting position, the user needs to provide a FEN string to set the board.
- `go`: This asks the engine to search and suggest the best move.
- `quit`: This ends the game and quits the interface.

The sample gameplay with the UCI engine is shown in the following code:

```
> uci
id name ChessZero
id author ChessZero
uciok

> isready
readyok

> ucinewgame

> position startpos moves e2e4

> go
bestmove e7e5

> position rnbqkbnr/pppp1ppp/8/4p3/4P3/8/PPPP1PPP/RNBQKBNR w KQkq - 0 1
moves g1f3

> go
```

```
bestmove b8c6

> quit
```

> To quickly generate the FEN string for any board position, you can use the board editor at https://lichess.org/editor/.

Now, let's talk about the Flask server script and how to deploy it on a GCP instance.

Deployment on GCP

This chess engine program requires the presence of a GPU. Thus, we have to follow additional steps before we can deploy the script on a GCP instance.

The rough workflow here is as follows:

1. Request for a quota increase on the GPU instances that are available to your account.
2. Create a GPU-based compute engine instance.
3. Deploy the script.

We'll look at these steps in detail in the following sections.

Request for a quota increase on GPU instances

The first step will be to request a quota increase on GPU instances. By default, the number of GPU instances you can have on your GCP account is 0. This limit is set by the quotas configuration for your account, and you need to request an increase. To do so, follow these steps:

1. Open your Google Cloud Platform console at https://console.cloud.google.com/.
2. On the left menu, click on **IAM & Admin** | **Quotas**, as shown in the following screenshot:

3. Click on the **Metrics** filter and type in **GPU** to find the entry reading GPU (all regions), as shown in the following screenshot:

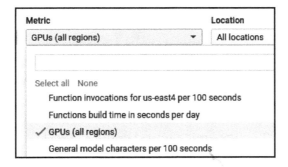

4. Select the entry and click on **Edit Quotas**.
5. You'll be asked for your identification, including your phone number. Fill in the details and click **Next**.
6. Enter the limit that you want to set your GPU quota to (preferably 1 in order to avoid misuse). Also, provide a reason for your requests, such as academic research, machine learning exploration, or anything that suits you!
7. Click on **Submit**.

After requesting, it should take around 10-15 minutes for your quota to be increased/set to the number you specified. You will receive an email informing you about the update. Now, you're ready to create a GPU instance.

Creating a GPU instance

The next step is to create a GPU instance. The process of creating a GPU instance is very similar to that of creating a non-GPU instance but requires one additional step. Let's quickly go through all these steps:

1. On your Google Cloud Platform dashboard, click on **Compute Engine | VM instances** from the left navigation menu.
2. Click on **Create Instance**.
3. Click on **CPU platform and GPU**, right below the **Machine type** selection section, as shown in the following screenshot:

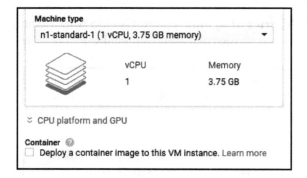

4. Click on **Add GPU** (the large plus (+) button). Select the GPU type and number of GPUs to be attached to this VM.
5. Change the Boot disk operating system to Ubuntu version 19.10.
6. In the **Firewall** section, check both HTTP and HTTPS traffic permissions, as shown in the following screenshot:

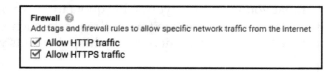

7. Click on **Create** at the bottom of the form.

After a few seconds, your instance will be successfully created. If you face any errors, such as zone resource limit exceeded, try changing the zone/region you're creating your instance in. This is usually a temporary issue.

Now, we can deploy the Flask server script.

Deploying the script

Now, we will deploy the Flask server script. But before we do so, let's go through what this script does:

1. The first few lines of the script import the necessary modules for the script to work:

```
from flask import Flask, request, jsonify
import os
import sys
import multiprocessing as mp
from logging import getLogger

from chess_zero.agent.player_chess import ChessPlayer
from chess_zero.config import Config, PlayWithHumanConfig
from chess_zero.env.chess_env import ChessEnv

from chess_zero.agent.model_chess import ChessModel
from chess_zero.lib.model_helper import load_best_model_weight

logger = getLogger(__name__)
```

2. The rest of the code is put into the `start()` function, which is instantiated with a `config` object:

```
def start(config: Config):
    ## rest of the code
```

3. The following lines create instances of the engine and human player and reset the game environment when the script starts working:

```
def start(config: Config):
    ...
    PlayWithHumanConfig().update_play_config(config.play)

    me_player = None
    env = ChessEnv().reset()
    ...
```

4. The model is created and the best weights of the model are loaded into it with the following code:

```
def start(config: Config):
    ...
    model = ChessModel(config)

    if not load_best_model_weight(model):
        raise RuntimeError("Best model not found!")
    player = ChessPlayer(config,
model.get_pipes(config.play.search_threads))
    ...
```

5. The last line in the preceding code creates an instance of the chess engine player with the configurations specified and with the model's knowledge:

```
def start(config: Config):
    ...
    app = Flask(__name__)

    @app.route('/play', methods=["GET", "POST"])
    def play():
        data = request.get_json()
        print(data["position"])
        env.update(data["position"])
        env.step(data["moves"], False)
        bestmove = player.action(env, False)
        return jsonify(bestmove)
    ...
```

The preceding code creates an instance of a Flask server app. The /play route is defined so that it accepts the position and moves parameters, which is the same as the commands we used in the UCI gameplay we defined previously.

6. The game state is updated and the chess engine is asked to calculate the next best move. This is returned to the user in JSON format:

```
def start(config: Config):
    ...
    app.run(host="0.0.0.0", port="8080")
```

The last line of the script starts the Flask server at host 0.0.0.0, which means that the script listens to all open IPs of the device it is running on. The port specified is 8080.

7. Finally, we will deploy the script to the VM instance we created. To do this, perform the following steps:

   1. Open the VM instances page of your GCP console.
   2. Click on the **SSH** button upon entering the VM you created in the previous section.
   3. Once your SSH session is active, update the repositories on the system by running the following command:

      ```
      sudo apt update
      ```

   4. Next, clone the repository using the following command:

      ```
      git clone
      https://github.com/PacktPublishing/Mobile-Deep-Learning-Project
      s.git
      ```

   5. Change the current working directory to the `chess` folder, as shown here:

      ```
      cd Mobile-Deep-Learning-Projects/Chapter8/chess
      ```

   6. Install PIP for Python3:

      ```
      sudo apt install python3-pip
      ```

   7. Install all the required modules for the project:

      ```
      pip3 install -r requirements.txt
      ```

   8. Provide a training PGN for the initial supervised learning. You can download a sample PGN from `https://github.com/xprilion/ficsdata`. The `ficsgamesdb2017.pgn` file contains 5,000 stored games. You need to upload this file to the `data/play_data/` folder.
   9. Run the supervised learning command:

      ```
      python3 src/chess_zero/run.py sl
      ```

   10. Run the self-learning command:

      ```
      python3 src/chess_zero/run.py self
      ```

When you're satisfied with the time you've given for the program to self-play, stop the script using *Ctrl + C/Z*.

11. Run the following command to start the server:

```
python3 src/chess_zero/run.py server
```

Now, you should be able to send positions and moves to the server and get responses. Let's quickly test this. Using Postman, or any other tool for API testing, we will make a request to the API with a FEN string to set a position and the move we're playing.

Say your VM instance is running on the public IP address (visible on the instance entry in your VM instances dashboard) 1.2.3.4. Here, we send the following POST request:

```
endpoint: http://1.2.3.4:8080/play
Content-type: JSON
Request body:
{
    "position": "r1bqk2r/ppp2ppp/2np1n2/2b1p3/2B1P3/2N2N2/PPPPQPPP/R1B1K2R w
KQkq - 0 1",
    "moves": "f3g5"
}
```

The output of the preceding code is "h7h6". Let's understand this interaction visually. The board, as defined in the FEN, looks as follows:

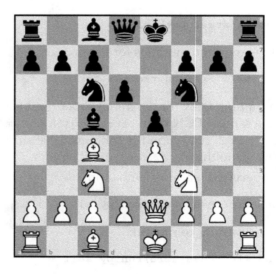

We told the server it was White's move, and the move that was made by the White player was f3g5, which means to move the White Knight to position G5 on the board. The 'w' in the FEN string of the board that we pass to the API indicates that the next turn will be made by the White player.

The engine responds by moving the pawn at H7 to H6, threatening the advance of the Knight, as shown in the following screenshot:

Now, we can integrate this API with the Flutter app!

Creating a simple chess UI on Android

Now that we understand reinforcement learning and how to use it to develop a chess engine that can be deployed to GCP, let's create a Flutter application for the game. The application will have two players – the user and the server. The user is the person playing the game, while the server is the chess engine that we have hosted on GCP. First, the user makes a move. This move is recorded and is sent to the chess engine in the form of a POST request. The chess engine then responds with its own movement, which is then updated on the screen.

We will create a simple single-screen application with a chessboard placed at the center, as well as the chess pieces. The application would appear as follows:

The widget tree of the application will look as follows:

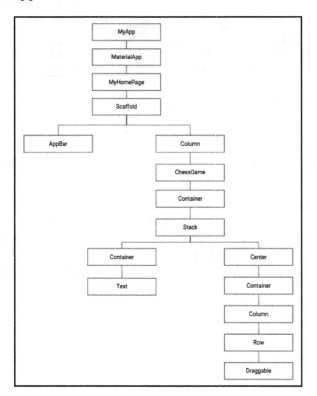

Let's start coding the application.

Adding dependencies to pubspec.yaml

We will start by adding the `chess_vectors_flutter` package to the `pubspec.yaml` file in order to display actual chess pieces on the chessboard we will be building. Add the following line to the dependencies section of `pubspec.yaml`:

```
chess_vectors_flutter: ">=1.0.6 <2.0.0"
```

Run `flutter pub get` to install the package.

Placing the chess pieces at the correct positions might be a bit tricky. Let's understand the convention we will use to place all the pieces at the correct positions.

Understanding the mapping structure

We'll start by creating a new dart file called `chess_game.dart`. This will contain all the game logic. Inside the file, let's declare a stateful widget called `ChessGame`:

1. To map pieces to the squares of the chessboard, we will use the same notation we used to build the model so that each square is represented by a letter and a number. We will create a list, `squareList`, inside `ChessGameState` so that we can store all the indexed squares, as follows:

```
var squareList = [
  ["a8","b8","c8","d8","e8","f8","g8","h8"],
  ["a7","b7","c7","d7","e7","f7","g7","h7"],
  ["a6","b6","c6","d6","e6","f6","g6","h6"],
  ["a5","b5","c5","d5","e5","f5","g5","h5"],
  ["a4","b4","c4","d4","e4","f4","g4","h4"],
  ["a3","b3","c3","d3","e3","f3","g3","h3"],
  ["a2","b2","c2","d2","e2","f2","g2","h2"],
  ["a1","b1","c1","d1","e1","f1","g1","h1"],
];
```

2. To store the correct pieces in the correct squares and update them according to a player's moves, we will create a HashMap called `board`:

```
HashMap board = new HashMap<String, String>();
```

The key of the HashMap will contain the indexes of the squares, while the value will be the pieces that the square will hold. We will denote a particular piece using a string that will contain a single letter according to the name of the piece. For example, a K will represent a King and a B will represent a Bishop. We distinguish between the White and Black pieces by using uppercase and lowercase letters. The uppercase letters will represent the White pieces, while the lowercase letters will represent the Black pieces. For example, a "K" will represent a White King and a "b" will represent a Black Bishop. `board['e7'] = "P"` would mean that the box with index `'e7'` currently has a White Pawn.

3. Now, let's place the pieces in their initial positions. For this, we need to define the `initializeBoard()` method, as follows:

```
void initializeBoard() {
  setState(() {
    for(int i = 8; i >= 1; i--) {
      for(int j = 97; j <= 104; j++) {
        String ch = String.fromCharCode(j)+'$i';
        board[ch] = " ";
      }
    }

    //Placing White Pieces
    board['a1'] = board['h1']= "R";
    board['b1'] = board['g1'] = "N";
    board['c1'] = board['f1'] = "B";
    board['d1'] = "Q";
    board['e1'] = "K";
    board['a2'] = board['b2'] = board['c2'] = board['d2'] =
    board['e2'] = board['f2'] = board['g2'] = board['h2'] = "P";
    //Placing Black Pieces
    board['a8'] = board['h8']= "r";
    board['b8'] = board['g8'] = "n";
    board['c8'] = board['f8'] = "b";
    board['d8'] = "q";
    board['e8'] = "k";
    board['a7'] = board['b7'] = board['c7'] = board['d7'] =
    board['e7'] = board['f7'] = board['g7'] = board['h7'] = "p";
  });
}
```

In the preceding method, we initialize all the indexes of the hashmap board with blank strings by using a simple nested loop to go through all the rows starting from a to h and all the columns starting from 1 to 8. Next, we place the chess pieces on their initial positions, as described in *step 2*. To make sure that the UI is redrawn when the board is initialized, we enclose the whole assignment inside `setState()`.

4. The board will be initialized as soon as the screen is launched. To ensure this, we need to override `initState()` and call `initializeBoard()` from there:

```
@override
void initState() {
  super.initState();
  initializeBoard();
}
```

Now that we have a better understanding of mapping the chess pieces, let's start placing actual images of the chess pieces on the screen.

Placing the images of the actual pieces

After mapping the pieces to their initial positions, we can start placing actual image vectors:

1. We begin by defining a function called `mapImages()` that takes the index of the square, that is, the key value of the hashmap board, and returns the image:

```
Widget mapImages(String squareName) {
  board.putIfAbsent(squareName, () => " ");
  String p = board[squareName];
  var size = 6.0;
  Widget imageToDisplay = Container();
  switch (p) {
    case "P":
      imageToDisplay = WhitePawn(size: size);
      break;
    case "R":
      imageToDisplay = WhiteRook(size: size);
      break;
    case "N":
      imageToDisplay = WhiteKnight(size: size);
      break;
    case "B":
      imageToDisplay = WhiteBishop(size: size);
      break;
    case "Q":
```

```
            imageToDisplay = WhiteQueen(size: size);
            break;
        case "K":
            imageToDisplay = WhiteKing(size: size);
            break;
        case "p":
            imageToDisplay = BlackPawn(size: size);
            break;
        case "r":
            imageToDisplay = BlackRook(size: size);
            break;
        case "n":
            imageToDisplay = BlackKnight(size: size);
            break;
        case "b":
            imageToDisplay = BlackBishop(size: size);
            break;
        case "q":
            imageToDisplay = BlackQueen(size: size);
            break;
        case "k":
            imageToDisplay = BlackKing(size: size);
            break;
        case "p":
            imageToDisplay = BlackPawn(size: size);
            break;
    }
    return imageToDisplay;
}
```

In the preceding function, we build a switch case block corresponding to the piece name contained in the square. We use the hashmap to find the piece in a particular square and then return the corresponding image. For example, if a value of a1 is passed into squareName and the hashmap board has the value "P" corresponding to the key-value a1, the image of a White Pawn will be stored in the imageToDisplay variable.

Note that out of 64 chessboard squares, only 32 of them will contain pieces; the rest will be blank. Therefore, in the hashmap, board, there will be keys that don't have a value. If a squareName does not have a piece, this is passed the imageToDisplay variable, which will just have an empty container.

2. In the previous step, we built widgets – either an image or an empty container – corresponding to each square on the chessboard. Now, let's arrange all of the widgets into rows and columns. A particular element in `squareName` – for example, `[a1,b1,....,g1]` – contains the squares that should be placed side by side. Therefore, we will wrap them into a row and wrap each of these rows into columns.

3. Let's start by defining the `buildRow()` method, which takes in a list. This is essentially an element list from `sqaureName` and builds a complete row. This method will look as follows:

```
Widget buildRow(List<String> children) {
    return Expanded(
      flex: 1,
      child: Row(
        children: children.map((squareName) =>
getImage(squareName)).toList()
      ),
    );
  }
```

In the preceding code snippet, we iterate through each of the elements of the list that was passed using the `map()` method. This makes a call to `getImage()` to get the appropriate image corresponding to a square. Then, we add all of these returned images as the children of a row. The row added a child to an expanded widget and returned it.

4. The `getImage()` method is defined as follows:

```
Widget getImage(String squareName) {
    return Expanded(
      child: mapImages(squareName),
    );
  }
```

This simply takes in the value of `squareName` and returns an expanded widget that will contain the image returned by `mapImages`, which we defined earlier. We will modify this method later to make sure each of the images can be dragged by the player so that they can make a move on the chessboard.

5. Now, we need to build the columns that will comprise the rows that have been built. For this, we need to define the `buildChessBoard()` method, as follows:

```
Widget buildChessBoard() {
  return Container(
    height: 350,
    child: Column(
        children: widget.squareList.map((row) {
            return buildRow(row,);
            }).toList()
    )
  );
}
```

In the preceding code, we iterated through each of the rows inside `squareList`, which is represented as a list. We built the rows by calling `buildRow()` and added them as children to a column. This column is added as a child to a container and returned.

6. Now, let's put all the pieces together, along with an actual chessboard image, on the screen. We will override the `build()` method to build a stack of widgets consisting of an image of a chessboard and its pieces:

```
@override
 Widget build(BuildContext context) {
   return Container(
       child: Stack(
         children: <Widget>[
           Container(
             child: new Center(child:
Image.asset("assets/chess_board.png", fit: BoxFit.cover,)),
             ),
           Center(
             child: Container(
               child: buildChessBoard(),
             ),
           )
         ],
       )
   );
 }
```

The preceding method builds a stack with a container that adds the image of a chessboard that was stored in the `assets` folder. The next child of the stack is the centrally aligned container with all the piece images that were added as widgets wrapped in rows and columns through the call to `buildChessBoard()`. The whole stack is added as a child to a container and returned so that it appears on the screen.

At this point, the application shows the chessboard, along with all the pieces placed at their initial positions. This looks as follows:

Now, let's make the pieces movable so that we can play an actual game.

Making the pieces movable

In this section, we will wrap each piece with a draggable so that the user is able to drag the chess pieces to their desired position. Let's look at the implementation in detail:

1. Recall that we declared a hashmap to store the positions of the pieces. A move will consist of moving a piece from one box and placing it in another. Suppose we have two variables, `'from'` and `'to'`, that store the indexes of the boxes for moving a piece. When a move is made, we pick up the piece that was at `'from'` and put it in `'to'`. Due to this, the box at `'from'` becomes empty. Following the same logic, we'll define the `refreshBoard()` method, which is called every time a move is made:

```
void refreshBoard(String from, String to) {
  setState(() {
    board[to] = board[from];
    board[from] = " ";
  });
}
```

The `from` and `to` variables store the indexes of the source and destination squares. These values are used as keys in the `board HasMhap`. When a move is made, the piece at `from` goes to `to`. After this, the square at `from` should become empty. This is enclosed inside `setState()` to make sure that the UI is updated after each move.

2. Now, let's make the pieces draggable. For this, we'll attach a draggable to each image widget of the board pieces that are returned by the `getPieceImage()` method. We do this by modifying the method like so:

```
Widget getImage(String squareName) {
    return Expanded(
        child: DragTarget<List>(builder: (context, accepted, rejected)
{
                return Draggable<List>(
                    child: mapImages(squareName),
                    feedback: mapImages(squareName),
                    onDragCompleted: () {},
                    data: [
                      squareName,
                    ],
                );
        }, onWillAccept: (willAccept) {
          return true;
        }, onAccept: (List moveInfo) {
          String from = moveInfo[0];
          String to = squareName;
         refreshBoard(from, to);
        })
    );
}
```

In the preceding function, we start by wrapping the image of a particular square in `Draggable`. This class is used to sense and follow drag gestures on the screen. The child property is used to specify the widget that is being dragged, while the widget inside feedback is used to track the movement of the finger over the screen. When the dragging is complete and the user lifts their finger, the target is given the opportunity to accept the data carried. Since we are making moves between a source and a target, we will add `Draggable` as a child of `DragTarget` so that the widget can be moved between the source and target. `onWillAccept` is set to true so that all the movements are possible.

This property can be modified so that it holds a function that can distinguish between legal chess moves and does not allow dragging for illegal movements. Once the piece has been dropped and the drag is complete, `onAccept` is called. The `moveInfo` list holds information about the source of the drag. Here, we make a call to `refreshBoard()` and pass in the values of `from` and `to` so that the screen can reflect the movement. At this point, we are done displaying an initial chessboard to the user and giving the pieces the ability to move between boxes.

In the next section, we will add interactivity to the application by making API calls to the hosted chess server. These will bring the game to life.

Integrating the chess engine API with a UI

The hosted chess server will be added to the application as an opponent player. The user will be the white side, while the server will be the black side. The game logic to be implemented here is very simple. The first move is given to the application user. When the user makes a move, they change the state of the chessboard from state X to state Y. The state of the board is represented by a FEN string. Also, they move a piece `from` a particular square `to` a particular square, which contributes to their move. When the user has completed a move, the FEN string for state X and their current move, which is obtained by concatenating the `from` and `to` squares, is sent to the server in the form of a `POST` request. The server, in return, responds with the next move from its side, which is then reflected on the UI.

Let's look at the code for this logic:

1. First, we define a method called `getPositionString()` to generate a FEN string for a particular state of the application:

```
String getPositionString(String move) {
    String s = "";
    for(int i = 8; i >= 1; i--) {
        int count = 0;
        for(int j = 97; j <= 104; j++) {
            String ch = String.fromCharCode(j)+'$i';
            if(board[ch] == " ") {
                count += 1;
                if(j == 104)
                    s = s + "$count";
            } else {
                if(count > 0)
                    s = s + "$count";
                s = s + board[ch];count = 0;
```

```
            }
        }
        s = s + "/";
    }
    String position = s.substring(0, s.length-1) + " w KQkq - 0 1";
    var json = jsonEncode({"position": position, "moves": move});
}
```

In the preceding method, we take in `move` as a parameter, which is a concatenation of the `from` and `to` variables. Next, we create the FEN string for the current state of the chessboard. The logic behind creating the FEN string is that we iterate through each row of the board and create a string for the row. The generated string is then concatenated to the final string.

Let's understand this in a better way with the help of an example. Consider a FEN string of `rnbqkbnr/pp1ppppp/8/1p6/8/3P4/PPP1PPPP/RNBQKBNR w KQkq - 0 1`. Here, each row can be represented by eight or fewer characters. The state of a particular row is separated from another one by the use of a deliminator, "/". For a particular row, each piece is represented by its assigned notation, where "P" means a White Pawn and `b` represents a Black Bishop. Each occupied square is explicitly represented by the piece notation. For example, `PpkB` indicates that the first four squares on the board are occupied by a White Pawn, Black Pawn, Black King, and White Bishop. For the empty boxes, an integer number is used and the number represents the count of contagious empty boxes. Notice the 8 in the example FEN string. This indicates that all 8 squares of the row are empty. `3P4` means the first three squares are empty, the fourth box is occupied by a White Pawn, and that four squares are empty.

In the `getPositionString()` method, we iterate through each of the rows, counting down from 8 to 1, and generate a state string for each of them. For each non-empty box, we simply add a character denoting the piece to the `'s'` variable. For each empty box, we increment the value of count by 1 and concatenate it to the `'s'` string either when a non-empty box is found or when we reach the end of the row. After iterating through each row, we add "/" to separate two rows. Finally, we generate the position string by concatenating the generated `'s'` string with `w KQkq - 0 1`. Then, we generate the required JSON object by using `jsonEncode()` with key-value pairs

2. We use the `from` and `to` variables from *Step 1* of the *Making the pieces movable* section to save the current move of the user. We can achieve this by adding two lines to the `refreshBoard()` method:

```
void refreshBoard(String from, String to) {
    String move= from + to;
    getPositionString(move);
    . . . . .
}
```

In the preceding code snippet, we concatenate the values of `from` and `to` and store them in a string variable called `move`. Then, we make a call to `getPositionString()` and pass the value of `move` to the parameter.

3. Next, we make a POST request to the server using JSON we generated in the previous step inside the `makePOSTRequest()` method:

```
void makePOSTRequest(var json) async{
    var url = 'http://35.200.253.0:8080/play';
    var response = await http.post(url, headers: {"Content-Type":
"application/json"} ,body: json);
    String rsp = response.body;
    String from = rsp.substring(0,3);
    String to = rsp.substring(3);
}
```

We start by storing the IP address of the chess server in the `url` variable. Then, we make an HTTP POST request using `http.post()` and pass the proper values for the URL, headers, and body. The response from the POST request contains the next move from the server-side and is stored in the variable response. We parse the body of the response and store it in a string variable called `rsp`. The response is basically a string, which is a concatenation of the source and destination squares from the server-side. For example, a response string of `f4a3` means that the chess engine wants to move the piece at square `f4` to square `a3`. We separate the source and destination using `substring()` and store the value in the `from` and `to` variables.

4. Now, we make the POST request from `getPositionString()` by adding the call to `makePOSTrequest()`:

```
String getPositionString(String move) {
    .....
    makePOSTRequest(json);
}
```

The call to `makePOSTrequest()` is added at the very end of the function after the FEN string generates the given state of the board.

5. Finally, we refresh the board to reflect the server's move on the board with the `refreshBoardFromServer()` method:

```
void refreshBoardFromServer(String from, String to) {
    setState(() {
        board[to] = board[from];
        board[from] = " ";
    });
}
```

The logic in the preceding method is very simple. First, we move the piece mapped at the `from` indexed square to the `to` indexed square and then empty the `from` indexed square.

6. Finally, we make calls to the appropriate methods to update the UI with the latest moves:

```
void makePOSTRequest(var json) async{
    ......
    refreshBoardFromServer(from, to);
    buildChessBoard();
}
```

After the post request has completed successfully and we have the response from the server, we make a call to `refreshBoardFromServer()` to update the mapping on the board. Finally, we call `buildChessBoard()` to reflect the latest move that was made by the chess engine on the app screen.

The following screenshot shows an updated UI after a move was made by the chess engine:

Notice that the black piece moved after the white piece. That is how the code works. First, the user makes a move. This is sent to the server with the initial state of the board. The server then responds with its move, which the UI is updated on. As an exercise, you can try to implement some logic to differentiate between valid and invalid moves.

> The code for this can be found at `https://github.com/PacktPublishing/`
> `Mobile-Deep-Learning-Projects/blob/master/Chapter8/flutter_`
> `chess/lib/chess_game.dart`.

Now, let's wrap up the application by creating the material app.

Creating the material app

Now, we're going to create the final material app inside `main.dart`. Let's start with the following steps:

1. First, we create stateless widget, `MyApp`, and override its `build()` method, as follows:

```
class MyApp extends StatelessWidget {
    @override
    Widget build(BuildContext context) {
        return MaterialApp(
            title: 'Chess',
            theme: ThemeData(primarySwatch: Colors.blue,),
            home: MyHomePage(title: 'Chess'),
        );
    }
}
```

2. We create a separate `StatefulWidget` called `MyHomePage` in order to place the UI at the center of the screen. The `build()` method of `MyHomePage` will look as follows:

```
@override
Widget build(BuildContext context) {
    return Scaffold(
        appBar: AppBar(title: Text('Chess'),),
        body: Center(
            child: Column(
                mainAxisAlignment: MainAxisAlignment.center,
                children: <Widget>[ChessGame()
                ],
            ),
        ),
    );
}
```

3. Finally, we execute the whole code by adding the following line in `main.dart`:

```
void main() => runApp(MyApp());
```

That's it! Now, we have an interactive chess game application that you can play with an intelligent opponent. I hope you win!

 The code for the entire file can be found at `https://github.com/PacktPublishing/Mobile-Deep-Learning-Projects/blob/master/Chapter8/flutter_chess/lib/main.dart`.

Summary

In this project, we covered the concepts of reinforcement learning and why they're popular among developers for creating game-playing AIs. We discussed AlphaGo and its sibling projects by Google DeepMind and studied their working algorithms in depth. Next, we created a similar program for playing Connect 4 and then for chess. We deployed the AI-powered chess engine to GCP on a GPU instance as an API and integrated it with a Flutter-based app. We also learned about how UCI is used to facilitate stateless gameplay for chess. After this project, you are expected to have a good understanding of how we can convert games into reinforcement learning environments, how to define gameplay rules programmatically, and how to create self-learning agents for playing these games.

In the next chapter, we will create an app that can make low-resolution images very high-resolution images. We'll do this with the help of AI.

9
Building an Image Super-Resolution Application

Remember the last time you went on a trip with your loved ones and took some nice photos to keep as memories, but when you went back home and swiped through them, you found they were very blurry and low quality? Now, all you have remaining of those beautiful moments are your own mental memories and those blurry photos. Wouldn't it be great if your photos could be made crystal clear and you could see every detail in them?

Super-resolution is the process of converting low-resolution images into high-resolution images based on the approximation of pixel information. While it may not be entirely magical today, it will certainly be a life-saver in the future when the technology has progressed enough to become a common AI application.

In this project, we will build an app that uses a deep learning model hosted on **DigitalOcean Droplet** that compares both the low-resolution and high-resolution images side by side to give us a good idea of how effective the technology is today. We shall be using a **Generative Adversarial Network (GAN)** to generate the super-resolution images.

In this chapter, we will cover the following topics:

- Basic project architecture
- Understanding GANs
- Understanding how image super-resolution works
- Creating a TensorFlow model for super-resolution
- Building the UI for the application
- Getting pictures from the device's local storage
- Hosting a TensorFlow model on DigitalOcean
- Integrating a hosted custom model on Flutter
- Creating the Material app

Let's begin by understanding the project's architecture.

Basic project architecture

Let's start by understanding the project's architecture.

The project we'll be building in this chapter is mainly divided into two parts:

- The Jupyter Notebook, which creates the model that performs super-resolution.
- The Flutter app that uses the model, which, after being trained on the Jupyter Notebook, is hosted on a Droplet in DigitalOcean.

From a bird's-eye view, the project can be described with the following diagram:

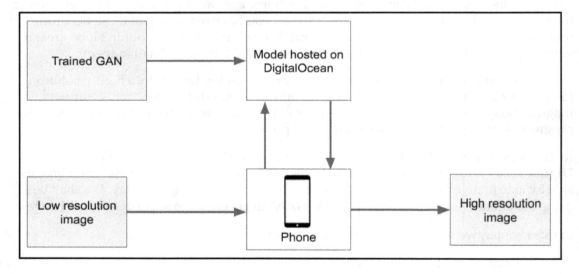

The low-resolution image is put into the model, which is fetched from the ML Kit instance hosted on Firebase and put into the Flutter app. The output is generated and displayed to the user as a high-resolution image. The model is cached on the device and only updates when the model is updated by the developer, hence allowing for faster predictions by cutting down on network latency.

Now, let's try understanding GANs in more depth.

Understanding GANs

GANs, which were introduced by Ian Goodfellow, Yoshua Bengio, and others in NeurIPS 2014, took the world by storm. GANs, which can be applied to all sorts of domains, generate new content or sequences based on the model's learned approximation of real-world data samples. GANs have been used heavily for generating new samples of music and art, such as the faces shown in the following image, none of which existed in the training dataset:

Faces generated by GAN after 60 epochs of training. This image has been taken from `https://github.com/gsurma/face_generator`.

The amount of realism that's present in the preceding faces demonstrates the power of GANs – they can pretty much learn to generate any sort of pattern when they've been given a good training sample size.

The core concept of GANs revolves around the idea of two players playing a game. In this game, one person says a random sentence and the other person points out whether it's a fact or fake simply by considering the words used by the first person. The only knowledge the second person can use is of the words (and how they're being used) that are commonly used in fake and real sentences. This can be described as a two-player game being played by a minimax algorithm where each player tries to counter the move that was made by the other player to the best of their ability. In GANs, the first player is the **generator** (**G**) and the second player is the **discriminator** (**D**). Both G and D are neural networks in regular GANs. The generator learns from the samples given in the training dataset and generates a new sample based on what it believes it can pass off as a real sample when viewed by an observer.

The discriminator learns from the training samples (positive samples) and the samples generated by the generator (negative samples) and attempts to classify which images are present in the dataset and which are generated. It takes the generated images from G and tries to classify them as real (present in the training samples) or generated (not present in the database).

Through backpropagation, the GAN tries to continuously reduce the number of times the discriminator is able to classify the images that the generator generates correctly. After some time, we hope to reach a stage where the discriminator starts performing poorly when identifying the generated images. This is where the GAN stops learning, and the generator can then be used to generate as many new samples as needed. Thus, training a GAN means to train the generator to produce outputs from random inputs so that the discriminator fails to identify them as generated images.

The discriminator classifies all the images that are passed to it into two categories:

- **Real images**: Images that are present in the dataset or are otherwise taken using a camera
- **Fake images**: Images that have been generated using a piece of software

The better the generator gets at deceiving the discriminator, the more realistic the outputs it produces will be when any random input sequence is provided to it.

Let's summarize the preceding discussion regarding how a GAN works as a diagram:

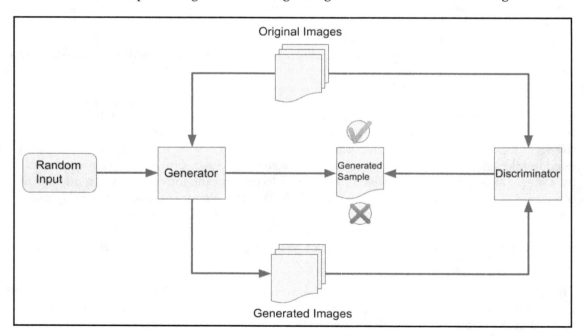

GANs have many different variations, all of which depend on the task they are performing. Some of them are as follows:

- **Progressive GANs**: Presented in a paper at ICLR 2018, a progressive GAN is where both the generator and discriminator start with low-resolution images and are progressively trained with increasing layers of the image, enabling the system to generate very high-resolution images quickly. For example, the image generated in the first iteration is 10x10 pixels, in the second generation it becomes 20x20, and so on until a very high-resolution image is obtained. The generator and the discriminator both grow in depth together.

- **Conditional GANs**: Say you have a GAN that can generate samples of 10 different classes, but at some point, you wish it to generate a sample within a given class or set of classes. This is when conditional GANs kick in. Conditional GANs allow us to generate samples of any given label, among all the labels that the GAN has been trained to generate. A very popular application of conditional GANs has been done in the realm of image-to-image translation, where one image is generated into another more realistic image of a similar or the same domain. You can try doodling some cats and getting a photorealistic version of your doodles by playing through the demos at `https://affinelayer.com/pixsrv/`.

- **Stacked GANs**: The most popular application of stacked GANs is in generating images based on text descriptions. In the first stage, the GAN generates an outline of the described items and in the second stage, it adds colors, as per the description. Then, the GAN in subsequent layers adds more details to the image to produce a photorealistic version of the image, as provided in the description. Stacked GANs can be differentiated from progressive GANs by observing that the images in the first iteration of a stacked GAN are already in the dimensions that the final output would be made in. However, similar to progressive GANs, in the first iteration the details in the image are minimal and need further layers before it can be fed to the discriminator.

In this project, we'll be discussing yet another variant of GANs called a **Super-Resolution GAN (SRGAN)**. We'll learn more about this variant in the next section.

Understanding how image super-resolution works

The pursuit and desire to be able to make **low-resolution** images more detailed and of a **higher resolution** has been around for several decades. **Super-resolution** is a collection of techniques that are used to convert low-resolution images into very high-resolution images and is one of the most exciting fields of work for image processing engineers and researchers. Several approaches and methods have been built to achieve super-resolution of images, and they have all had varying levels of success toward their goal. However, in recent times, with the development of SRGANs, there has been a significant improvement regarding the amount of super-resolution that can be possible using any low-resolution image.

But before we discuss SRGANs, let's learn about some concepts related to image super-resolution.

Understanding image resolution

In qualitative terms, the resolution of an image is determined by its clarity. Resolution can be classified as one of the following:

- Pixel resolution
- Spatial resolution
- Temporal resolution
- Spectral resolution
- Radiometric resolution

Let's take a look at each.

Pixel resolution

One of the most popular formats for specifying resolution, pixel resolution most commonly refers to the number of pixels involved in forming an image. A single pixel is the smallest individual unit that can be displayed on any given viewing device. Several pixels can be combined to form an image. Previously in this book, we talked about image processing and referred to a pixel as an individual unit of color information stored in the matrix and that it represents an image. The pixel resolution defines the total number of pixel elements required to form a digital image, which may differ from the effective number of pixels visible on the image.

A very common notation of marking the pixel resolution of an image is to express it in terms of megapixels. Given an image of NxM pixel resolution, its resolution can be written as (NxM / 1000000) megapixels. Thus, an image that's 2,000x3,000 in dimension would have 6,000,000 pixels in it and its resolution can be expressed as 6 megapixels.

Spatial resolution

This is the measure of the degree to which lines that have been put closely together in an image can be resolved by a person who is looking at the image. Here, the idea that the more pixels an image has, the better it appears in terms of clarity, isn't strictly true. This is due to the lower spatial resolution of the image with a higher number of pixels. Hence, a good spatial resolution is necessary along with having a good pixel resolution for images to render in good quality.

It can also be defined as the amount of distance one side of a pixel represents.

Temporal resolution

Resolution can also depend on time. For instance, images of the same region taken by a satellite or using an **Unmanned Aerial Vehicle (UAV)** drone might differ through time. The amount of time needed to recapture an image of the same region is called temporal resolution.

Temporal resolution primarily depends on the device that is capturing the images. This may be variant, as in the case of an image capture, which is performed when a specific sensor is triggered, say, in a speed trap camera on the side of a road. It can also be constant; for example, in a camera that's been configured to take photos at every x interval.

Spectral resolution

Spectral resolution refers to the number of bands that an image capturing device can record. It can also be defined as the width of the bands or the range of the wavelengths of each band. In terms of digital imaging, spectral resolution is analogous to the number of channels in the image. Another way of understanding spectral resolution is the number of distinguishable bands in any given image or recording of bands.

The number of bands in black and white images is 1, while the number of bands in a color (RGB) image is 3. It is possible to capture the images of hundreds of bands, wherein the other bands provide different kinds of information about the image.

Radiometric resolution

Radiometric resolution is the ability of a capturing device to represent the intensity received on any band/channel. The higher the radiometric resolution, the more accurately the device can capture the intensities on its channels and the more realistic that image will be.

Radiometric resolution is analogous to the bits per pixel of an image. While an 8-bit image pixel can represent 256 different intensities, a 256-bit image pixel can represent 2^256 different intensities. A black and white image has a 1-bit radiometric resolution, which means it can only have two different values in each pixel, namely 0 and 1.

Now, let's try to understand SRGANs.

Understanding SRGANs

SRGANs are a class of GANs that focuses on creating super-resolution images from low-resolution images.

The functionality of an SRGAN algorithm is described as such: the algorithm picks a high-resolution image from the dataset and samples it down to a low-resolution image. Then, the generator neural network tries to produce a higher resolution image from the low-resolution image. We will call this a super-resolution image from now on. The super-resolution image is sent to the discriminator neural network, which has already been trained on samples of high-resolution images and some basic super-resolution images so that they can be classified.

The discriminator classifies the super-resolution image sent to it by the generator as either a valid high-resolution image, a fake high-resolution image, or a super-resolution image. If the image is classified as a super-resolution image, the GAN loss is backpropagated through the generator network so that it produces a better fake next time. Over time, the generator learns how to create better fakes and the discriminator begins failing to correctly identify super-resolution images. The GAN stops learning here and is classed as trained.

This can be summarized with the following diagram:

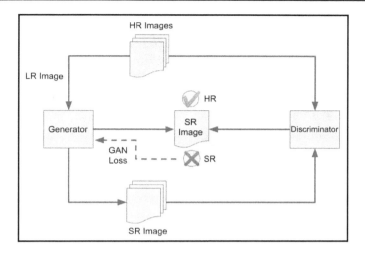

Now, let's start creating an SRGAN model for super-resolution.

Creating a TensorFlow model for super-resolution

Now, we'll start building a GAN model that performs super-resolution on images. Before we dive into the code, we need to understand how the project's directory will be organized.

Project directory structure

The following files and folders are present in this chapter:

- api/:
  - model /:
    - __init __.py: This file indicates that the parent folder of this file can be imported like a module.
    - common.py: This contains common functions that are required for any GAN model.
    - srgan.py: This contains functions that are required for developing the SRGAN model.

- weights/:
    - gan_generator.h5: A pre-trained weights file for the model. Feel free to use this to quickly run and check out how the project works.
- data.py: Utility functions for downloading, extracting, and loading the images in the DIV2K dataset.
- flask_app.py: We will be using this file to create a server that will be deployed on DigitalOcean.
- train.py: The model training file. We will discuss this file in greater depth in this section.

 You can find the source code for this part of the project at https://github.com/PacktPublishing/Mobile-Deep-Learning-Projects/tree/master/Chapter9/api.

The **Diverse 2K (DIV2K)** dataset was introduced in the **New Trends in Image Restoration and Enhancement (NTIRE)** 2017 Challenge on Single Image Super-Resolution and was also used in the 2018 version of the challenge.

In the next section, we will work on building the SRGAN model script.

Creating an SRGAN model for super-resolution

First, we'll begin by working on the train.py file:

1. Let's start by importing the necessary modules into the project:

```
import os

from data import DIV2K
from model.srgan import generator, discriminator
from train import SrganTrainer, SrganGeneratorTrainer
```

The preceding imports bring in some ready-made classes, such as SrganTrainer, SrganGeneratorTrainer, and so on. We will discuss each of them in detail after we've finished working on this file.

2. Now, let's create a directory for the weights. We shall use this directory to store intermediate models as well:

```
weights_dir = 'weights'
weights_file = lambda filename: os.path.join(weights_dir, filename)

os.makedirs(weights_dir, exist_ok=True)
```

3. Next, we'll download and load images from the DIV2K dataset. We will download the training and validation images separately. For both sets, the images can be found in two pairs – high resolution and low resolution. However, these are downloaded separately:

```
div2k_train = DIV2K(scale=4, subset='train', downgrade='bicubic')
div2k_valid = DIV2K(scale=4, subset='valid', downgrade='bicubic')
```

4. Once the dataset has been downloaded and loaded into the variables, we need to transform both the train and validation images into TensorFlow dataset objects. This step also clubs the high-resolution and low-resolution images together in both datasets:

```
train_ds = div2k_train.dataset(batch_size=16,
random_transform=True)
valid_ds = div2k_valid.dataset(batch_size=16,
random_transform=True, repeat_count=1)
```

5. Now, recall the definition of a GAN we provided in the *Understanding GANs* section. In order to make the generator start producing fakes that the discriminator can evaluate, it needs to learn to create basic fakes. To do this, we will quickly train a neural network so that it can generate basic super-resolution images. We'll name it the **pre-trainer**. Then, we'll transfer the weights of the **pre-trainer** to the actual SRGAN so that it can learn more by using the discriminator. Let's build and run the **pre-trainer**:

```
pre_trainer = SrganGeneratorTrainer(model=generator(),
checkpoint_dir=f'.ckpt/pre_generator')
pre_trainer.train(train_ds,
                  valid_ds.take(10),
                  steps=1000000,
                  evaluate_every=1000,
                  save_best_only=False)

pre_trainer.model.save_weights(weights_file('pre_generator.h5'))
```

Now, we've trained a basic model and saved its weights. We can always change the SRGAN and restart from the basic training by loading its weights.

6. Now, let's load the **pre-trainer** weights into an SRGAN object and perform the training iterations:

```
gan_generator = generator()
gan_generator.load_weights(weights_file('pre_generator.h5'))

gan_trainer = SrganTrainer(generator=gan_generator,
discriminator=discriminator())
gan_trainer.train(train_ds, steps=200000)
```

Note that the training operation in the preceding code might take a large amount of time on an average machine with 8 GB RAM and an Intel i7 processor. It is recommended that this training be performed in a cloud-based virtual machine with **Graphics Processing Units** (**GPUs**) available.

7. Now, let's save the weights for the GAN generator and discriminator:

```
gan_trainer.generator.save_weights(weights_file('gan_generator.h5')
)
gan_trainer.discriminator.save_weights(weights_file('gan_discrimina
tor.h5'))
```

Now we are ready to move on to the next section, where we'll build the UI of the Flutter app that will be using this model.

Building the UI for the application

Now that we understand the basic functionality of the image super-resolution model and have created a model for it, let's do a deep dive into building the Flutter application. In this section, we will build the UI of the app.

The UI of the app will be very simple: it will contain two image widgets and button widgets. When the user clicks on the button widget, they will be able to pick an image from the device's gallery. The same image will be sent as input to the server hosting the model. The server will return an enhanced image. The two image widgets that will be placed on the screen will be used to display the input to the server and the output from the server.

The following images illustrate the basic structure and the final flow of the application:

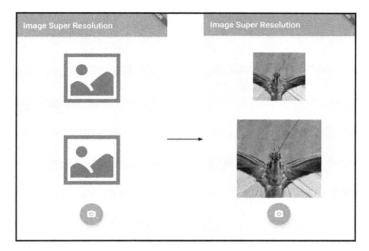

The three primary widgets of the application can be simply arranged in a column. The widget tree for the application will look as follows:

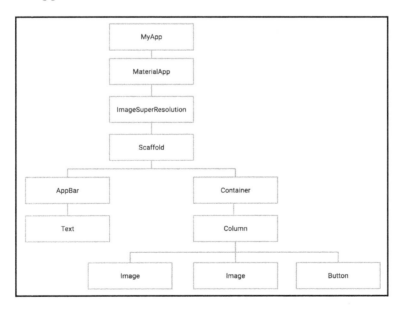

Now, let's write the code to build the primary screen. The following steps discuss the creation and placement of widgets for the app:

1. First of all, we create a new file named `image_super_resolution.dart`. This will contain a stateless widget called `ImageSuperResolution`. This widget will contain the code for the main screen of the application.

2. Next, we will define a function called `buildImageInput()` that returns a widget that's responsible for displaying the image that was selected by the user:

```
Widget buildImage1() {
    return Expanded(
        child: Container(
            width: 200,
            height: 200,
            child: img1
        )
    );
}
```

This function returns an `Expanded` widget with a `Container` as its `child`. The `width` and `height` of the `Container` are 200. The child of the `Container` is initially a placeholder image stored in the assets folder that can be accessed through the `img1` variable, as follows:

```
var img1 = Image.asset('assets/place_holder_image.png');
```

We'll also add the path to the image inside the `pubspec.yaml` file, as follows:

```
flutter:
    assets:
        - assets/place_holder_image.png
```

3. Now, we will create another function, `buildImageOutput()`, that returns a widget that's responsible for displaying the enhanced image that's returned by the model:

```
Widget buildImageOutput() {
    return Expanded(
        child: Container(
            width: 200,
            height: 200,
            child: imageOutput
        )
    );
}
```

This function returns an `Expanded` widget with a `Container` as its child. The width and height of the `Container` are set to `200`. The child of the `Container` is a widget called `imageOutput`. Initially, `imageOutput` will also contain a placeholder image, as follows:

```
Widget imageOutput = Image.asset('assets/place_holder_image.png');
```

We will update `imageOutput` after we've integrated the model into the application.

4. Now, we will define our third function, `buildPickImageButton()`, which returns a `Widget` that we can use to select an image from the device's gallery:

```
Widget buildPickImageButton() {
    return Container(
        margin: EdgeInsets.all(8),
        child: FloatingActionButton(
            elevation: 8,
            child: Icon(Icons.camera_alt),
            onPressed: () => {},
        )
    );
}
```

This function returns a `Container` with a `FloatingActionButton` as its child. The `elevation` property of the button controls the size of the shadow below it and is set to `8`. To reflect that the button is used to select an image, it has been given an icon of a camera through the `Icon` class. Currently, we've set the `onPressed` property of the button to blank. We will define a function in the next section that will enable the user to choose an image from the device's gallery when the button is pressed.

5. Finally, we'll override the build method to return the `Scaffold` for the app:

```
@override
Widget build(BuildContext context) {
    return Scaffold(
        appBar: AppBar(title: Text('Image Super Resolution')),
        body: Container(
            child: Column(
                crossAxisAlignment: CrossAxisAlignment.center,
                children: <Widget>[
                    buildImageInput(),
                    buildImageOutput(),
```

```
                                            buildPickImageButton()
                            ]
                        )
                    )
                );
        }
```

`Scaffold` contains an `appBar` with its title set to **Image super Resolution**. The body of `Scaffold` is a `Container` with its child as a `Column`. The children of the column are the three widgets that we built in the previous steps. Also, we set the `crossAxisAlignment` property of `Column` to `CrossAxisAlignment.center` to make sure that the column is placed at the center of the screen.

At this point, we have successfully built the initial state of the application. The following screenshot shows how the app looks right now:

Although the screen looks perfect, it isn't functional right now. Next, we'll add functionality to the app. We will add the ability to let the user choose an image from the gallery.

Getting pictures from the device's local storage

In this section, we will add the functionality of `FloatingActionButton` to let the user choose an image from the gallery of the device. This will eventually be sent to the server so that we can receive a response.

The following steps describe how to launch the gallery and let the user choose an image:

1. To allow the user to choose an image from the device's gallery, we will use the `image_picker` library. This launches the gallery and stores the image file selected by the user. We will start by adding a dependency in the `pubspec.yaml` file:

   ```
   image_picker: 0.4.12+1
   ```

   Also, we fetch the library by running `flutter pub get` on the Terminal.

2. Next, we import the library inside the `image_super_resolution.dart` file:

   ```
   import 'package:image_picker/image_picker.dart';
   ```

3. Now, let's define the `pickImage()` function, which lets the user choose an image from the gallery:

   ```
   void pickImage() async {
       File pickedImg = await ImagePicker.pickImage(source:
   ImageSource.gallery);
    }
   ```

4. From inside the function, we simply make a call to `ImagePicker.pickImage()` and specify `source` as `ImageSource.gallery`. The library itself handles the complexity of launching the device's gallery. The image file chosen by the user is eventually returned by the function. We store the file returned by the function in the `pickedImg` variable, which is of the `File` type.

5. Next, we define the `loadImage()` function in order to display the image selected by the user on the screen:

   ```
   void loadImage(File file) {
       setState(() {
           img1 = Image.file(file);
       });
    }
   ```

   This function takes in the image file selected by the user as input. Inside the function, we set the value of the `img1` variable we declared earlier to `Image.file(file)`, which returns an `Image` widget built from `'file'`. Recall that, initially, `img1` was set to a placeholder image. To re-render the screen and show the image that was chosen by the user, we enclose the new assignment of `img1` inside `setState()`.

6. Now, let's add `pickImage()` to the `onPressed` property of `FloatingActionButton` inside `builtPickImageButton()`:

```
Widget buildPickImageButton() {
    return Container(
        ....
        child: FloatingActionButton(
            ....
            onPressed: () => pickImage(),
        )
    );
}
```

The preceding addition makes sure that when the button is clicked, the gallery is launched so that an image can be selected.

5. Finally, we'll add a call to `loadImage()` from `pickImage()`:

```
void pickImage() async {
    ....
    loadImage(pickedImg);
}
```

Inside `loadImage()`, we pass in the image selected by the user that's stored in the `pickedImage` variable so that it can be viewed on the screen of the application.

After following all the preceding steps, the app will look as follows:

At this point, we have structured the user interface of the application. We have also added some functionality that lets the user choose an image from the device's gallery and show it on the screen.

In the next section, we'll learn how to host the model we built in the *Creating a TensorFlow model for super-resolution* section as an API so that we can use it to perform super-resolution.

Hosting a TensorFlow model on DigitalOcean

DigitalOcean is an amazing, low-cost cloud solutions platform that is very easy to get started with and offers nearly everything that an app developer might need for powering the backend of their app out of the box. The interface is very simple to use, and DigitalOcean boasts some of the most extensive documentation around getting started with setting up different types of application servers on the cloud.

In this project, we shall be using DigitalOcean's Droplet to deploy our super-resolution API. A Droplet in DigitalOcean is simply a virtual machine that usually runs on a shared hardware space.

First, we'll create the `flask_app.py` file in the project directory and add the code required for the server to work.

Creating a Flask server script

In this section, we shall work on the `flask_app.py` file, which will be running on the cloud virtual machine as a server. Let's get started:

1. First, we'll make the necessary imports to the file:

```
from flask import Flask, request, jsonify, send_file
import os
import time

from matplotlib.image import imsave

from model.srgan import generator

from model import resolve_single
```

2. Now, we'll define the `weights` directory and load the generator weights into the file:

```
weights_dir = 'weights'
weights_file = lambda filename: os.path.join(weights_dir, filename)

gan_generator = generator()
gan_generator.load_weights(weights_file('gan_generator.h5'))
```

3. Next, we'll instantiate the `Flask` app using the following line of code:

```
app = Flask(__name__)
```

4. Now, we are ready to build the routes the server will listen to. First, we'll create the `/generate` route, which takes an image as input, generates a super-resolution version of it, and returns the filename of the generated high-resolution image to the user:

```
@app.route('/generate', methods=["GET", "POST"])
def generate():

    global gan_generator
    imgData = request.get_data()
    with open("input.png", 'wb') as output:
        output.write(imgData)

    lr = load_image("input.png")
    gan_sr = resolve_single(gan_generator, lr)
    epoch_time = int(time.time())
    outputfile = 'output_%s.png' % (epoch_time)
    imsave(outputfile, gan_sr.numpy())
    response = {'result': outputfile}

    return jsonify(response)
```

Let's try to understand what's happening in the preceding code block. The `/generate` route has been set to listen to only the GET and POST methods of HTTP requests. First, the method fetches the image that was provided to it in the API request, converts it into a NumPy array, and then feeds it into the SRGAN model. The SRGAN model returns a super-resolution image, which is then assigned a unique name and stored on the server. The user displays the name of the file, using which they can call another endpoint to download the file. Let's build this endpoint now.

5. To create an endpoint in order to download the generated files, we can use the following code:

```
@app.route('/download/<fname>', methods=['GET'])
def download(fname):
    return send_file(fname)
```

Here, we created an endpoint called `/download` that, when appended with a filename, fetches it and sends it back to the user.

6. Finally, we can write the code that executes this script and sets up the server:

```
app.run(host="0.0.0.0", port="8080")
```

Save this file. Make sure to push your repository to a GitHub/GitLab repository at this point.

Now, we are ready to deploy this script to a `DigitalOcean` Droplet.

Deploying the Flask script to DigitalOcean Droplet

To deploy the Flask script to a DigitalOcean Droplet, you'll have to create a DigitalOcean account and create a Droplet. Follow these steps to do so:

1. Head on over to `digitalocean.com` in your preferred web browser.

 You can also go to `https://m.do.co/c/ca4f8fcaa7e9` if you wish to receive $100 credit upon adding your billing details. We'll do this later.

2. Fill in your details on the registration form of DigitalOcean and proceed to the next step by submitting the form.
3. You will be asked to verify your email and add a billing method for your DigitalOcean account.

4. In the next step, you will be prompted to create your first project. Enter the required details and submit the form to create your project:

5. Once your project has been created, you'll be taken to the DigitalOcean dashboard. You will be able to see a prompt to **Create a Droplet**, as shown in the following screenshot:

6. Click on the prompt to bring up the Droplet creation form. Choose the options described in the following table:

Field	Description	Value to use
Choose an image	The operating system that your Droplet will run on.	Ubuntu 18.04 (or the latest available version)
Choose a plan	Choose the configuration for your Droplet.	4 GB RAM or higher
Add block storage	Additional persistent, detachable storage volume for your Droplet.	Leave as the default
Choose a datacenter region	The region where your Droplet is served from.	Choose any according to your preference
Select additional options	Choose any additional features that will work along with your Droplet.	Leave as the default
Authentication	Choose the method of authentication for your VM.	One-time password
Finalize and create	Some additional settings and options for your Droplet.	Leave as the default

7. Click on Create Droplet and wait for DigitalOcean to provision your Droplet.

8. Once your Droplet has been created, click on its name to bring up the Droplet management console, which should look as follows:

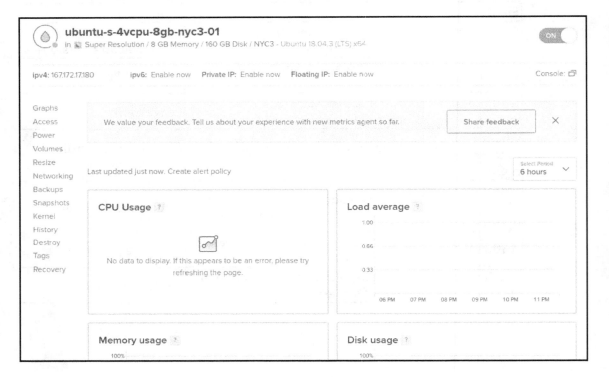

9. Now, we can log in to the Droplet using the **Access** tab on the left navigation menu of the Droplet console shown in the previous screenshot. Click on **Access** and then **Launch Console**.

10. A new browser window will open up displaying a VNC view of your Droplet. You'll be asked to enter the username and password for your Droplet. The username you must use here is **root**. The password can be found in your registered email's inbox.

11. When you log in for the first time, you'll be asked to change your Droplet password. Make sure that you choose a strong password.

12. Once you've logged into your Droplet, you'll see some Ubuntu welcome text on the VNC Terminal, as shown in the following screenshot:

```
Welcome to Ubuntu 18.04.3 LTS (GNU/Linux 4.15.0-66-generic x86_64)

 * Documentation:  https://help.ubuntu.com
 * Management:     https://landscape.canonical.com
 * Support:        https://ubuntu.com/advantage

 System information as of Wed Mar 18 18:16:10 UTC 2020

 System load:  0.18              Processes:             111
 Usage of /:   0.7% of 154.90GB  Users logged in:       0
 Memory usage: 2%                IP address for eth0: 167.172.17.180
 Swap usage:   0%

111 packages can be updated.
63 updates are security updates.


root@ubuntu-s-4vcpu-8gb-nyc3-01:~# _
```

13. Now, carry out the steps to set up a deep learning environment on a cloud VM, as provided in the *Appendix* of this book.

14. Next, clone the project repository to your Droplet and change your working directory to the `api` folder of the repository using the following command:

```
git clone https://github.com/yourusername/yourrepo.git
cd yourrepo/api
```

15. Use the following command to run the server:

```
python3 flask_app.py
```

Besides some warning messages from TensorFlow, at the end of the Terminal's output you should see the following lines indicating that the server has started successfully:

```
 * Serving Flask app "flask_app" (lazy loading)
 * Environment: production
   WARNING: This is a development server. Do not use it in a
   production deployment.
   Use a production WSGI server instead.
 * Debug mode: off
 * Running on http://0.0.0.0:8080/ (Press CTRL+C to quit)
```

Now, your server is live and running on the IP of the Droplet, as can be seen in your Droplet console.

In the next section, we will learn how to use the Flutter app to make a POST request to the server and show the response of the server on the screen.

Integrating a hosted custom model on Flutter

In this section, we will make a POST request to the hosted model and pass it in the image selected by the user. The server will respond with a `NetworkImage` in PNG format. Then, we'll update the image widget we added earlier to show the enhanced image that's returned by the model.

Let's start integrating the hosted model into the application:

1. First of all, we will need two more external libraries to make a successful POST request. Therefore, we'll add the following libraries as dependencies to the `pubspec.yaml` file:

   ```
   dependencies:
       flutter:
             http: 0.12.0+4
             mime: 0.9.6+3
   ```

   The `http` dependency contains a set of classes and functions that make consuming HTTP resources very convenient. The `mime` dependency is used for processing streams of MIME multipart media types.

   Now, we need to run `flutter pub get` to make sure all the dependencies have been installed into our project properly.

2. Next, we import all the newly added dependencies into the `image_super_resolution.dart` file:

   ```
   import 'package:http/http.dart' as http;
   import 'package:mime/mime.dart';
   ```

3. Now, we need to define `fetchResponse()`, which takes in the selected image file and creates a POST request to the server:

   ```
   void fetchResponse(File image) async {
       final mimeTypeData =
           lookupMimeType(image.path, headerBytes: [0xFF,
   0xD8]).split('/');
   ```

```
        final imageUploadRequest = http.MultipartRequest('POST',
Uri.parse("http://x.x.x.x:8080/generate"));

        final file = await http.MultipartFile.fromPath('image',
image.path,
            contentType: MediaType(mimeTypeData[0], mimeTypeData[1]));
        imageUploadRequest.fields['ext'] = mimeTypeData[1];
        imageUploadRequest.files.add(file);
        try {
          final streamedResponse = await imageUploadRequest.send();
          final response = await
http.Response.fromStream(streamedResponse);
          final Map<String, dynamic> responseData =
json.decode(response.body);
          String outputFile = responseData['result'];
        } catch (e) {
          print(e);
          return null;
        }
    }
```

In the preceding method, we find the MIME type of the selected file by using the `lookupMimeType` function using the file's path and its headers. Then, we initialize a multipart request, as expected by the server hosting the model. We do this using HTTP. We use `MultipartFile.fromPath` and set the value of `image` to the path that gets attached as the `POST` parameter. We explicitly pass the extension of the image to the request body since `image_picker` has some bugs. Due to this, it mixes up image extensions with filenames such as `filenamejpeg`, which creates problems on the server side when it comes to managing or verifying the file extension. The response from the server is then stored in the `response` variable. The response is in JSON format, so we need to decode it using `json.decode()`. The function takes in the body of the response, which can be accessed using `response.body`. We store the decoded JSON in the `responseData` variable. Finally, the output of the server is accessed using `responseDate['result']` and is stored in the `outputFile` variable.

4. Next, we define the `displayResponseImage()` function, which takes in the name of the PNG file that's returned by the server inside the `outputFile` parameter:

```
void displayResponseImage(String outputFile) {
    print("Updating Image");
    outputFile = 'http://x.x.x.x:8080/download/' + outputFile;
    setState(() {
        imageOutput = Image(image: NetworkImage(outputFile));
```

```
        });
    }
```

As per the customization of the server, we need to append a string before the name of the file to display it on the screen. The string should contain the port address where the server is running, followed by `'/download/<outputFile>'`. Then, we set the value of the `imageOutput` widget to a `NetworkImage` using the final value of `outputFile` as the `url` value. Also, we enclose it inside `setState()` so that we can refresh the screen after the response is fetched properly.

5. Next, we make a call to `displayResponseImage()` at the very end of `fetchResponse()` and pass in the `outputFile` received from the hosted model:

```
void fetchResponse(File image) async {
    . . . .
    displayResponseImage(outputFile);
}
```

6. Finally, we add the call to `fetchResponse()` from `pickImage()` by passing in the image that was initially selected by the user:

```
void pickImage() async {
    . . . .
    fetchResponse(pickedImg);
}
```

In the preceding steps, we started by making a POST request to the server hosting the model. Then, we decoded the response and added code to display it on the screen. The addition of `fetchResponse()` at the end of `pickImage()` makes sure that the POST request is made only after the user has chosen an image. Also, to ensure that an attempt to display the response image has been made after successfully decoding the output from the server, `displayImageResponse()` is called at the end of `fetchResponse()`. The following screenshot shows the final expected state of the screen:

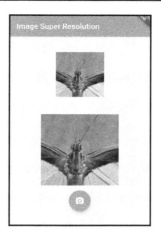

Thus, we've finished building the application so that we can display the output of the model. We've kept the two images together on the screen so that we can see the difference between them.

The code for the image_super_resolution.dart file can be accessed at https://github.com/PacktPublishing/Mobile-Deep-Learning-Projects/tree/master/Chapter9/flutter_image_super_resolution.

Creating the Material app

Now, we will add main.dart in order to create the final Material app. We'll create a stateless widget called MyApp and override the build() method:

```
class MyApp extends StatelessWidget {
    @override
    Widget build(BuildContext context) {
        return MaterialApp(
            title: 'Flutter Demo',
            theme: ThemeData(
                primarySwatch: Colors.blue,
            ),
            home: ImageSuperResolution(),
        );
    }
}
```

Finally, we execute the code, as follows:

```
void main() => runApp(MyApp());
```

With that, we've finished creating an application that lets the user choose an image and modify its resolution.

Summary

In this chapter, we studied super-resolution images and how we can apply them using a SRGAN. We also studied other types of GANs and how GANs work in general. Then, we discussed how to create a Flutter application that can be integrated with an API hosted on a DigitalOcean Droplet so that we can perform image super-resolution when an image has been picked from the gallery. Next, we covered how to use DigitalOcean Droplets and how it is a good choice for hosting the backends of applications due to its low cost and easy-to-use interface.

In the next chapter, we will discuss some popular applications that have seen great improvements by integrating deep learning into their functionality. We will also explore some hot research areas in deep learning for mobile phones, and briefly discuss the latest work that has been done on them.

10
Road Ahead

The most important part of a journey is knowing where to go next once it ends. We have covered some unique and powerful **deep learning** (**DL**) applications related to Flutter apps so far in this series of projects, but it is important for you to know where you can find more such projects, inspiration, and knowledge to build your own cool projects. In this chapter, we shall briefly cover the most popular applications using DL on mobile apps today, the current trends, and what is expected to come in this field in the future.

In this chapter, we will cover the following topics:

- Understanding recent trends in DL on mobile applications
- Exploring the latest developments in DL on mobile devices
- Exploring current research areas for DL in mobile apps

Let's begin by studying some of the trends in the world of DL mobile apps.

Understanding recent trends in DL on mobile applications

DL specifically, and **Artificial Intelligence** (**AI**) more broadly, are becoming more and more mobile with the latest technology and hardware advancements. Organizations have been using intelligent algorithms to provide a personalized user experience and increase app engagement. With technologies such as face detection, image processing, text recognition, object recognition, and language translations, mobile applications have become much more than just a medium to provide static information. They are capable of adapting to the user's personal preferences and choices, as well as the present and past environment situations, to provide a seamless user experience.

Let's look at some trending applications and the methods they deploy to provide a good user experience, alongside increasing app engagement.

Math solver

Launched by Microsoft on January 16, 2020, the Math solver application helps students complete their mathematical assignments by simply clicking on pictures in questions on their smartphones. The application provides support for both basic and advanced mathematical problems, covering a wide range of topics, including elementary arithmetic, quadratic equations, calculus, and statistics. The following screenshot shows how the application works:

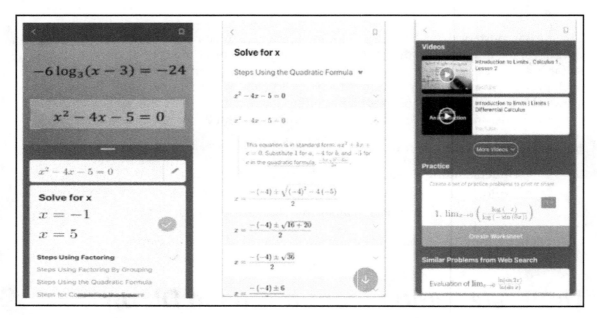

The user can click a picture of a handwritten or printed problem on their smartphone, or directly scribble or type it on the device. The application makes use of AI to recognize the problem and solve it accurately. Additionally, it is equipped to provide a step-by-step explanation, with additional learning materials such as worksheets and video tutorials relating to the problem.

Netflix

Netflix's recommendation system is one of the biggest success stories of using DL on mobile applications. Netflix utilizes a number of algorithms to understand users' preferences and comes up with a list of recommendations they might be interested in. All content is tagged with labels that provide an initial set of data from which the algorithms can learn. Further, the system monitors over 100 million user profiles to analyze what people watch, what they might watch later, what they have watched before, what they watched a year ago, and so on. All of the data collected is brought together to learn the kind of content a user might be interested in.

The data collected using the tags and user behavior is then brought together and fed into complex ML algorithms. This data helps explain the factors that might hold the most importance—for example, if a movie that a user watched a year ago should be counted twice compared to a series they watched last week. The algorithms also learn from user behavior, such as whether the user liked or disliked particular content, or the shows the user binged on and watched in 2 nights. All of the factors are brought together and analyzed carefully, resulting in a list of recommendations users might be interested in the most.

Google Maps

Google Maps has helped commuters to travel to new places, explore new cities, and monitor daily traffic. In early June 2019, Google Maps released a new feature to enable users to monitor bus travel times in 10 major cities across India, as well as get live updates from Indian Railways. The feature, live in Bengaluru, Chennai, Coimbatore, Delhi, Hyderabad, Lucknow, Mumbai, Pune, and Surat, makes use of Google's live traffic data and public bus schedules to calculate accurate travel times and delays. The algorithm supporting the feature learns from the sequence of bus positions over time. This data is further combined with the speed of cars on the bus's path at the time of the commute. The data is also used to capture the unique properties of a specific street. Researchers have also simulated the possibility of queries that pop up about an area, to make the model much more robust and accurate.

Tinder

The world's most popular application for meeting new people, Tinder deploys a number of learning models to increase the number of people liking a particular profile. The **Smart Photos** feature increases a user's probability to find a correct match. The feature randomly orders the pictures of a particular user and shows them to others. The algorithm supporting the feature analyzes the frequency of the pictures being swiped left or right. It uses the knowledge to reorder the pictures according to their popularity. The algorithm's accuracy has been constantly increasing with the collection of more and more data.

Snapchat

The filters used by Snapchat are design overlays added on top of pictures and videos, with the capability of following face movements. These filters are made possible by computer vision. The first step of the algorithm being used by the application is to detect the faces present in an image. It outputs boxes bounding the detected faces. It then marks the facial landmarks—such as eyes, nose, and lips—for each of the detected faces. The output here is generally a two-dimensional point containing x-coordinates and y-coordinates. After the faces and facial features have been detected properly, it uses image processing to correctly place or apply filters on the whole face. The algorithm goes one step further to analyze the key facial features, using the Active Shape Model. The model, after being trained by the manual marking of the boundaries of key facial features, creates an average face that aligns with a face appearing on the screen. The model creates a mesh to correctly place the filters and track their movements.

Now, we'll take a look at the research areas in the field of DL.

Exploring the latest developments in DL on mobile devices

With the complexities of DL and AI combining with mobile applications, software and hardware optimizations are being constantly made to run the models efficiently on devices. Let's look at some of them.

Google's MobileNet

Google's MobileNet was launched in 2017. It is a set of mobile-first computer vision models based on TensorFlow, very carefully optimized to run efficiently within a restrictive mobile environment. It acts as a bridge between accuracy in complex neural network structures and performance constraints on mobile runtimes. Since the models have the capability to run locally on the device itself, MobileNet has the advantages of security, privacy, and flexible accessibility. The two most important goals of MobileNet are reduced size and minimal complexity when dealing with computer vision models. The first version of MobileNet offered low-latency models capable of working smoothly with restrictive resources. They can be used for classification, detection, embeddings, and segmentation, supporting a wide range of use cases.

MobileNetV2, released in 2018, is a significant enhancement to the first version. It can be used for semantic segmentation, object detection, and classification. MobileNetV2, launched as a part of the TensorFlow-Slim image classification library, can be directly accessed from Colaboratory. It can also be downloaded locally, explored using Jupyter, and can be accessed from TF-Hub and GitHub. The two most important features added to the architecture are linear bottlenecks between the layers and shortcut connections between the bottlenecks. The bottlenecks encode intermediate inputs and outputs, and the inner layers support the ability to convert from lower-level concepts to higher-level descriptors. The traditional residual connections and shortcuts help to reduce training time and increase accuracy. MobileNetV2 is faster, more accurate, and requires fewer operations and parameters compared to the first version. It works very efficiently for object detection and segmentation to extract features.

 You can read more on this research work here: `https://arxiv.org/abs/1905.02244`.

Alibaba Mobile Neural Network

Alibaba **Mobile Neural Network (MNN)** is an open sourced lightweight DL inference engine. Jia Yangqing, the Vice President of Engineering at Alibaba, says: "*Compared with general-purpose frameworks like TensorFlow and Caffe2 that cover both training and inference, MNN focuses on the acceleration and optimization of inference and solves efficiency problems during model deployment so that services behind models can be implemented more efficiently on the mobile side. This is actually in line with ideas in server-side inference engines like TensorRT. In large-scale machine learning applications, the number of computations for inference are usually 10+ times more than that for training. Therefore, optimization for inference is especially important.*"

The main focus areas of MNN are running and inference of **Deep Neural Network** (**DNN**) models. It concentrates on the optimization, conversion, and inference of the models. MNN has been adopted to run successfully in a number of mobile applications of Alibaba Inc, such as Mobile Tmall, Mobile Taobao, Fliggy, UC, Qianniu, and Juhuasuan. It covers search recommendation, short video capture, live broadcast, equity distribution, security risk control, interactive marketing, product search by image, and many other real-life scenarios. **Internet of Things** (**IoT**) devices such as Cainiao call cabinets are also making greater use of technology. MNN has great stability and can run more than 100 million times per day.

MNN is highly versatile and provides support for most of the popular frameworks in the market such as TensorFlow, Caffe, and **Open Neural Network Exchange** (**ONNX**). It is equally compatible with common neural networks such as **Convolutional Neural Networks** (**CNNs**) and **Relational Neural Networks** (**RNNs**). MNN is lightweight and highly optimized for mobile devices and has no dependencies. It can be easily deployed to mobile devices and a variety of embedded devices. It also supports the major mobile operating systems Android and iOS, along with embedded devices, with the **Portable Operating System Interface** (**POSIX**). MNN, being independent of any external library, delivers very high performance. Its core operations are implemented through large volumes of handwritten assembly code to take maximum advantage of **Advanced RISC Machine** (**ARM**) CPUs. With the efficient **image processing module** (**IPM**), speeding up affine transform and color space transform without libyuv or OpenCV, MNN is easy to use.

While these products are under active development and research, let's now look at some of the areas that are expected to grow in importance in the future.

Exploring current research areas for DL in mobile apps

It is crucial for the healthy growth of any field of study that an active community of researchers invests time and effort into it. Fortunately, the application of DL on mobile devices has gathered strong attention from developers and researchers worldwide, with many mobile handset manufacturers, such as Samsung, Apple, Realme, and Xiaomi, integrating DL right into the system **user interface** (**UI**) they produce for all their devices. This gives a huge boost to the speed at which the models run, and their accuracy is regularly improved by system updates.

Let's look at some of the most popular research areas in the field and how they've been progressing.

Fashion images

In 2019, the DeepFashion2 dataset was presented by Yuying Ge, Ruimao Zhang, and others. The dataset is an improvement on the DeepFashion dataset and includes 491,000 images from both sellers and consumers. The dataset identifies 801,000 clothing items. Each item in the dataset is marked with a scale, occlusion, zoom-in, viewpoint, category, style, a bounding box, dense landmarks, and a per-pixel mask.

The dataset has 391,000 images in the training set, 34,000 images in the validation set, and 67,000 images in the test set. This dataset offers the possibility of coming up with better models that are able to identify fashion clothing and different clothing items from images. One could easily imagine the range of applications this dataset could lead to—including online stores recommending products to buy according to what consumers often wear together, complete with the preferred brands and expected price range of the products. It is also likely to identify the profession any person may be involved in and their financial, religious, and geographical details, simply by identifying the clothing items and brands they wear.

You can read more about the DeepFashion2 dataset here: `https://arxiv.org/abs/1901.07973`.

Self-Attention Generative Adversarial Networks

We discussed an application of **Generative Adversarial Networks** (**GANs**) in Chapter 9, *Building an Image Super-Resolution Application*, where we generated high-resolution images from low-resolution images. GANs do a fairly good job of learning to mimic art and patterns. However, they fail to perform well where longer sequences need to be remembered and in instances where there are multiple parts of the sequence that are important toward making a generated output. Hence, we look toward **Self-Attention GANs** (**SAGANs**), introduced by Ian Goodfellow and his team, which are GAN systems that allow attention-driven, long-range dependency modeling for image-generation tasks. This system has had better performance on the ImageNet dataset and is expected to be adopted widely in the future.

A derivate of the works done using SAGANs is the DeOldify project by Jason Antic. This project aims to bring color into old images and videos, so that it seems that they never lacked color in the first place. An example from the DeOldify project is shown in the following screenshot:

Migrant Mother by Dorothea Lange (1936). Image taken from DeOldify GitHub repository at `https://github.com/jantic/DeOldify`. The project is available for testing and demo at `https://deoldify.ai/`. You can read more about SAGANs at `https://arxiv.org/abs/1805.08318`.

Image animation

Facebook, a popular social media platform with a dedicated app for several platforms, has been working on creating tools that allow you to produce 3D images by using normal cameras that would otherwise only produce 2D images. Image animation is a similar technology that allows us to bring animation into static images. A very exciting usage of this technology can be imagined as people taking selfies and then choosing from a library of motions to animate their images as if they were making those motions themselves.

While yet at a very nascent stage, image animation is something that can become a popular and fun application, considering similar applications featuring deepfake technologies have made it into a successful business—for example, the Zao app in China.

 You can read the image animation research paper here: `https://arxiv.org/abs/2003.00196v1`.

Summary

In this chapter, we discussed some of the most popular mobile applications that are famous for their cutting-edge usage of DL in their business products, and also about the way DL has impacted their growth. We also discussed the current latest developments in the field of DL for mobile applications. Finally, we discussed some exciting research areas for the field, and how they could grow into potential popular apps in the future. We believe that by now, you will have a very good idea about how DL can be deployed on mobile applications, and how, using Flutter, you can build cross-platform mobile applications that run on all popular mobile platforms.

We conclude this chapter with the hope that you'll make the best use of the ideas and knowledge presented in this project series and build something awesome that brings about a revolution in this space of technology.

Appendix

The world of computer science is exciting in the way that it allows several software components to come together and work toward building something new. In this short appendix, we've covered the tools, software, and online services that you'll need to set up before you can embark on your journey of deep learning on mobile devices.

In this chapter, we will cover the following topics:

- Setting up a deep learning environment on Cloud VM
- Installing Dart SDK
- Installing Flutter SDK
- Configuring Firebase
- Setting up **Visual Studio** (**VS**) Code

Setting up a deep learning environment on Cloud VM

In this section, we will present a quick guide on how to set up an environment on a **Google Cloud Platform** (**GCP**) Compute Engine **Virtual Machine** (**VM**) instance in order to perform deep learning. You can easily extend the methods described here to other cloud platforms as well.

We will begin with a quick guide on how to create your GCP account and enable billing on it.

Creating a GCP account and enabling billing

To create a GCP account, you will need a Google Account. If you have an email address ending in `@gmail.com` or an account on G Suite, you already have a Google Account. If not, you can create a Google Account by visiting `https://accounts.google.com/sigNup`. Once you are logged in to a Google Account, perform the following steps:

1. Visit `console.cloud.google.com` on your browser.
2. Accept any terms and conditions that are presented to you in popups.
3. You will be able to view your GCP Console dashboard. You can get up to speed with this dashboard by reading through the support document at `https://support.google.com/cloud/answer/3465889`.
4. On the left-hand navigation menu, click on **Billing** to open the billing management dashboard. You will be prompted to add a billing account, as shown in the following screenshot:

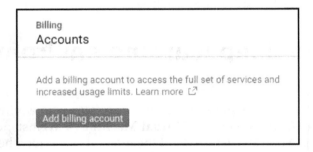

5. Click on **Add billing account**. You will be redirected to the `GCP Free Trial` registration page if you're eligible for it. You can read more about the free trial at `https://cloud.google.com/free/docs/gcp-free-tier`. You should see a screen similar to the one in the following screenshot:

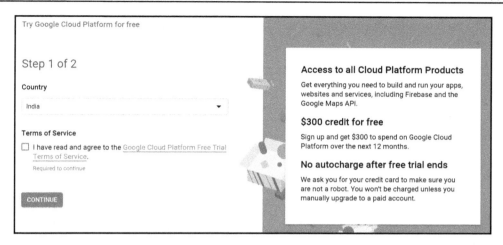

6. Fill in the form as required. Once you've finished creating the billing, return to the GCP Console dashboard.

You have successfully created your GCP account and enabled billing on it. Next, you'll be able to create a project in your GCP console and allocate resources to the project. We will demonstrate this in the upcoming section.

Creating a project and GCP Compute Engine instance

In this section, you'll be creating a project on your GCP account. All resources in GCP are encapsulated under projects. Projects may or may not belong to an organization. An organization can have multiple projects under it, and a project may have multiple resources inside it. Let's begin by creating the project, as shown in the following steps:

1. In the top left of the screen, click on the **Select a project** drop-down menu.
2. In the dialog box that appears, click on **New project** in the top right of the dialog box.

3. You'll be shown the new project creation form, as shown in the following screenshot:

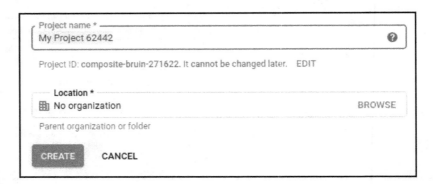

4. After filling in the requisite details, click on **CREATE** to finish creating your project. Once you have created your project, you'll be taken to the project's dashboard. Here, you'll be able to view some basic logging and monitoring related to the currently selected project. You can read more about how GCP resources are organized at `https://cloud.google.com/docs/overview`.

5. On the left navigation pane, click on **Compute Engine**. You'll be prompted to create a VM instance.

6. Click on **CREATE** to bring up the Compute Engine instance creation form. Fill in the form as needed. We'll assume you've chosen the Ubuntu 18.04 LTS distribution while creating the instance.

7. Make sure that you enable access for the HTTP and HTTPS connections to your VM instance in the firewall settings, as shown in the following screenshot:

8. Click on **CREATE**. GCP begins provisioning a VM instance for you. You'll be taken to the VM instances management page. You should see your VM listed on this page, as shown in the following screenshot:

You're now ready to start configuring this VM instance to perform deep learning. We will cover this in the next section.

Configuring your VM instance to perform deep learning

In this section, we'll guide you through how to install the packages and modules for performing deep learning on the VM instance you have created. These instructions for the installation of the packages and modules will be similar across any cloud service provider of your choice.

 You could also use similar commands on your local system as well, in order to set up a local deep learning environment.

Let's begin by invoking the terminal of the VM:

1. Click on the **SSH** button on the VM instances page to start a terminal session to your VM.

2. You should see the terminal session start, with some general information relating to the system and details of the last login, as shown in the following screenshot:

```
Welcome to Ubuntu 18.04.4 LTS (GNU/Linux 5.0.0-1033-gcp x86_64)

 * Documentation:  https://help.ubuntu.com
 * Management:     https://landscape.canonical.com
 * Support:        https://ubuntu.com/advantage

  System information as of Thu Mar 19 23:28:40 UTC 2020

  System load:  0.0              Processes:            92
  Usage of /:   12.1% of 9.52GB  Users logged in:      0
  Memory usage: 6%               IP address for ens4:  10.128.0.39
  Swap usage:   0%

0 packages can be updated.
0 updates are security updates.



The programs included with the Ubuntu system are free software;
the exact distribution terms for each program are described in the
individual files in /usr/share/doc/*/copyright.

Ubuntu comes with ABSOLUTELY NO WARRANTY, to the extent permitted by
applicable law.

xprilion@instance-1:~$
```

3. Now, let's perform an update on the package repositories of this newly created instance:

```
sudo apt update
```

4. Next, we will install **Anaconda** on this VM. Anaconda is a popular collection of packages for performing deep learning and data science-related tasks using Python. It comes packaged with the conda package manager, which makes it very easy to manage different versions of Python packages installed on the system. To install it, we first need to get the Anaconda installer download link. Head over to https://www.anaconda.com/distribution/#download-section. You will be taken to a page offering you a choice of which Anaconda version you want to install, as shown in the following screenshot:

Anaconda 2020.02 for Linux Installer

Python 3.7 version	Python 2.7 version
Download	Download
64-Bit (x86) Installer (522 MB)	64-Bit (x86) Installer (477 MB)
64-Bit (Power8 and Power9) Installer (276 MB)	64-Bit (Power8 and Power9) Installer (295 MB)

5. It is recommended that you choose the Python 3.7 version. Right-click on the **Download** button and find the option in the menu that allows you to copy the link address.

6. Switch to the terminal session of your VM instance. Use the following command to replace the placeholder text with the link you have copied by pasting it in the command, as shown here:

```
curl -O <link_you_have_copied>
```

7. The preceding command will download the Anaconda installer to your current user's home directory. To verify it, you can use the `ls` command. Now, to set this file to be executable, we will use the following command:

```
chmod +x Anaconda*.sh
```

8. Now, the installer file can be executed by your system. To start its execution, use the following command:

```
./Anaconda*.sh
```

9. Installation should begin. You should be presented with a prompt asking you whether you accept the license agreement of the Anaconda software, as shown here:

```
Welcome to Anaconda3 2020.02

In order to continue the installation process, please review the license
agreement.
Please, press ENTER to continue
>>>
```

10. Hit *Enter* to continue reviewing the license. You'll be shown the license file.

11. Hit the down arrow key to read through the agreement. Enter `yes` to accept the license.

12. You'll be asked to confirm the location of your Anaconda installation, as shown in the following screenshot:

```
Anaconda3 will now be installed into this location:
/home/xprilion/anaconda3

  - Press ENTER to confirm the location
  - Press CTRL-C to abort the installation
  - Or specify a different location below

[/home/xprilion/anaconda3] >>>
```

13. Hit *Enter* to confirm the location. Package extraction and installation will begin. Once this is complete, you'll be asked whether you want to initialize the Anaconda environment; enter `yes` here, as follows:

```
Do you wish the installer to initialize Anaconda3
by running conda init? [yes|no]
[no] >>> yes
```

14. Now, the installer will complete its tasks and exit. To activate the Anaconda environment, use the following command:

```
source ~/.bashrc
```

15. You've successfully installed the Anaconda environment and activated it. To check whether the installation has been successful, enter the following command in the terminal:

```
python3
```

If the output of the following command includes the words **Anaconda, Inc.** on the second line, your installation has been successful. You can see it in the following screenshot:

```
(base) xprilion@instance-1:~$ python3
Python 3.7.6 (default, Jan  8 2020, 19:59:22)
[GCC 7.3.0] :: Anaconda, Inc. on linux
Type "help", "copyright", "credits" or "license" for more information.
>>>
```

Now, you can start running deep learning scripts on this environment. However, you might want to add more utility libraries to this environment in the future, such as PyTorch or TensorFlow, or any other package. Since this book assumes familiarity with Python, we'll not discuss the `pip` tool in much detail.

Let's now look at how you can install TensorFlow on your VM.

Installing TensorFlow on a VM

TensorFlow is a great framework to perform deep learning.

To install it, you can use the following commands:

```
# TensorFlow 1 with CPU only support
python3 -m pip install tensorflow==1.15

# TensorFlow 1 with GPU support
```

```
python3 -m pip install tensorflow-gpu==1.15

# TensorFlow 2 with CPU only support
python3 -m pip install tensorflow

# Tensorflow 2 with GPU support
python3 -m pip install tensorflow-gpu
```

Another popular library in Python, which is often installed, is the Natural Language Toolkit (NLTK) library. We will demonstrate its installation process in the upcoming section.

Installing NLTK on a VM and downloading packages

To install NLTK on the VM and to download the data packages for it, perform the following steps:

1. Install NLTK using `pip`:

```
python3 -m pip install nltk
```

2. There are several different data packages available for NLTK. In most use cases, you won't need them all. To list all of the available data packages for NLTK, use the following command:

```
python3 -m nltk.downloader
```

The output of the preceding command will allow you to interactively view all of the available packages, select the ones you require, and then download them.

3. However, if you wish to download only one package, use the following command:

```
python3 -m nltk.downloader stopwords
```

The preceding command will download the `stopwords` data package of NLTK. In very rare circumstances, you might find yourself needing or using all of the data packages available in NLTK.

With this amount of setup, you should be able to run most deep learning scripts on your cloud VM.

In the next section, we will look at how to install Dart on your local system.

Installing Dart SDK

Dart is an object-oriented language developed by Google. It is used for mobile and web application development. Flutter is built with Dart. Dart has a **Just In Time** (JIT)-based development cycle that is compatible with stateful hot reload and an ahead-of-time compiler for fast startup and predictable performance, which makes it suitable for Flutter.

The following sections discuss how to install Dart on Windows, macOS, and Linux.

Windows

The easiest way to install Dart in Windows is by using Chocolatey. Simply run the following command in the terminal:

```
C:\> choco install dart-sdk
```

Next, we will look at how to install Dart on Mac systems.

macOS

To install Dart on macOS, perform the following steps:

1. Install Homebrew by running the following command in the Terminal:

    ```
    $ /usr/bin/ruby -e "$(curl -fsSL
    https://raw.githubusercontent.com/Homebrew/install/master/install)"
    ```

2. Run the following command to install Dart:

    ```
    $brew tap dart-lang/dart
    $brew install dart
    ```

Next, we will look at how to install Dart on a Linux system.

Linux

Dart SDK can be installed in Linux as follows:

1. Perform the following one-time setup:

    ```
    $sudo apt-get update
    $sudo apt-get install apt-transport-https
    $sudo sh -c 'wget -qO-
    https://dl-ssl.google.com/linux/linux_signing_key.pub | apt-key add
    -'
    ```

```
$sudo sh -c 'wget -qO-
https://storage.googleapis.com/download.dartlang.org/linux/debian/d
art_stable.list > /etc/apt/sources.list.d/dart_stable.list'
```

2. Install the stable release:

```
$sudo apt-get update
$sudo apt-get install dart
```

Next, we'll look at how to install the Flutter SDK on our local machines.

Installing Flutter SDK

Flutter is a toolkit by Google used to build natively compiled Android, iOS, and web applications with a single code base. Features such as fast development with hot reload, an expressive UI that is simple to build, and native performance have all made Flutter a preferable choice for application developers.

The following sections discuss how to install Flutter SDK on Windows, macOS, and Linux.

Windows

The following steps outline, in detail, how to install Flutter on Windows:

1. Download the latest stable release of Flutter SDK from `https://storage.` `googleapis.com/flutter_infra/releases/stable/windows/flutter_windows_` `v1.9.1+hotfix.6-stable.zip`.
2. Extract the ZIP folder, and navigate to the directory where you want to install Flutter SDK in order to place the `flutter` folder.

 Avoid placing `flutter` in a directory that might require special privileges such as `C:\Program Files\`.

3. Type `env` into the **Start** search bar and select **Edit Environment Variables**.
4. Append the full path to `flutter/bin` to **Path** under **User Variables** using `;` as a separator.

If the **Path** entry is missing, simply create a new **Path** variable and set `path` to `flutter/bin` as its value.

5. Run `flutter doctor` in the terminal.

`flutter doctor` analyzes the entire Flutter installation to check whether more tools are needed to run Flutter successfully on the machine.

Next, we will look at how to install Flutter on a Mac system.

macOS

Flutter can be installed on macOS as follows:

1. Download the latest stable SDK from `https://storage.googleapis.com/flutter_infra/releases/stable/macos/flutter_macos_v1.9.1+hotfix.6-stable.zip`.
2. Extract the downloaded ZIP folder to a suitable location, like so:

```
$cd ~/
$unzip ~/Downloads/flutter_macos_v1.9.1+hotfix.6-stable.zip
```

3. Add the `flutter` tool to the path variable: `$ export PATH=`pwd`/flutter/bin:$PATH`.
4. Open `bash_profile` to permanently update `PATH`:

```
$cd ~
$nano .bash_profile
```

5. Add the following line to `bash_profile`:

```
$export PATH=$HOME/flutter/bin:$PATH
```

6. Run `flutter doctor`.

Linux

The following steps outline how to install Flutter on Linux:

1. Download the latest stable version of the SDK from `https://storage.googleapis.com/flutter_infra/releases/stable/linux/flutter_linux_v1.9.1+hotfix.6-stable.tar.xz`.

2. Extract the file to a suitable location:

```
$cd ~/development
$tar xf ~/Downloads/flutter_linux_v1.9.1+hotfix.6-stable.tar.xz
```

3. Add `flutter` to the `path` variable:

```
$export PATH="$PATH:`pwd`/flutter/bin"
```

4. Run `flutter doctor`.

Next, we'll look at how to configure Firebase for serving ML Kit and custom models.

Configuring Firebase

Firebase offers tools that facilitate application development and helps in supporting a large user base. Firebase can easily be used for Android, iOS, and web applications. The products offered by Firebase, such as Cloud Firestore, ML Kit, Cloud Functions, Authentication, Crashlytics, Performance Monitoring, Cloud Messaging, and Dynamic Links, help to build apps, thus improving app quality in a growing business.

To integrate a Firebase project, you need to create a Firebase project and integrate it into your Android or iOS application. The subsequent sections discuss how to create a Firebase project and integrate it into your Android and iOS projects.

Creating a Firebase project

First of all, we need to create a Firebase project and link it to our Android and iOS projects. This linkage helps us to utilize the functionalities provided by Firebase.

To create a Firebase project, perform the following steps:

1. Visit the Firebase console at `https://console.firebase.google.com`.
2. Click on **Add project** to add a new Firebase project:

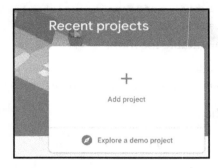

3. Provide a name for your project:

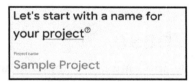

4. Enable/disable Google Analytics as per your requirements. It is generally recommended that you keep it enabled.

 Google Analytics is a free and unlimited analytics solution that enables targeting, reporting, and more in Firebase Crashlytics, Cloud Messaging, In-App Messaging, Remote Config, A/B Testing, Predictions, and Cloud Functions.

4. If you choose Firebase Analytics, you will also need to select an account:

After creating the project on the Firebase console, you will need to configure it separately for Android and iOS platforms.

Configuring the Android project

The following steps discuss how to configure your Android project to support Firebase:

1. Navigate to the app on the Firebase console. In the center of the project overview page, click on the Android icon to launch the workflow setup:

2. Add the package name to register the app on the Firebase console. The package name that is filled in here should match the package name of your application. The package name provided here acts as a unique key for identification:

Additionally, you can provide a nickname and a debug signing certificate, SHA-1.

3. Download the `google-services.json` file and place it inside the `app` folder:

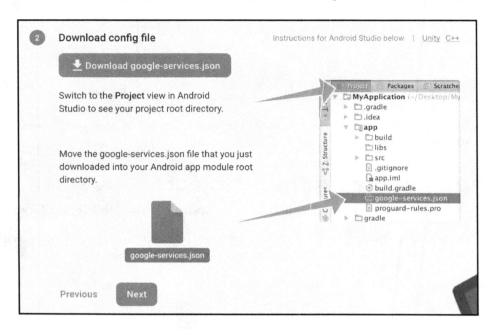

The `google-services.json` file stores the developer credentials and configuration settings and acts as a bridge between the Firebase project and the Android project.

4. The Google services plugin for Gradle loads the `google-services.json` file that you just downloaded. The project-level `build.gradle` (`<project>/build.gradle`) should be modified, as follows, to use the plugin:

```
buildscript {
  repositories {
    // Check that you have the following line (if not, add it):
    google()  // Google's Maven repository
  }
  dependencies {
    ...
    // Add this line
    classpath 'com.google.gms:google-services:4.3.3'
  }
}

allprojects {
  ...
```

```
repositories {
  // Check that you have the following line (if not, add it):
  google()  // Google's Maven repository
  ...
}
}
```

5. Here is the app-level `build.gradle` (`<project>/<app-module>build.gradle`):

```
apply plugin: 'com.android.application'
// Add this line
apply plugin: 'com.google.gms.google-services'

dependencies {
  // add SDKs for desired Firebase products
  //
https://firebase.google.com/docs/android/setup#available-libraries
}
```

Now, you are all set to use Firebase in your Android project.

Configuring the iOS project

The following steps demonstrate how to configure your iOS project to support Firebase:

1. Navigate to the app on the Firebase console. In the center of the project overview page, click on the iOS icon to launch the workflow setup:

2. Add the **iOS bundle ID** name to register the app on the Firebase console. You can find your **bundle identifier** in the **General** tab for your app's primary target in Xcode. It is used as a unique key for identification:

Additionally, you can provide a nickname and App Store ID.

3. Download the `GoogleService-Info.plist` file:

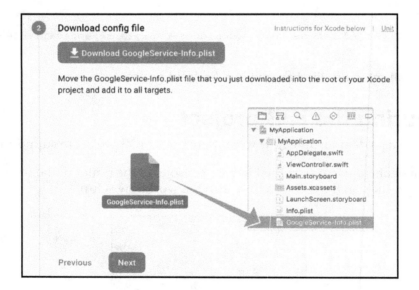

4. Move the `GoogleService-Info.plist` file that you just downloaded into the root of your Xcode project and add it to all the targets.

Google Services uses CocoaPods to install and manage dependencies.

5. Open a terminal window and navigate to the location of the Xcode project for your app. In this folder, create a Podfile if you don't have one:

```
pod init
```

6. Open your Podfile and add the following:

```
# add pods for desired Firebase products #
https://firebase.google.com/docs/ios/setup#available-pods
```

7. Save the file and run it:

```
pod install
```

This creates a `.xcworkspace` file for your app. Use this file for all future developments of your application.

8. To connect to Firebase when your app starts up, add the following initialization code to your main `AppDelegate` class:

```
import UIKit
import Firebase

@UIApplicationMain
class AppDelegate: UIResponder, UIApplicationDelegate {

  var window: UIWindow?

  func application(_ application: UIApplication,
    didFinishLaunchingWithOptions launchOptions:
      [UIApplicationLaunchOptionsKey: Any]?) -> Bool {
    FirebaseApp.configure()
    return true
  }
}
```

Now, you are all set to use Firebase in your Android project.

Setting up VS Code

Visual Studio (**VS**) Code is a lightweight code editor developed by Microsoft. Its simplicity and expansive repository of plugins make it a convenient tool for developers. With its Dart and Flutter plugins, along with app execution and debug support, Flutter applications are very easy to develop.

In the upcoming sections, we will demonstrate how to set up VS Code to develop Flutter applications. We will start by downloading the latest version of VS Code from `https://code.visualstudio.com/`.

Installing the Flutter and Dart plugins

First of all, we need to install the Flutter and Dart plugins on VS Code.

This can be done as follows:

1. Load VS Code on your machine.
2. Navigate to **View** | **Command Palette**.
3. Start typing in `install`, and select **Extensions: Install Extensions**.
4. Type `flutter` into the **Extensions** search field, select **Flutter** from the list, and then click on **Install**. This also installs the required Dart plugin.
5. Alternatively, you can navigate to the sidebar to install and search for **Extensions**:

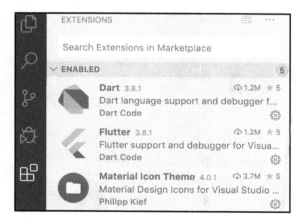

After successfully installing the Flutter and Dart extensions, we need to validate the setup. This is described in the next section.

Validating the setup with flutter doctor

It is generally recommended that you validate the setup to ensure that everything works fine.

The Flutter installation can be validated as follows:

1. Navigate to **View** | **Command Palette**.
2. Type in `doctor`, and then select `Flutter: Run Flutter Doctor`.
3. Look at the output inside the **OUTPUT** pane. Any errors or missing libraries are listed in the output.
4. Alternatively, you can run `flutter doctor` on the terminal to check whether everything is working fine:

```
Doctor summary (to see all details, run flutter doctor -v):
[✓] Flutter (Channel stable, v1.12.13+hotfix.8, on Mac OS X 10.14.6 18G3020, locale en-IN)

[!] Android toolchain - develop for Android devices (Android SDK version 29.0.3)
    ! Some Android licenses not accepted.  To resolve this, run: flutter doctor --android-licenses
[!] Xcode - develop for iOS and macOS
    ✗ Xcode installation is incomplete; a full installation is necessary for iOS development.
      Download at: https://developer.apple.com/xcode/download/
      Or install Xcode via the App Store.
      Once installed, run:
        sudo xcode-select --switch /Applications/Xcode.app/Contents/Developer
        sudo xcodebuild -runFirstLaunch
[!] Android Studio (version 3.5)
    ✗ Flutter plugin not installed; this adds Flutter specific functionality.
    ✗ Dart plugin not installed; this adds Dart specific functionality.
[✓] Connected device (1 available)

! Doctor found issues in 3 categories.
```

The preceding screenshot shows you that, while Flutter is good to go, some other related configurations are missing. In such a situation, you might want to install all of the supporting software and rerun `flutter doctor` to analyze the setup.

After successfully setting up Flutter on VS Code, we can proceed to create our first Flutter app.

Creating the first Flutter app

Creating the first Flutter app is very simple. Perform the following steps:

1. Navigate to **View** | **Command Palette**.
2. Start typing in `flutter`, and select **Flutter: New Project**.

3. Enter a project name, such as `my_sample_app`.
4. Click on **Enter**.
5. Create or select the parent directory for the new project folder.
6. Wait for project creation to complete and the `main.dart` file to appear.

 For more details, you can refer to the documentation, at `https://flutter.dev/docs/get-started/test-drive`.

In the next section, we will discuss how to run your first Flutter application.

Running the app

The creation of a new Flutter project comes with a template code that we can run directly on mobile devices. After creating your first template application, you can try to run it as follows:

1. Navigate to the VS Code status bar (that is, the blue bar at the bottom of the window):

2. Select your preferable device from the device selector area:

   - If no device is available and you want to use a device simulator, click on No Device and launch a simulator:

   - You can also try setting up a real device for debugging.

3. Click on the **Settings** button—a cog icon gear in the top-right corner (now marked with a red or orange indicator) that is next to the **DEBUG** textbox that reads **No Configuration**. Select **Flutter** and choose the debug configuration to create your emulator if it is closed or to run the emulator or device that is now connected.

4. Navigate to **Debug | Start Debugging** or press F5.

5. Wait for the app to launch—progress is printed in the **DEBUG CONSOLE** view:

Once the app build is complete, you should see the initialized app on your device:

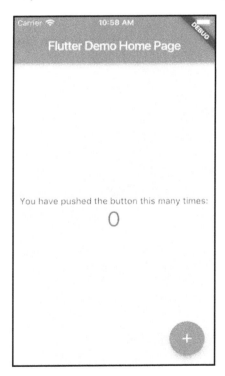

In the next section, we will look at the hot reload feature of Flutter, which helps in fast development.

Trying hot reload

The fast development cycle offered by Flutter makes it suitable for time-optimized development. It supports **Stateful Hot Reload**, which means that you can reload the code of a live running application without having to restart or lose the app state. Hot reloading can be described as a method by which you can make changes to your app source, tell your command-line tool that you want to hot reload, and view the changes within seconds on your device or emulator.

In VS Code, hot reloading can be performed as follows:

1. Open `lib/main.dart`.
2. Change the `You have pushed the button this many times:` string to `You have clicked the button this many times:`. Do *not* stop your app. Let your app run.

3. Save your changes: Invoke **Save All**, or click on **Hot Reload**.

Other Books You May Enjoy

If you enjoyed this book, you may be interested in these other books by Packt:

Machine Learning for Mobile
Revathi Gopalakrishnan, Avinash Venkateswarlu

ISBN: 978-1-78862-935-5

Learn how to clean your data and ready it for analysis

- Build intelligent machine learning models that run on Android and iOS
- Use machine learning toolkits such as Core ML, TensorFlow Lite, and more
- Learn how to use Google Mobile Vision in your mobile apps
- Build a spam message detection system using Linear SVM
- Using Core ML to implement a regression model for iOS devices
- Build image classification systems using TensorFlow Lite and Core ML

Mobile Artificial Intelligence Projects
Karthikeyan NG, Arun Padmanabhan, Et al

ISBN: 978-1-78934-407-3

- Explore the concepts and fundamentals of AI, deep learning, and neural networks
- Implement use cases for machine vision and natural language processing
- Build an ML model to predict car damage using TensorFlow
- Deploy TensorFlow on mobile to convert speech to text
- Implement GAN to recognize hand-written digits
- Develop end-to-end mobile applications that use AI principles
- Work with popular libraries, such as TensorFlow Lite, CoreML, and PyTorch

Leave a review - let other readers know what you think

Please share your thoughts on this book with others by leaving a review on the site that you bought it from. If you purchased the book from Amazon, please leave us an honest review on this book's Amazon page. This is vital so that other potential readers can see and use your unbiased opinion to make purchasing decisions, we can understand what our customers think about our products, and our authors can see your feedback on the title that they have worked with Packt to create. It will only take a few minutes of your time, but is valuable to other potential customers, our authors, and Packt. Thank you!

Index

W

webhook
  deploying, to Cloud Functions for Firebase 68,
    69
  implementing 67, 68

widgets 38
Windows
  Dart SDK, installing 340
  Flutter SDK, installing 341
Wit.ai
  used, for creating chatbots 53

www.ingramcontent.com/pod-product-compliance
Lightning Source LLC
Chambersburg PA
CBHW080612060326
40690CB00021B/4666